Substance Abuse, Family Violence, and Child Welfare

Bridging Perspectives

Editors

Robert L. Hampton
Vincent Senatore
Thomas P. Gullotta

Vol. 10 *Issues in Children's and Families' Lives*

SAGE Publications
International Educational and Professional Publisher
Thousand Oaks   London   New Delhi

For information:

 SAGE Publications, Inc.
2455 Teller Road
Thousand Oaks, California 91320
E-mail: order@sagepub.com

SAGE Publications Ltd.
6 Bonhill Street
London EC2A 4PU
United Kingdom

SAGE Publications India Pvt. Ltd.
M-32 Market
Greater Kailash I
New Delhi 110 048 India

Printed in the United States of America

Library of Congress Cataloging-in-Publication Data

Main entry under title:

Substance abuse, family violence & child welfare: Bridging perspectives /
editors, Robert L. Hampton, Vincent Senatore, Thomas P. Gullotta.
    p.   cm. — (Issues in children's and families' lives; v. 10)
Includes bibliographical references (p.) and index.
ISBN 0-7619-1457-9 (cloth: acid-free paper).
ISBN 0-7619-1458-7 (pbk.: acid-free paper)
    1. Parents—Substance abuse—United States.   2. Substance abuse—
United States.   3. Child welfare—United States.   4. Child abuse—
United States.   5. Family violence—United States.   6. Family
social work—United States.   I. Hampton, Robert L.   II. Senatore,
Vincent.   III. Gullotta, Thomas, 1948- .   IV. Title: Substance
abuse, family violence, and child welfare.   V. Series.
HV4999.P37S83   1998
362.29'085—dc21   97-45256

This book is printed on acid-free paper.

98   99   00   01   02   03   10 9 8 7 6 5 4 3 2 1

Acquiring Editor:	C. Deborah Laughton
Editorial Assistant:	Eileen Carr
Production Editor:	Astrid Virding
Production Assistant:	Lynn Miyata
Book Designer/Typesetter:	Janelle LeMaster
Cover Designer:	Ravi Balasuriya
Print Buyer:	Anna Chin

Contents

GIMBEL '96 PARTICIPANTS

Martin Bloom
Suzanne M. Colby
David F. Duncan
Laura Feig
Thomas P. Gullotta
Robert L. Hampton
James Maffuid
Micah L. McCreary
Thomas J. McMahon
Wilbert Murrell
Hank Resnik
Vincent Senatore
Janice Shafer

This work is dedicated to Amanda, Brittany,
Jimmy, Becca, Ceama, Sydney, Spencer,
and all children and their families that they
might be ever free from all forms of abuse.

Foreword

Children are the most vulnerable members of our society. We all share a special obligation to ensure their physical and psychological well-being. Properly nurtured in a supportive environment, their potential knows no limit. However, far too many of them are denied such an environment in which to grow. Instead, neglect and abuse leave emotional scars which often last a lifetime. Protecting children from such maltreatment is one of government's foremost responsibilities.

One of the contributing factors most frequently present in these troubled homes is serious substance abuse. While drug or alcohol addiction can have a tragic impact on the abusing adult, it can have an even more devastating impact on a child forced to live with that adult.

Since 1976, child welfare departments across this country have seen an increase of more than 330% in child abuse and neglect reports. Studies indicate that chemical dependency is present in at least two thirds of the families known to public child welfare agencies. Substance abusers are more likely than other parents to abuse and neglect their children, and maltreating parents are more likely than other parents to abuse alcohol and other drugs. It is essential that this link between parental substance abuse and child maltreatment be better understood. For this reason, I have co-sponsored legislation recently introduced in the Senate directing the Department of Health and Human Services to conduct a study of the impact of adult substance abuse on child neglect and abuse.

I commend the Gimbel Child and Family Program for addressing this growing societal problem. Located in New London, Connecticut, the Gimbel Child and Family Program recognizes the efforts of non-tenured scholars and practitioners in developing initiatives for children, adolescents, and their families that are designed to promote emotional and physical health and family stability. Over the past year, scholars from across the country have come together to better understand the relationship between substance abuse and threats to child welfare. Importantly, they have been seeking out more effective and efficient ways of integrating the fields of substance abuse prevention and treatment and child welfare. As is stated in the White House 1997 *National Drug Control Strategy:* "We are a great nation with tremendous capacity for organizational innovation and focused commitment of integrated, systematic, problem-solving initiatives. However, we are up against ruthless elements that threaten to undermine our social fabric and harm our citizens. By thoughtful, creative, and energetically applied programs, we can overcome virtually any challenge." There are few elements more ruthless, more threatening to our social fabric than substance abuse which contributes to child endangerment. It is important for the professionals in these two fields to work together, to share research, to develop integrated approaches to prevention and treatment programs, and to receive interdisciplinary training.

I commend the authors of this book for their energy, their time, and their intellectual commitment to seeking ways of bringing together two fields that so touch the lives of many of our children and their families. Many innovative program designs based on theory and research are presented in the forthcoming chapters. The importance of integrating substance abuse and child welfare prevention and treatment interventions is clearly an important theme of this book. Share this information with your elected officials, community leaders, teachers, and parents . . . all who are concerned about the well-being of our children. Better understanding of the problem is the first essential step to the solution.

—Edward M. Kennedy
Senator, Massachusetts

Introduction

It is hard to understand how society could have gone so long without recognizing that children in abusive situations often live in families in which alcohol and other drugs are abused. It is embarrassing that fields of study have developed so narrowly that they are not conscious of the life circumstances of all family members. It is inexcusable that bridges between the fields of substance abuse and child welfare have not been established sooner.

This book is the result of these failings. It is the fruit of a unique continuing study underwritten by the Gimbel Foundation. Recognizing that practitioners and scholars seldom interact and that multidisciplinary discussions are rarer still, the Gimbel Foundation, working with the Child and Family Agency of Southeastern Connecticut and the *Journal of Primary Prevention,* is experimenting with a biennial program intended to identify promising scholars and practitioners working on issues vital to the health and well-being of children and families in the United States. This effort not only recognizes the next generation of social service leaders in this country but identifies promising approaches that exist to improve our nation's health and the gaps that need to be bridged in order for meaningful improvement to occur.

The program is demanding. It entails three weekend study groups over a period of 18 months with serious individual study occurring between meetings. Recognized Gimbel Scholars work with a select multidisciplinary faculty who graciously donate their time to challenge time-honored thinking and stimulate new, more effective ways to address recalcitrant problems. In the chapters that follow, Gimbel scholars and faculty present a beginning framework for serving the multiple needs of families with substance-abusing members.

Using literary examples to illustrate the social history of children, women, and men, Gullotta, Hampton, Senatore, and Eismann remind us that abusive behavior and intoxication are not limited to recent times. Huckleberry Finn's drunken and abusive father and the morphine-addicted Mrs. Tyrone in Eugene O'Neill's (1989) autobiographical play, *Long Day's Journey Into Night,* have long exposed the plight of children and other family members living in these circumstances.

In Chapter 2, Jones examines the literature on drug-exposed children in the child welfare system and the interventions that facilitate their optimum development. Reviewing the developmental outcomes for children with prenatal and postnatal substance exposure, she describes the environments in which these children are reared. Her chapter concludes with a discussion of strategies that address the needs of these children and their caregivers.

In "Understanding the Problem: The Gap Between Substance Abuse Programs and Child Welfare Services," Feig describes the legislative and policy contexts in which potential collaborations between the fields of substance abuse and child welfare are being developed or abandoned. She offers direction to practitioners in both fields as they seek to better address the needs of these families.

In Chapter 4, Gardner, Resnik, and Rogers describe the damaging effects that parental and family substance abuse add to a host of child welfare problems. These scholars then examine these interrelationships and their implications for effective interventions and policies, using initiatives of the Center for Substance Abuse Prevention (CSAP) to illustrate their points. The authors conclude their chapter by discussing approaches for improving the coordination of prevention efforts in this area.

Chapter 5, by Bloom, provides a transition from foundational perspectives to an applied examination of the issues. In his chapter appropriately titled "The Bridges of Child Welfare/Substance Abuse County," Bloom uses the bridge metaphor to examine: what is important in the fields of substance abuse and child welfare; how do we begin to link them; what would the linkage look like; who would control access to this bridge; what would be some of the stresses on this bridge; and why would anyone want to cross the bridge?

In the next chapter, McMahon and Luthar discuss the right that children have to be raised in a safe, structured family environment with biological parents whose day-to-day functioning is not compromised by substance abuse. The authors discuss what can be done within drug abuse treatment systems to develop services that directly affect quality of life for children living with a drug-dependent parent. This chapter challenges us to think of innovative ways to deliver family-oriented substance abuse interventions so that the children of substance-abusing parents will receive the assistance they need.

In "Child Welfare and Substance Abuse Services: From Barriers to Collaboration," Colby and Murrell examine the institutional, professional, and interpersonal barriers to collaboration between the fields of child welfare and substance abuse. Using examples of successful collaborative efforts, the authors offer principles for overcoming these barriers.

Drawing from their experience as family therapists working with this population, McCreary, Maffuid, and Stepter discuss the need for clinicians to develop a sound therapeutic foundation to enhance their effectiveness with clients. The authors suggest that a family-based psychoeducational program that empowers these families to live healthy and drug-free lives is an effective treatment intervention.

The volume concludes with a provocative chapter by Duncan that reminds readers that not all substance abusers are child abusers. There are parents who, although severely impaired, care deeply for their children. Further, Duncan wonders whether it is wise to lump together those who misuse drugs with those who abuse them. He joins others, such as conservative pundit William F. Buckley, Jr., Nobel laureate economist Milton Friedman, and former Secretary of State George Schultz, in calling for a critical reanalysis of America's drug policies.

We offer this book to policymakers, to graduate students, but most of all to those working in the child welfare and substance abuse fields. We hope that policymakers will use this volume's findings to craft laws and funding opportunities that go beyond bridging the gap, and actually fill the gap between these fields. Children should not be lost in the chasm between two service systems that should, but too often do not, work effectively together. Children should not have to fall into this chasm, which hides too many cases from the view of those who might otherwise be able to intervene in a timely and family-sensitive manner. We hope that graduate students will resist the pull of monolithic practices that do not stress interdisciplinary collaboration. Because such monolithic practices address only a narrow portion of the problem, with little if any effort to address the whole family, they have left gaping holes in the service system into which children and their parents fall. Finally, we urge our colleagues to join us in a continued search for unified approaches for prevention and treatment for children and their parents who find themselves in these circumstances.

—Robert L. Hampton
Vincent Senatore
Thomas P. Gullotta

Reference

O'Neill, E. (1989). *Long day's journey into night.* New Haven, CT: Yale University Press. (Original work published 1955)

Acknowledgments

Many people contributed to this volume. On behalf of my coeditors, I thank the outstanding authors of the nine chapters. These individuals are committed to understanding and improving the lives of children and families by building bridges and through scholarship, dialogue, and action.

First, I want to thank Joan Kim who, by taking care of the details throughout this project, allowed me to work on its conceptual issues and other day-to-day responsibilities in the office. Next, I want to thank the many individuals who have assisted with the research and other tasks that go into sustaining a learning community and into completing an edited volume: Sondra Alexis, Marianne Eismann, Diane Gaboury, Tawanna Gaines, Mary Lou Gayda, Ginny Heredita, Judy Lovelace, and Wendy Traub. I also want to thank my colleagues in the Department of Family Studies and in the Division of Undergraduate Studies at the University of Maryland who understand my need for ongoing intellectual and professional engagement in this field of inquiry. Finally, I want to thank our colleagues at Sage Publications, C. Deborah Laughton and Eileen Carr, who have always made our work easier.

—Robert L. Hampton
The University of Maryland

When Pap Gets Too Handy With His Hick'ry:[1] A Selected Literary and Social History of Substance Abuse and Child Abuse

THOMAS P. GULLOTTA

ROBERT L. HAMPTON

VINCENT SENATORE

MARIANNE EISMANN

This is a book of science. Its chapters contain facts, theories, and findings. This information leads its contributing authors to assumptions about how we must bring two disparate fields closer together. It is a travesty that child welfare has not grappled with substance abuse when nearly two thirds of child protection cases involve substance-abusing caretakers. The connection was noted at least 120 years ago when English essayist Frances Power Cobbe (1878/1996, p. 302) described mothers who "keep their houses in a miserable state of dirt and disorder, neglect their children, and sell their clothes and furniture for gin" and fathers who on "reeling home from the gin-shop" hear the "baby cry in the cradle . . . [and] stamps on it." It is just as much a travesty that substance abuse interventions ignore all but the abusing individual. But this first chapter is not about science. In the discussion that follows, we refer to literary and historical instances of substance and child abuse to introduce the reader to some of the reasons

1

young people are mistreated. This review is not intended to be exhaustive. Rather, its purpose is to sensitize readers and provide images with which they may already be familiar but not have thought of as examples of substance and child abuse. Many readers may be surprised by some of the selections we have chosen to create these mental images.

That surprise comes from nearly extinguished memories of stories readers recall had happier beginnings, middles, and endings. In fact, this is not always the case. As when we ignore a friend's propensity for a second and then a third drink, or the coarseness with which he or she speaks to children or spouse, we wish to recall these stories' better moments. We begin this chapter with an exploration of female and male relationships, for how man has treated woman is repeated in their treatment of the child.

A Historical Overview
of the Sexes

In a sense, the history of the sexes is a reflection on the treatment of the child. While women and men have occupied the same time, they have experienced that time differently. While women and men shared experiences, those experiences were perceived differently by each. In this section we examine how some of those experiences changed and, in so doing, paint an impressionistic picture of life in the past. We discern several general trends, but the reader is cautioned to remember that there are exceptions to each generalization. The relationship changes that we identify cannot be tied to absolute historical dates, nor did they occur everywhere at the same time. Changes like the decline of community control over relationships and the rise of romantic love and the treatment of offspring as human beings and not as property tended to occur first among the upper classes and in urban areas and then to spread slowly, often taking centuries, to the general populace and into less urban areas. These changes were not fully accepted by everyone at the time or now, for that matter. However, our purpose in this section is to show how Western female and male adult roles have evolved, and such exceptions do not alter the direction those roles have taken. Finally, much of that discussion takes place within the context of couple relationships, for the sexes are linked, if for no other reason, out of biological necessity.

Children in Past Times

Recall the story of the infant Christ, wrapped in swaddling clothes and laid in a manger. What image does this story suggest to you? Does it suggest an image of a newborn infant wrapped in a clean cloth for warmth and yet able to move his arms freely inside that cloth? And your image of the stable—is it clean, with barn animals pressed tightly together, providing warmth for the infant? If those are your impressions, few infants before the 18th century enjoyed such luxury. For most, being swaddled meant that a strip of cloth some 2 inches across was wrapped around the infant's legs, arms, torso, and head until only a small part of the face remained exposed. Encased in its cocoon, the living infant mummy was then hung from a peg, laid on a table, or left on the floor near the hearth while mother worked. Left in its excrement for hours, an infant was lucky if the peg did not break, the wrappings were not ignited by a stray spark, or a barnyard hog did not supplement its diet with an infant morsel (deMause, 1988; Shorter, 1977).

Until very recent times, children have existed at the bottom of the human hierarchy. Not coming into existence, figuratively speaking, until sometime between their fourth and seventh birthdays, many were treated no better than, and most worse than, barnyard animals (Aries, 1962; deMause, 1988; Shorter, 1977). Two explanations for this nonexistent position have been put forth.

The first is that high child mortality discouraged adults from attaching much importance to children until they were old enough to have a reasonable chance of survival. It was a common occurrence, for example, not to name a child until that infant was 2 or more years old, which explains why many old European and, in the United States, New England cemeteries (prior to 1700) have nameless gravestones marking the burials of young children. Until the mid-19th century, with unspeakable sanitation conditions and with medical care that more often hastened death than prolonged life, many young individuals fought a losing battle with such illnesses as diphtheria, typhoid, measles, and mumps (McLaughlin, 1971; Shorter, 1977). To illustrate this last statement, consider these entries in the 1713 diary of the Boston minister Cotton Mather that detail the effects of a common childhood illness on his household:

> October 18, 1713. The Measles coming into the Town, it is likely to be a Time of Sickness. . . .

> November 4, 1713. In my poor family, now, first my wife has the Measles appearing on her; we know not yet how she will be handled. My daughter Nancy is also full of them. . . . [as is] Lissy . . . Jerusha, [and my maid servant]. Help Lord; and look mercifully on my poor, sad, sinful family. . . .

> [November 9, 1713] On Monday . . . my dear, dear, dear [wife] expired.

> November 14, 1713. [my maid servant has died]. The two newborns are languishing in the Arms of Death.

> November 17-18, 1713. About midnight, little Eleazar died.

> November 20, 1713. Little Martha dies, about ten o'clock a.m.

> November 21, 1713. This Day, I attended the Funeral of my two: Eleazar and Martha. Betwixt 9h. and 10h. at night, my lovely Jerusha expired. She was two years and about seven months . . . Lord, I am oppressed; undertake for me! (Cotton Mather, 1713, cited in Bremner, 1970, pp. 46-48)

As these diary entries suggest, Cotton Mather cared deeply for his wife and children. This was a caring attitude that was becoming increasingly prevalent among the upper classes in the 18th century, especially in the North American colonies.

The second argument is that adult indifference, more than natural conditions, explains the general lack of value attached to children prior to the 18th century. This view proposes that adults regarded children as greedy, gluttonous creatures sucking mother's substance from her breast (Yalom, 1997). Hunt (1970) suggests that women and men saw infants "prosper at the expense of the female, from whose body the child sucked the precious substance he needed for his own survival" (p. 120). In a society that held the similar view that a woman's intake of a man's vital fluids (semen) into her body weakened him, resentment rather than love may have been nurtured. Indeed, during the mid 1800s, Tannahill (1980) reports that dispassionate mechanical sex with a prostitute was viewed by many in the medical profession as less harmful to a male's health than loving emotional sex with his wife. Sex with a prostitute (and without emotional feeling) was viewed by medical authorities as less of a strain on the male's fragile physical health.

In support of this second position, that children were held with indifference, consider the life situation of a woman during those times. Pregnancy was a near-universal constant, with the possibility of death for the mother, as well as infant, ever present. Even as late as the 1870s when birthrates had significantly declined, English middle-class families still averaged six (6) children with a risk of death in childbirth or shortly thereafter calculated at 1 in 10.[2] That is, with each childbirth experience the woman ran a 10% risk of death. Poverty and famine were constant companions except for the wealthy, and a woman's work responsibilities did not vanish with the birth of a child. Until this century, she was expected to return to work as quickly as possible.

Evidence of gross indifference abounds. For instance, rocking an infant to sleep in days past more resembled a televised wrestling match than a soothing lullaby. Before the 18th century, rocking, it is reported, meant literally knocking a child unconscious (Shorter, 1977). The poorest children were likely to receive the worst treatment. In *Oliver Twist* (Dickens, 1837/1985), Charles Dickens writes of children in the care of the parish who "sickened from want and cold, or fell into the fire from neglect, or got half smothered by accident," or were "overlooked in turning up a bedstead, or inadvertently scalded to death when there happened to be a washing," though he adds, facetiously, that "the latter accident was very scarce" (pp. 48-49).

Two additional examples suggest not mere indifference but real resentment toward children. The first was the common practice by the middle and upper classes of sending away their infants to be wet-nursed (breast-fed) by strangers. As late as 1777, evidence shows that one sixth of the infants residing in or around Paris were nursed this way (Shorter, 1977). With the exception of the Dutch and the American Colonies, this practice was common in Western society (Yalom, 1997). Wet-nursing sealed for many infants a premature death warrant. Many wet nurses were "desperately poor, harried creatures who generally lived in rural hovels," with milk too scarce to nurse one child, let alone two or three (Shorter, 1977).

> Several [wet nurses] have only a single room, in which are crowded together a number of beds and chests. Some have but a single bed, and three nurslings. . . . [Wet nurses] most often just dumped their water on the dirt floor [of their cottage], "unable to take the trouble to throw it outside." The domestic livestock of pigs, goats, sheep, and poultry lived right with the family. . . . Right at the door was the fertilizer pile, and rotting straw was stuffed around the place in nooks and crannies [as insulation from the cold]. Underfoot there squished, "a sort of black water, greenish, and fetid." Just the place for a baby, in other words. (p. 179)

For a period lasting up to 2 years, the infant would be left with a wet nurse out of the sight and care of its parents. The mortality rate, as one might expect, was high. Wet-nursed infants were at least twice as likely to die as infants who remained home. In some parts of France, mortality rates of wet-nursed infants approached 90% (Shorter, 1977).

And yet, the wet-nursed infant might be considered better off than the infant abandoned on a garbage heap or in street gutter to perish. This last example of gross indifference can again be explained by the poverty and famine that periodically swept across Europe (Murstein, 1974).

How many of the approximately 33,000 children abandoned in France each year as late as the mid-19th century were abandoned for reasons of love, indifference, or resentment cannot be determined. Poverty, pestilence, famine, and war certainly separated parents from children who, if times and conditions had been different, would have remained with them. Still, these conditions alone do not adequately account for the treatment many young children received at the hands of their parents. Clearly, young children held little value in premodern times.

Women in Past Times

In the hierarchy of the premodern couple, a woman occupied a position slightly above that of a child but far beneath that of a man.

A woman was prized but, more often than not, prized less than a horse.[3] She had no formal recognition by society. She could not hold property, bring matters to court for settlement, or decide whom to marry. Until Victorian times, generally speaking, for the lower and middle classes, a woman's position in the couple relationship is well summed up by the following observation:

> The wives are the first servants in the household: they plow the soil, care for the house, and eat after their husbands, who address them only in harsh, curt tones, even with a sort of contempt. If the horse and the wife fall sick at the same time, the . . . [husband] rushes to the blacksmith to care for the animal and leaves the task of healing his wife to nature. (Hugo, 1835, cited in Shorter, 1977, p. 56)

We believe there were four factors that created this intolerable set of circumstances. The first is the nature of the marriage contract. In premodern times, regardless of social class, men and women had little to do with the establishment of their own marriages. The decision was made by the couple's fathers and was based on property and class. The notion that affection might enter into the arrangement was never considered. Love was an unaffordable luxury for individuals engaged in a struggle of survival (Murstein, 1974; Shorter, 1977; Stone, 1977).

Further restricting women's freedom was Christianity's subjection of women to men. Man was made in the image of God, woman was made from Adam. Milton (1667/1962, p. 93) captures this imbalance in *Paradise Lost* when he compares Adam's and Eve's relationships to God. Adam's relationship is direct; Eve's is mediated through Adam: "Hee for God only, shee for God in him." It is Eve who, misled by Satan, tempts Adam with the fruit of the tree of knowledge of good and evil and initiates their banishment from Eden. Church teachings by scholars like Augustine created an image of women as "lecherous temptresses" possessing "feeble intellects" who could be inhabited by spirits and demons (Murstein, 1974). From that point of view, these contemptible individuals deserved treatment inferior to that given a barn animal, and they needed to be broken, as Katherine was in *The Taming of the Shrew*, of any idea of equality. A woman's role was to bow to her husband as "thy lord, thy life, thy keeper, thy head, thy sovereign" (Shakespeare, 1969, p. 113).

Next, women, until very recently in this century, have been the victims of their own bodies. Physical sex differences exposed women to a host of diseases, injuries, and other dangers that males could escape. For example, men could escape the responsibility of a sexual liaison that produced a child.

Women suffered the pains, hazards, and effects of childbirth and suffered through the medical treatments afforded them at that time. For example (and bear with us for this illustration is a bit complicated), remember the common practice of swaddling infants? One outcome of wrapping these infants like mummies was to deprive them of the sun. Deprived of sunlight, a primary source of vitamin D in past times, children ran a high risk of developing a disease called rickets, one outcome of which was the development of a small pelvic structure. For women, who would conceive, bear, and be in delivery with a child, this outcome often proved fatal.

Imagine a time before 1867 when Joseph Lister introduced the then radical idea that an individual should wash his or her hands before touching the sick. Imagine a time when the afterbirth (the placenta) was ripped from a mother's insides if it did not slough off quickly enough following birth. Imagine a time when caesarean deliveries were performed only on dead women.

Now picture a woman in the birthing process who has suffered rickets as a child. Her pelvic structure is too small to permit the passage of an infant—her infant. Days have gone by and the midwife pushing and pulling, yanking and shoving, has been decidedly unsuccessful in dislodging the infant. It would be at this point and after consultation with the village womenfolk that the midwife would reach into her satchel and remove a curved hook, most often made of iron. This hook would be used to extract the infant. If the head were too large for a pelvis that was too small, the hook would be used to puncture the skull, "through the eye or the mouth, in order to haul it out. If the child presented buttocks first, the hooks would go into its back or ribcage" (Shorter, 1982, p. 87). This action of puncturing an infant's skull to facilitate delivery (needless to say killing the infant) was called a craniotomy. The death of the mother after a craniotomy was not an infrequent occurrence.

Further, from the magic of her menstrual blood to her milk, she was a mysterious creature whom man both desired and feared. In the mythology that rose about her, she could be the cause of war (Helen of Troy), the origin of the world's plagues (Pandora's box), and responsible for man's fall from God's grace (Eve). Clearly, this was a dangerous creature, threatening man's survival.

A final factor, mentioned earlier, concerns beliefs about vital body fluids. Man's vital fluids were contained, in part, in his semen. Until early in the 20th century he was warned to conserve those precious fluids lest he experience a plague of misfortune. Tempting him to spill his seed and waste his health was the lecherous creature, woman—yet another reason for him to resent her.

Is this to say that all female-male relationships were forged in hell? No, many examples of caring relationships in premodern times can be observed. However, even Cotton Mather's love for his wife was within the context of a time that placed very little value on the female.

Men in Past Times

"Thy husband is thy lord, thy life, thy keeper, thy head, thy sovereign" (Shakespeare, 1969, p. 133). Assuming that a male survived childhood, he was assured of sitting atop the hierarchy of the couple relationship. Though not able to arrange his own marriage (this was his father's task), he was assured of the dowry that his wife would bring to their marriage. Should she be unpleasing to the eye, he could seek outside female companionship. She had no recourse to such behavior. Rather, he viewed her as a baby machine with little other value (Murstein, 1974; Shorter, 1977, 1982; Stone, 1977).

Of course, exceptions existed in which the ruler of the household did show appreciation, concern, and care for other members of the household. Nevertheless, he did so always within the context of his recognized position as the leader and ruler of the relationship.

Couple Relationships in Past Times

Given the roles that women and men fulfilled in premodern times, it is not surprising that, by modern standards, these relationships left much to be desired. Children were treated with, at best, indifference. Women held a position nearly equivalent to a slave's, and men ruled the roost. Intimacy and romanticism were given short shift.

In addition, these relationships are described by social historians as more community-centered than couple-centered. Shorter (1977) provides one example of community control over behavior. For example, townsfolk might hold demonstrations around a couple's cottage to bring public attention to the man's failure to control his wife. The hooting and hollering and burning of straw figures in effigy were attempts to maintain community standards of approved behavior (norms). In Charles Dickens's novel *Great Expectations* (1861/1948), Joe Gargery, the blacksmith, shares such an experience with his young ward, Pip. Joe's mother has broken community norms by leaving her abusive, drunken husband:

> "My father, Pip, he were given to drink, and when he were overtook with drink, he hammered away at my mother most onmerciful. It were a'most the only hammering he did, indeed, 'xcepting at myself. And he hammered at me with a wigour only to be equalled by the wigour with which he didn't hammer at his anwil.—You're a-listening and understanding, Pip?"
>
> "Yes, Joe."
>
> " 'Consequence, my mother and me we ran away from my father several times; and then my mother she'd go out to work, and she'd say, 'Joe,' she'd say, 'now, please God, you shall have some schooling, child,' and she'd put me to school. But my father were that good in his hart that he couldn't abear to be without us. So, he'd come with a most tremenjous crowd and make such a row at the doors of the houses where we was, that they used to be obligated to have no more to do with us and to give us up to him. And then he took us home and hammered us. Which, you see, Pip," said Joe, pausing in his meditative raking of the fire, and looking at me, "were a drawback on my learning." (Dickens, 1861/1948, pp. 45-46)

Reconsider this fictional passage against the points made in the preceding sections. Dickens describes the man as the unquestioned ruler of his family in the eyes of the "crowd." Unlike other fictional women in Dickens's stories, who were known for their abuse of children, Mrs. Gargery flees from her abusive husband with her son only to find neighbors joining with her husband in the condemnation of her action.[4] Community pressure in support of the husband's control over the family forces her return to this abusive relationship where she and young Joe are again battered. Notice that community concern is not focused on the welfare of either the mother or her child. Rather, the focus of attention is on maintaining the power structure that saw the wife and son as the property of an alcoholic, abusive father.

The Transition to Modern Families

Three gradual changes from the 1700s forward altered the behavior of the sexes toward each other. The first was a movement away from family arranged to individually arranged marriages. As couples acquired more decision-making power, the influence of property and lineage declined and that of intimacy, romance, and love rose. In this new couple arrangement, the value of a woman increased beyond that of a servant or a slave, and the occasional practice of buying and selling wives ceased.[5]

The next change involved the value attached to children. Maternal indifference and resentment of the infant was replaced by recognition. Do not confuse this recognition, however, with the acquisition of full human status. The child was still the property of its parents and still at tremendous risk of cruelty. Indeed, it would not be until the late 1800s in the United States that child welfare would begin to emerge as a concern.

For example, in 1874, after being told that a child, Mary Ellen, was being horribly mistreated, a mission worker appealed to the New York City Society for the Prevention of Cruelty to Animals (SPCA) to intercede on the child's behalf. The mission worker had tried to get the police and other institutions to intervene but had been unsuccessful in her attempts. To the credit of the SPCA, it went to court to protect the child on the grounds that Mary Ellen was an animal and thus was deserving of the protections horses and other beasts of burden had from maltreatment. The SPCA won their suit. Mary Ellen was removed by authorities from this situation and placed in a home for delinquent girls! Is it not ironic that the birth of the child protective services movement in the United States was occasioned by its first of many inept decisions (Levine & Levine, 1992).[6]

Interestingly, 10 years later, Mark Twain (1884/1962), living in Connecticut and upper New York State, publishes *Huckleberry Finn*.[7] Huck is a remarkable young man who despite a cruel drunken father and an initially rejecting community has not lost his innate goodness. As that goodness emerges and Huck starts to "civilize," his alcoholic father (Pap) emerges from obscurity to claim Huck so as to access Huck's newfound wealth. In a custody hearing, the common law principle that the child is the property of the parent asserts itself:

> The judge and the widow went to the law to get the court to take me away from him and to let one of them be my guardian; but it was a new judge that had just come, and he didn't know the old man; so he said courts mustn't interfere and separate families if they could help it; he said he druther not take a child away from its father. . . . That pleased the old man till he couldn't rest. He said he'd cowhide me till I was black and blue if I didn't raise some money for him. I borrowed three dollars . . . and pap took it and got drunk and went a-blowing . . . till most midnight; then they jailed him. . . . But he said he was satisfied; said he was the boss of his son, and he'd make it warm for him. (Twain, 1884/1962, p. 42)

It would not be until the 1960s that child protective services would reemerge in reaction to a paper by Kempe and his colleagues (Kempe, Silverman, Steele, Droegemuller, & Silver, 1962) titled, "The Battered Child Syndrome." It would be during this same decade that in the United States young people would be extended for the first time the protection offered by the Bill of Rights and the Constitution.[8]

The final change propelled by the industrial revolution was a movement away from an identification with the community to a closer, more intimate bonding with each other. Community involvement and control over women and men weakened, to be replaced with an image of the couple in the context of the family as a "haven in a heartless world" (Lasch, 1977). This gave rise to the "Cult of Domesticity" forever immortalized in Currier and Ives' prints of domestic life, Norman Rockwell's cover art for *The Saturday Evening Post,* and in those 1950s television shows like *Father Knows Best* and *The Donna Reed Show.*

While the Cult of Domesticity spoke of chocolate cookies and warm bread baking in the oven, for many children ovens remained cool to the touch while the smell of stale beer filled the air. In *Sweet Mystery: A Book of Remembering,* Judith Paterson (1996), through a child's eyes, chronicles the decline of her parents into alcoholism. The reader twinges in pain when she recalls her mother

> totter[ing] toward the house in her bathing suit, a beer in one hand, a cigarette in the other, almost too wobbly to walk. . . . I run toward my mother. She looks strange. Her eyes shrink to slits and her face goes murderous at the sight of me.
>
> "What are you doing out here, Judy?" she asks, stressing my name like a dirty word.
>
> "I want to swim."
>
> "Get back in the house where you belong."
>
> I stand in memory, a small child wearing only underpants waiting to be taken in her mother's arms. A woman stands before me, slinging her head from side to side like a colt in a burning barn. . . . I want my parents to stop turning into monsters. (Paterson, 1996, pp. 107-108)

Like many children, Paterson wonders how she has contributed to her parents' alcoholism. Like many children, she reaches out to a God who has apparently lost interest in his blemished enterprise.

> I learned how to pray, sitting in an alcove before a dark window . . . looking into the street and saying to myself, "God, bring my father back. Bring him back, and I will always be good and never wish for another thing."
>
> Stop my heart from pounding in my chest. Stop my fear. Stop my loneliness. Stop Momma's drinking. Stop my father from leaving. Stop our family from being the way it is. (Paterson, 1996, pp. 167-168)

While the Cult of Domesticity spoke of fathers like Atticus Finch in Harper Lee's hauntingly beautiful novel *To Kill a Mockingbird* (1960), it generally hid from view fathers like Robert Ewell. Robert Ewell is a racist subsistence farmer who is both a coward and a drunkard. His treatment of his daughter Mayella is the cause for her troubled behavior. In the courtroom passage of that book, Tom Robinson, a black man accused of molesting Mayella, is questioned by Atticus on the circumstances leading to his being inside the Ewell home. In the passage that follows, we believe that more than drunken, inappropriate parenting has occurred. We believe Robert Ewell has sexually molested Mayella:

[On the stand Tom Robinson is asked what Mayella Ewell after hugging him did next] "She reached up an' kissed me 'side of the face. She says she never kissed a grown man before an' she might as well kiss a nigger. She says what her papa do to her don't count. She says, 'Kiss me back, nigger.' " (Lee, 1960, p. 194)

What powerful language: "What her papa do to her don't count." If we are correct in our interpretation of this passage, we are witnessing the disintegration of a character. It matters not that she does not know Tom Robinson other than as a friendly neighbor. A warm body offers a moment of sanctuary but no protection from the trauma she has experienced.

Contemplate the thought of a warm body that provides a moment of feeling. There is no commitment, only an exhausted emptiness that remains after the body expends its sexual heat. In *Long Day's Journey Into Night*, Eugene O'Neill (1955/1989) writes of Jamie Tyrone's doomed attempt to find a moment of sanctuary in liquor and prostitutes. Jamie is no child nor is any other character in this painful autobiographical portrait of O'Neill's life, as the inscription to his wife reflects on his boyhood:

Dearest: I give you the original script of this play of old sorrow, written in tears and blood. . . . [I give this play to you] as a tribute to your love and tenderness which gave me the faith in love that enabled me to face my dead at last and write this play—write it with deep pity and understanding and forgiveness for all the four haunted Tyrones. (O'Neill, 1955/1989)

This powerful play chronicles a single day emblematic of the life of the Tyrone family. In the agonizing passage from morning to night, alcohol numbs the males to their anguish and serves as the disinhibiter necessary to reveal the personality flaws of each character. It exposes the elder James Tyrone's cheapness—his disrespect—for all save himself. It robs Edmund, as does consumption, of the will to write or to live. It numbs Jamie from thoughts that he is responsible for killing a younger brother whom he exposed to the measles. As we see in the next passage, Jamie, speaking to Edmund, carries the emotional pockmarks of his family as he reels toward destruction, convinced that he can touch nothing, be involved with no one, nor can he act without harm resulting:

But don't get the wrong idea, Kid. I love you more than hate you . . . But you'd better be on your guard. Because I'll do my damnedest to make you fail. Can't help it. I hate myself. Got to take revenge. (O'Neill, 1955/1989, p. 166)

Then, of course, there is Mary, wife to James, mother of Edmund and Jamie and the dead infant, Eugene. Mary who after the birth of Edmund was treated by a quack doctor and under his charge transformed into a morphine addict. Mary is like the fog that drapes their New London cottage: present and blurring the landscape, influencing the behavior all around her yet drifting into fancies, fragile and delicate but blemished and spoiled like all the Tyrones.

From the fictional characters of Huckleberry Finn, Joe Gargery, and Mayella Ewell to the all-too-real pain of Judith Paterson and Eugene O'Neill, we witness the hurt that alcohol and other drugs inflicts on children. Are drugs solely responsible for the pain that twists and distorts the lives of these fictional and nonfictional characters? No, clearly there are other imperfections to be found in these parents and in a society that established the rules of behavior that enabled men, women, and children to interact in this manner. In these fictional, real, and semi-fictional stories, alcohol and other drugs loosen the slim veneer of restraint, enabling cruelty to occur.

We ask you to remember these images of children and gender as you read this volume. Use the suffering that these characters felt to discover ways to link the fields of substance abuse and child welfare. Join us as we try to find routes to diminishing the number of children sitting alone in some alcove praying for intervention.

Notes

1. This statement is taken from Twain's (1884/1962, p. 47) *Huckleberry Finn*.

2. Assuming the woman did not die in childbirth, which was a common occurrence, horrific death rates resulted from "milk fever." The belief was that the production of milk in some women led to high fever, infection, and death. The reality was that septic conditions around the new mother and invasive after-birth medical practices were the culprits.

3. "The notion that a man's wife is PROPERTY, in the sense in which a horse is his property (descended to us rather through the Roman law than the customs of

our Teuton ancestors), is the fatal root of incalculable evil and misery" (Cobbe, 1878/1996, p. 293).

4. For an example of one of Dickens's meaner women, one need look no further than Pip's sister in *Great Expectations,* who raises him "by hand" and continues the childhood abuse of Joe Gargery in their marriage.

5. Tannahill (1980) reports the story of a Scotsman purchasing another man's wife from him for twopence a pound. See Thomas Hardy's (1886/1966) *The Life and Death of the Mayor of Casterbridge* for a description of wife-selling.

6. This incredible story does have a positive ending. The mission worker, Mrs. Wheeler, did not abandon Mary Ellen. She returned to court and received custody of the child, who grew to womanhood, married, and had two children (Lazoritz, 1990).

7. The authors are not aware of whether Twain was influenced by the Mary Ellen case, but the similarities between the two give cause to wonder, considering the publicity given the case and Twain's residence.

8. The Gault decision, which extended these rights to young people, was a remarkable case. Francis Gault at age 14 was accused of making an obscene phone call with a friend. Without a trial, in the sense we understand it today, he was sentenced to a reformatory until he turned 21. A partial transcript of the Supreme Court ruling can be found in Adams, Gullotta, and Markstrom-Adams (1994).

References

Adams, G. R., Gullotta, T. P., & Markstrom-Adams, C. (1994). *Adolescent life experiences* (3rd ed.). Pacific Grove, CA: Brooks/Cole.

Aries, P. (1962). *Centuries of childhood.* New York: Knopf.

Bremner, R. H. (1970). *Children and youth in America: Vol. 1. 1600-1865.* Cambridge, MA: Harvard University Press.

Cobbe, F. P. (1996). Wife-torture in England. In A. Broomfield & S. Mitchell (Eds.), *Prose by Victorian women: An anthology.* New York: Garland. (Original work by Cobbe published 1878)

deMause, L. (1988). *The history of childhood.* New York: Peter Bedrick Books.

Dickens, C. (1948). *Great expectations.* New York: Holt, Rinehart & Winston. (Original work published 1861)

Dickens, C. (1985). *Oliver Twist.* New York: Penguin. (Original work published 1837)

Hardy, T. (1966). *The life and death of the Mayor of Casterbridge.* New York: St. Martin's. (Original work published 1886)

Hunt, D. (1970). *Parents and children in history: The psychology of family life in early modern France.* New York: Basic Books.

Kempe, C. H., Silverman, F. H., Steele, B. F., Droegemuller, W., & Silver, H. K. (1962). The battered child syndrome. *Journal of the American Medical Association, 181,* 17-24.

Lasch, C. (1977). *Haven in a heartless world.* New York: Basic Books.

Lazoritz, S. (1990). Whatever happened to Mary Ellen? *Child Abuse & Neglect, 14,* 143-149.

Lee, H. (1960). *To kill a mockingbird.* New York: Warner.

Levine, M., & Levine, A. (1992). *Helping children: A social history.* New York: Oxford University Press.

McLaughlin, T. (1971). *Dirt: A social history as seen through the uses and abuses of dirt.* New York: Stein & Day.

Milton, J. (1962). *Paradise lost.* New York: Macmillan. (Original work published 1667)

Murstein, B. I. (1974). *Love, sex, and marriage through the ages.* New York: Springer.

O'Neill, E. (1989). *Long day's journey into night.* New Haven, CT: Yale University Press. (Original work published 1955)

Paterson, J. H. (1996). *Sweet mystery: A book of remembering.* New York: Farrar, Straus, & Giroux.

Shakespeare, W. (1969). *William Shakespeare: The complete works.* Baltimore, MD: Penguin.

Shorter, E. (1977). *The making of the modern family.* New York: Basic Books.

Shorter, E. (1982). *A history of women's bodies.* New York: Basic Books.

Stone, L. (1977). *The family, sex, and marriage in England, 1500-1800.* New York: Harper & Row.

Tannahill, R. (1980). *Sex in history.* New York: Stein & Day.

Twain, M. (1962). *The adventures of Huckleberry Finn.* San Francisco: Chandler. (Original work published 1884)

Yalom, M. (1997). *A history of the breast.* New York: Knopf.

CHAPTER 2

Building Bridges for Children: Addressing the Consequences of Exposure to Drugs and to the Child Welfare System

BRENDA JONES HARDEN

The metaphor in the subtitle of this volume evokes a compelling image of contemporary children in the child welfare system. These children must navigate the perilous waters of prenatal and postnatal substance exposure, as well as a child welfare system ill-equipped to handle the sheer size and the complexity of their population. They are children whose developmental context extends beyond the "double jeopardy" of exposure to drugs and poverty (Parker, Greer, & Zuckerman, 1988) to a third environmental risk—exposure to the child welfare system. The challenge, for those charged with these children's care, is to construct sturdy bridges over the hazardous waters they encounter, to ensure their safe passage into adulthood.

The numbers of American children exposed to substances prenatally and postnatally are staggering. Prevailing estimates suggest that up to 20% of newborns are affected by prenatal substance exposure and that 6 million children are being reared by substance using parents (U.S. Department of Health and Human Services,

AUTHOR'S NOTE: The author would like to thank the Smith-Richardson Foundation for financial support and Dr. Edward Zigler for intellectual support during the completion of her dissertation, which formed the basis of this chapter.

1992). Recent surveys of American households (U.S. Department of Health and Human Services [DHHS], 1994, 1995) revealed that 11.3% of parents overall, 5.5% of women who recently gave birth, and 2.3% of pregnant women reported illicit drug use.

Adults' use of legal substances affects many children as well. It is estimated that between 8% and 11% of women of childbearing age are alcoholics/problem drinkers and that 12.7% of mothers use alcohol weekly (U.S. Department of Health and Human Services, 1994). About one half of American children 5 and under experience postnatal tobacco exposure and one fourth have been prenatally exposed (Overpeck & Moss, 1991) (see Feig, Chapter 3, this volume, for further data on parental substance use).

The overarching goal of this chapter is to consider the unique needs of drug exposed children in the child welfare system, and the interventions that facilitate their optimum development. The first section delineates the developmental outcomes for children of prenatal and postnatal substance exposure. The second section describes the environments in which these children are reared, whether in or out of state custody. The chapter culminates with an exploration of strategies to address the needs of these children and their caregivers.

The Developmental Consequences of Drug Exposure

The transactional model, which accentuates the interaction between biology and environment, provides a framework for understanding the developmental sequelae of prenatal drug exposure (Sameroff & Fiese, 1990). The synergistic influences of perinatal events and the postnatal caretaking context are considered within a "continuum of caretaking casualty," highlighting the environmental contribution to child outcome. Studies of premature children have documented that there are multiple determinants of the developmental sequelae observed, including degree of biological insult and familial and socioeconomic factors (Sameroff, 1986). In research on low birth weight infants (Escalona, 1982), it has been found that biologically vulnerable infants are more affected by environmental stressors than are normal infants.

Variability in developmental outcome for drug exposed children has also been attributed to this confluence of multiple biological and environmental factors (e.g., Myers, Olson, & Kaltenbach, 1992). Prenatal drug exposure is a complex phenomenon that must be understood within an ecological context, including the uterine, familial, social, and economic environments in which the fetus, infant, and child develop (Weston, Ivins, Zuckerman, Jones, & Lopez, 1989).

The empirical literature on prenatal substance exposure reflects the tenor of the times. Current research focuses on the developmental outcomes of prenatal cocaine exposure, whereas research of over a decade ago addressed exposure to opiates. Methodological concerns continue to be raised about substance exposure studies, such as biased definitions of study populations, unreliable techniques for user identification, confounding effects of extent and duration of prenatal drug exposure, the polydrug use of substance users, and the narrow selection of developmental factors to be studied (cf. Mayes, Granger, Bornstein, & Zuckerman, 1992). Due to the difficulty of conducting longitudinal research with drug-involved populations, most studies of children have been limited to infancy and early childhood. In addition, there is a paucity of data concerning the effects of *paternal* substance use on children, despite evidence that males consistently have higher rates than females (U.S. Department of Health and Human Services, 1994).

Moreover, disentangling the biological and environmental effects of prenatal drug exposure is considered one of the major methodological challenges in this work (Mayes et al., 1992). For example, developmental outcome in drug exposed children has been found to be consistent with that of the children in the general impoverished population who have not been prenatally exposed to substances (cf. Chasnoff, Griffith, Freier, & Murray, 1992; Powell, 1991). Much of the variability found in outcome of drug exposed children is attributed to environmental factors (Parker et al., 1988). The distinction between immediate perinatal effects and long-term effects, perhaps due to the plasticity of the young brain, is another issue that emerges in this research.

Despite these caveats, a range of biopsychosocial outcomes for children exposed to substances in utero has been documented. In the paragraphs following, a review of the literature on the effects of prenatal substance exposure on physical health, cognition, and socioemotional functioning will be offered. The substances most commonly used by illicit drug-using women of childbearing age will be addressed—tobacco (nicotine and other substances), alcohol, marijuana, cocaine, and opiates (heroin and methadone). Although each substance will be treated separately, it should be underscored that the majority of drug exposed children will have encountered multiple substances in utero (Mayes et al., 1992).

Sequelae of Tobacco Exposure

Physical Health. The physical health outcomes of in-utero nicotine exposure have been widely documented and seem mostly to occur during the neonatal period. Cigarette smoking during pregnancy is associated with low birth weight, intrauterine growth retardation, low Apgar scores, and prematurity (Wen et al., 1990). Decreased height and weight persist in children prenatally exposed to nicotine (Coles, 1993; Fried, Watkinson, & Gray, 1992). There is also evidence of an association between prenatal and postnatal maternal cigarette smoking and the development of sudden infant death syndrome (SIDS) (Behnke & Eyler, 1993; Bergman & Weisner, 1976).

Other studies have reported respiratory difficulties during childhood due to prenatal and postnatal exposure to cigarette smoke (Behnke & Eyler, 1993). Studies investigating the link between asthma and tobacco exposure have suggested that prenatal exposure may affect airway responsiveness (Samet, Lewit, & Warner, 1994). Lower respiratory tract illness (e.g., bronchitis, pneumonia) have been found at higher rates in children whose parents smoke. Other physical health effects of involuntary smoking include middle ear disease, compromised pulmonary function, and increased general illness (Samet et al., 1994).

Mild neurologic dysfunction and neurobehavioral effects have been documented less consistently, but include such behaviors as poor habituation, increased crying, and increased tremors/startles (Jacobson, Fein, Jacobson, Schwartz, & Dowles, 1984; Picone, Allen, Olson, & Ferris, 1982). Studies exploring the association between maternal smoking and congenital malformations have had mixed results (Zuckerman, 1988).

Cognitive Development. It has been reported, albeit inconsistently, that heavy cigarette smoking (i.e., >10 cigarettes/day) during pregnancy leads to impaired cognitive functioning in affected children (Sexton, Fox, & Hebel, 1990). Academic difficulties, such as compromised verbal, perceptual, and memory skills, have been noted as well (Fried & Watkinson, 1990).

Socioemotional Functioning. There is limited data concerning the socioemotional functioning of tobacco exposed children. Neurobehavioral outcomes that have been inconsistently documented include compromised habituation and orientation, increased crying, as well as poorer performance on head-turning and sucking tasks (Zuckerman, 1988). Attentional problems and increased activity levels have been identified as consequences of prenatal nicotine exposure (Sexton et al., 1990; Streissguth, Martin, Barr, & Sandman, 1984).

Sequelae of Alcohol Exposure

Physical Health. The impact of alcohol consumption during pregnancy on the physical development of children is well established. Intrauterine growth retardation has been found in alcohol exposed infants, due to poor maternal nutrition, the direct toxic effects of alcohol on the fetus, and alcohol's interference with fetal nutritional intake (Coles, 1993; Zuckerman & Bresnahan, 1991). Alcohol exposed children are often diagnosed with failure to thrive (weight and height below the fifth percentile). Growth retardation is often sustained throughout childhood. Neurobehavioral outcomes include irritability, poorer habituation and orientation, increased tremors, poorer arousal, disturbances of sleep, poorer motor tone and development, and diminished spontaneous movement (Streissguth & Randels, 1989).

A spectrum of specific patterns of physical sequelae exists in children chronically exposed to alcohol in utero, ranging from fetal alcohol effects (FAE) to the more severe fetal alcohol syndrome (FAS). The three primary features of FAS are pre- and postnatal growth retardation, central nervous system dysfunction, and facial dysmorphology (Coles, 1993; McCance-Katz, 1991; Rosett, 1980). Other features of FAS are intraoral deformities, vision and hearing deficits, cardiac problems, hypotonia, poor coordination, and skeletal malformations. Neurobehavioral outcomes have been documented, such as feeding difficulties, sleep irregularities, and hyperactivity (Weiner & Morse, 1988). Long-term physical effects of FAS include persistent growth retardation, poor or delayed motor development, compromised immune systems, and cardiac problems (Coles, 1993; Weiner & Morse, 1988). Contrastingly, children with FAE usually do not have all three types of physical health impairment, and often do not display these difficulties throughout childhood.

Cognitive Development. The cognitive effects of alcohol consumption during pregnancy on children vary with the physical health outcomes found in affected children (i.e., more severe physical impairments are associated with more severe cognitive impairments). Children with FAS display severe cognitive impairments. Mild to moderate mental retardation is commonly found in these children, with accompanying language and perceptual difficulties (Rosett & Weiner, 1984; Streissguth et al., 1984). Children without the full-blown syndrome also have lower intelligence, language, and academic achievement scores on standardized tests. Factors that impede academic functioning have also been noted with these children, including difficulties in reasoning, problem solving, memory, and auditory and visual-motor processing (Coles, 1993; Streissguth & Randels, 1989).

Socioemotional Functioning. Emotional and behavior problems identified in alcohol exposed children include hyperactivity, distractibility, restlessness, lack of persistence, and impulsivity (Streissguth, 1986). Oppositionality, aggression, poor peer relationships, and other externalizing disorders have been reported in some studies (e.g., Earls, Reich, Jung, & Cloninger, 1988; Fitzgerald, Kaltenbach, & Finnegan, 1990). Other research has noted such outcomes as emotional reactivity, irritability, overdependence, and rigidity (Coles, 1993). Internalizing disorders (e.g., depression, anxiety) have also been reported at higher rates in children of alcoholics (Bennett, Wolin, & Reiss, 1988).

There is evidence that alcohol exposure during early childhood may result in the child's later alcohol use and other at-risk behaviors (e.g., delinquency). One study found that adolescents were four times more likely to become alcoholics if they had an alcoholic parent (Schuckit & Sweeney, 1987). Clearly, findings such as these must be considered within the context of the individual and interactional contribution of genetics and environment.

Sequelae of Marijuana Exposure

Physical Health. The literature on the effects of prenatal marijuana exposure is limited and inconsistent. There is some evidence that birth weight, length, and head circumference are compromised as a result of heavy marijuana use during pregnancy (Coles & Platzman, 1993; Zuckerman, 1988). Albeit inconsistently, neurobehavioral outcomes have been found, such as increased tremors; poorer habituation to visual stimuli; and shorter, higher pitched cries (Fried, 1980). Increased motility and decreased quiet sleep have also been observed. An association between prenatal marijuana use and later development of childhood leukemia has been suggested (Odom, Lampkin, Tannuous, Buckley, & Hammond, 1990; Robison et al., 1989).

Cognitive Development. The paucity and inconsistency of empirical documentation regarding prenatal marijuana exposure make it difficult to arrive at any conclusions about its effects on children's cognition. There is some indication that heavy marijuana use in pregnancy may lead to poorer memory, perceptual, and verbal abilities in children (Fried & Watkinson, 1990).

Socioemotional Functioning. Again, the dearth of empirical literature on prenatal marijuana exposure limits what conclusions can be drawn about its effects on the socioemotional functioning of children. Attentional difficulty is the only socioemotional factor that has been identified in children with marijuana exposure in utero (Fried et al., 1992).

Sequelae of Cocaine Exposure

Physical Health. Consistently reported physical health sequelae for prenatally cocaine exposed infants are low birth weight due to prematurity and/or maternal malnutrition, intrauterine growth retardation, and microcephaly (Bresnahan, Brooks, & Zuckerman, 1991; Myers et al., 1992; Neuspiel & Hamel, 1991). The evidence is inconclusive regarding other physiologic findings such as respiratory difficulties (Chasnoff, Griffith, MacGregor, Dirkes, & Burns, 1989), infections (Lindenberg, Alexander, Gendrop, Nencioloi, & Williams, 1991), and neurologic effects (Mayes, 1994; Neuspiel & Hamel, 1991).

Some studies have reported neurobehavioral abnormalities, including increased tremulousness, irritability, hypersensitivity, movement disorders, increased stiffness of tone, abnormal sleep/wake cycles, state disorganization, fine motor deficits, impaired orientation, and abnormal cry characteristics (Chasnoff et al., 1989; Lester & Tronick, 1994; Oro & Dixon, 1987; Van Baar, Fleury, Soepatmi, Ultee, & Wesselman, 1989).

Cognitive Development. Most research has documented that cocaine exposed children exhibit intellectual skills similar to nonexposed children (Azuma & Chasnoff, 1993; Chasnoff et al., 1992). A fairly consistent finding is that cocaine exposed children have low-average to average intellectual functioning (Freier, Griffith, & Chasnoff, 1991; Griffith, Zauma, & Chasnoff, 1994; Howard, Beckwith, Rodning, & Kropenske, 1989). One study documented that during the preschool years, cocaine exposed children perform within the borderline range of intelligence with scores significantly lower than their nonexposed counterparts (Beckwith et al., 1994).

More domain-specific cognitive effects have been reported among cocaine exposed children, particularly language delays (Freier et al., 1991; Griffith et al., 1994; Howard et al., 1989). Preliminary research has suggested the existence of perceptual and analytical deficits in cocaine exposed children, such as classification and categorization difficulties (Ahl, 1993; Rodning, Beckwith, & Howard, 1989b).

Socioemotional Functioning. There is emerging consensus that the more salient deficits associated with these children may fall in the behavioral domain (Lester & Tronick, 1994). Thus, in recent years, studies of cocaine effects on child behavior have increased. Affective dysregulation has been documented in several studies. Research on emotionality and temperament suggest that mothers and observers rate cocaine exposed children as having decreased positive and negative reactivity and fewer affective displays (Alessandri, Sullivan, Imaizumi, & Lewis, 1993). Cocaine exposed infants exhibit difficulties with state regulation and joint attention (Beeghly & Tronick, 1994; Brooks, Zuckerman, Bamforth, Cole, & Kaplan-Sanoff, 1994). The poorly modulated cry of cocaine exposed infants has also been documented (Lester et al., 1991). These early signs of dysregulation have been postulated to derive directly from the neurological effects of prenatal cocaine exposure (Lester & Tronick, 1994; Rodning et al., 1989b).

In older children, regulatory difficulties have been identified in the areas of irritability, attention deficits, hyperactivity, distractibility, and frustration (Azuma & Chasnoff, 1993; Barth, 1991; Freier et al., 1991; Powell, 1991). Aggression and impulsivity have emerged as salient behavioral problems (Griffith et al., 1994). Elevations in internalizing behaviors have been found with preschool-aged cocaine exposed children, including anxiety, depression, and withdrawn behaviors (Hawley & Disney, 1992). Potential evidence regarding the poor regulatory capacity of cocaine exposed children is also obtained through studies of their play behavior, which is characterized by less complexity, increased inattentiveness, less purposefulness, and precipitous shifts (Beeghly, Brilliant, Cabral, Tronick, & Frank, 1996; Rodning, Beckwith, & Howard, 1989a).

Sequelae of Opiate Exposure

Physical Health. The physiologic impact of opiate exposure seems to be limited to the period of early infancy. Unlike other substances, opiate use during pregnancy results in a salient experience of physiologic withdrawal from the substance for the neonate. Withdrawal experiences vary in intensity, delay to onset, and duration (Finnegan, 1988). Principal physiologic characteristics of neonatal abstinence syndrome (i.e., withdrawal) are gastrointestinal difficulties, respiratory distress, sleeping irregularities, poor feeding, tremors, sweating, hypertonicity, high-pitched crying, and abrasion of the extremities (Finnegan, 1988; Kaltenbach, 1994).

As with infants exposed to other substances, opiate exposed neonates display lower birth weights, heights, head circumference, and Apgar scores (Kaltenbach & Finnegan, 1989). Some studies have also reported a higher incidence of sudden infant death syndrome (Zuckerman & Bresnahan, 1991). Neurobehavioral symptoms include irritability, tremulousness, jitteriness, increased movement, difficulty alerting, restlessness, poor sleep patterns, and difficulty habituating to light (Kaltenbach & Finnegan, 1989).

Cognitive Development. Opiate exposed infants appear to function in the normal range of intelligence until approximately the age of 2 (Kaltenbach, 1994). There is evidence that older opiate exposed children score lower on developmental and intelligence tests (Rosen & Johnson, 1982). One study identified perceptual, quantitative, memory, auditory, and visual deficits in children exposed to heroin in utero (Wilson, McCreary, Kean, & Baxter, 1979). Compromised performance on fine and gross motor tests also has been found in this population of children (Strauss, Lesson-Firestone, Chavez, & Stryker, 1979). It should be noted that these findings have not been consistently reported in the literature. The variability found in outcome has been attributable to dosage and to environmental influence such as whether the mother was maintained on methadone or was an active heroin user (i.e., devoid of the support of a drug program) (Kaltenbach, 1994).

Socioemotional Functioning. Socioemotional outcomes of opiate exposure have not been measured to the same extent as cognitive outcomes. Behavioral outcomes such as unpredictability, irritability, inattentiveness, lack of social responsiveness, and conduct problems have been observed in some studies (Kaltenbach & Finnegan, 1988; Wilson, 1989).

Summary

There is great variability in the developmental sequelae of children exposed to substances in utero. Current research does point to some specific effects of substance exposure on the developing child. The most consistent finding across substances is low birth weight due to prematurity, maternal malnutrition, and other factors. Acute neurobehavioral sequelae are observed in the neonatal period for all substances, but tend to wane after early infancy. Two substances have unique outcomes that appear during the neonatal period. Opiate exposure results in a set of physiologic withdrawal symptoms termed neonatal abstinence syndrome. Severe alcohol exposure produces a pattern of physiologic and cognitive effects characterized as fetal alcohol syndrome.

As children become older and the environment has a greater impact on their functioning, it is difficult to separate which developmental outcomes result from prenatal substance exposure and which from a challenging postnatal environment. Developmental deficits have been found among children after infancy, including cognitive and learning impairments, attentional problems, and behavioral difficulties such as hyperactivity and impulsivity. The inconsistency of these findings and the lack of specificity of the effects (i.e., specific findings not associated with specific drug) suggest that factors other than prenatal substance exposure are more predictive of developmental outcome for older children, such as the caregiving environment.

Environmental Context and Drug Exposed Children

An ecological approach (Bronfenbrenner, 1979), which considers the multiple environmental systems that impinge upon the developing child, is instructive in the quest for knowledge about the effects of prenatal drug exposure. The transactional model suggests that although perinatal events have the largest impact during infancy, the environmental effects are more prominent in later childhood (Sameroff & Fiese, 1990). Clearly, the postnatal environments experienced by drug exposed children have a major influence on the children's outcomes. Although the evidence on prenatal drug exposure and the caretaking environment is limited, it is possible to derive a profile of the caretaking experiences of these children. Virtually all of the studies addressing this issue focus on the mother as caregiver, highlighting a clear need for more research on the role of the father in the drug involved family. There is some evidence citing the contribution of the alcoholic father to adverse outcomes in his children, such as externalizing behaviors. The limited research on paternal drug use suggests that it has less influence on child outcome than maternal drug use (Brook, Tseng, & Cohen, 1996; Kandel, 1990; Tubman, 1993).

Parental Functioning

Drug exposure in the postnatal environment is unquestionably damaging to the developing child. It is well documented that substance abuse is transmitted intergenerationally (cf. Luthar, Merikangas, & Rounsaville, 1993). This section, however, primarily addresses other psychosocial issues that arise from postnatal substance exposure. Parental drug use has implications for the nature of the parent-child dyad and ultimately for child development. There are bidirectional contributions to the negative interaction between the drug using mother and her child. The characteristics of the child (e.g., temperament, neurologic effects of drug exposure) can serve to exacerbate the mother's difficulty in caring for the child (Howard & Kropenske, 1991; Kaltenbach & Finnegan, 1989). It is suggested that the effects of drugs on neonatal behavior (which may disappear in later infancy) have implications for the developing attachment between the vulnerable mother and child.

Just as infants bring constitutional characteristics to the dyadic interaction, the mother's individual psychological characteristics greatly determine her availability to her child. The comorbidity of substance addiction and mental disorder has been widely reported (e.g., Bays, 1990; Chavkin, Paone, Friedmann, & Wilets, 1993; Luthar et al., 1993; Regier et al. 1990; Rivers, 1989), with a rate estimated to be as high as 90% (Bays, 1990). For example, depression, which may be preexisting or a residual of drug abstinence, has been observed in disproportionate rates in drug using mothers (estimates range from 50% to 80%) (Boyd, 1993; Frank et al., 1988; Woods, Eyler, Behnke, & Conlon, 1993). Depression has been documented as having a negative effect on maternal responsiveness and subsequent child growth, developmental outcome, and behavioral difficulty (Downey & Coyne, 1990; Field, 1992; Radke-Yarrow, Cummings, Kulzynski, & Chapman, 1985).

Other mental disorders found in clinical studies of drug using women include bipolar illness (Khantzian, 1985) and personality disorders (Rounsaville & Luthar, 1994; Zuckerman, Amara, & Beardslee, 1987). A fairly consistent finding in the literature is the increased incidence of anxiety among drug using women (Gawin & Kleber, 1988; Nunes, Quitkin, & Klein, 1989). Other psychological variables that have been reported to characterize drug using women include lowered self-esteem, guilt, anger, aggression, and irritability (Chavkin et al., 1993), as well as preexisting or residual attention deficit disorder (Khantzian, 1985). There is some evidence that the existence of these forms of psychopathology among drug using parents increases the likelihood that their children will exhibit similar psychopathology (Luthar et al., 1993).

Similarly, studies have documented that the drug-abusing mother's mental state, apart from her drug usage, affects her parenting capacity. For example, in a study of cocaine involved dyads, Griffith, Chasnoff, and Freier (1989) found that evidence of maternal psychopathology was correlated with child outcome, suggesting an effect of maternal emotional state on mother-child interaction and subsequent child outcome. In a study of mothers on methadone, Hans, Bernstein, and Henson (1990) found that those who had a diagnosis of antisocial personality disorder had more dysfunctional interactions with their children than those with no diagnosis of mental illness or with a diagnosis of an affective disorder.

Adverse emotional experiences in childhood, such as maltreatment and parental addiction, have been posited as an etiologic factor in adult psychopathology. Investigations of drug-abusing women have documented a high incidence of childhood sexual abuse and sexual trauma (estimates range from 30% to 75%) (cf. Boyd, 1993; Kaltenbach, 1994; Rohsenow, Corbett, & Devine, 1988; Root, 1989). Physical abuse has also been indicated in the childhood experiences of female substance users (Davis, 1990; Ladwig & Anderson, 1989; Regan, Ehrlich, & Finnegan, 1987).

Among drug-abusing women, family histories of substance addiction have been noted in a disproportionate number of cases (Boyd, 1993). For example, in one study of female crack cocaine addicts, family members introduced the drug to 21% of the population (Boyd & Mieczkowski, 1990). In addition to the impact that a childhood experience of parental substance use has on the parenting capacity of drug using mothers, it has major implications for the social supports available to them. Drug using women often have not had positive social supports at any point in their lives (Boyd & Mieczkowski, 1990; Daghestani, 1988; Davis, 1990).

The lifestyles of drug using mothers are incongruent with adequate parenting. Drug using mothers are more likely to have been exposed to violence and to have experienced negative life events (Amaro, Fried, Cabral, & Zuckerman, 1990). They exhibit maladaptive behavior patterns as a result of their addiction, such as prostitution and criminal involvement (Daghestani, 1988). Their irresponsibility and impulsivity (e.g., use of financial resources to purchase drugs instead of providing for their children's concrete needs) has also been documented (Tarter, Blackson, Martin, Loeber, & Moss, 1993; Brook, Brook, Gordon, Whiteman, & Dohen, 1990; Davis, 1990). The preoccupation with obtaining the drug leaves little time for more adaptive pursuits (Brooks et al., 1994) or for the development of supportive familial, spousal, and peer relationships (Office of Substance Abuse Prevention [OSAP], 1992). In addition, the deviant lifestyles and lack of emotional control that accompany their drug usage hinder their capacity to discipline and monitor their children appropriately (Patterson, 1982; Tarter et al., 1993).

Elevated levels of stress have been reported among parents of drug exposed children. The stress that a mother experiences deleteriously affects the mother-child dyad (Singer, Farkas, & Kleigman, 1992). Kelley (1992) compared biological and foster parents rearing cocaine exposed children, and parents of non-cocaine exposed children. She found that parents of drug exposed infants reported more child-related stress than controls, specifically in the areas of hyperactivity, distractibility, and adaptability. Biological mothers of drug exposed children had more elevated stress levels than foster mothers and comparison mothers.

Dyadic Relationships

The personal difficulties of the drug using woman seriously affect her relationship with her child. Because she often did not experience a nurturing parental figure herself, it is difficult for her to engage in positive parental behavior with her own children (Daghestani, 1988). A research group in Chicago has pointed to the early relationship dysfunction in cocaine involved dyads, citing maternal tendency toward rigidity and overcontrol, lack of pleasure, and limited emotional responsivity in their interactions with their infants (Burns, Chethick, Burns, & Clark, 1991; Chethick et al., 1990). Another study documented a noncontingent interaction between cocaine addicted mothers and their infants (Fitzgerald et al., 1990). In addition, the psychological deficits and inadequate parenting of cocaine abusers have been identified as precipitants to developmental difficulties in their children (Davis, 1990; Griffith et al., 1989).

Contrastingly, research exists that refutes the evidence that drug using parents have more problematic interactions with their children. Studies of the feeding interaction between cocaine using mothers and their children and a non drug using comparison group produced no findings of differences (Free, Russell, Mills, & Hathaway, 1990; Neuspiel & Hamel, 1991). In a descriptive study of methadone maintained mother-infant dyads, Johnson and Rosen (1990) reported no relation between intensity of maternal drug use and maternal responsiveness to her infant. However, the authors attributed this finding to a floor effect on their interaction scale. They did find an association between increased drug usage and decreased maternal ratings of "easy" infant temperament.

A higher proportion of insecure attachment has been documented among children exposed to cocaine and PCP, with most falling in the avoidant or disorganized category (Rodning et al., 1989a). These researchers also found poor interactions at home between drug using mothers and their infants, including increased restriction and punishment and less sensitivity toward the children. In a study of toddlers of drug using parents, Brook and colleagues (1996) found that maternal attachment and control behaviors, as well as personality factors, were related to toddlers' display of anxious/regressive and impulsive behaviors. An investigation of latency-aged children of drug users documented that maternal warmth, involvement, and appropriate discipline led to enhanced child adjustment (Kandel, 1990). The clinical literature has underscored the variability in the attachment experiences of drug exposed children, with differences attributed to factors such as infant temperament, extended family relationships, and community support (Davidson, 1991).

Researchers have also discussed the lack of mutual regulation in the drug involved dyad. The mother has poor affective regulation due to her drug use, while the baby may be dysregulated due to the neurological effects of prenatal drug exposure. Thus, the dyadic interaction is characterized by regulatory dysfunction, which may result in the infant's inability to accomplish developmental tasks such as state regulation and joint attention (Beeghly & Tronick, 1994; Brooks et al., 1994). In their work with cocaine using mothers and their infants, Freier and colleagues (1991) report two different patterns of maternal response. One set of mothers detached from their infants due to the infants' failure to respond. Another set presented as more intrusive and worked overly hard to get infants to respond. Kaltenbach and Finnegan (1988) found that infants experiencing neonatal abstinence syndrome as a result of prenatal opiate exposure are very difficult for their mothers to care for, due to state dysregulation, irritability, poor orientation, and inconsolableness.

Lester (1992) examined mother-infant communication in cocaine involved dyads. He reported two different cry characteristics in cocaine exposed neonates: (a) excitability syndrome (higher pitched, more variable, longer in duration); and (b) depressed (less energy, increased latency to cry onset, fewer cry bursts, more turbulence). He postulated that mothers using cocaine would find it difficult to modulate their response to these cry behaviors in order to regulate the infant. Similar abnormal cry behaviors have been found in children exposed to other substances. Drug using women have difficulty responding to their infants who exhibit such behaviors. In their work with adolescents with drug using parents, Brook and colleagues (1990) postulated that parent-child attachment is hindered in families in which parents exhibit less affectionate and child-centered behavior; the parent-child relationships are based on conflict; and the children are less likely to identify with their parents.

Decreased emotional responsiveness, availability, acceptance, and sensitivity, as well as a lack of commitment to their children, have been observed in drug using mothers (Howard & Kropenske, 1991). Similarly, decreased maternal physical involvement (Free et al., 1990) and poor quality involvement (Rodning, Beckwith, & Howard, 1991) with the child have been noted. It has also been suggested that the parenting of substance abusers is characterized by a lack of attentiveness and parental protection, which leads to the psychological isolation of the child (Boyd, 1993). Maternal lack of self-discipline and achievement orientation has been postulated to predict poor parenting style (i.e., inability to provide structure in life of child) (Bauman & Dougherty, 1983). Burns and Burns (1988) have described parenting dysfunction in chemically dependent women and suggest four factors from which the dysfunction stems: a negative parenting heritage; the emotional instability of the mother; lack of social support; and the high-risk child who is to be parented.

Child Maltreatment and Abandonment

Child maltreatment is the extreme of the continuum of problematic interactions between the drug using parent and the child. Due to the variability in child maltreatment reporting practices across the country, it is difficult to ascertain the numbers of children who are maltreated due to drug abuse. The National Committee for the Prevention of Child Abuse (1989) estimates that 675,000 children are maltreated annually by a substance-abusing caretaker. Current estimates based on protective service reports have a very wide range, indicating that substance abuse is implicated in 20% to 90% of cases (Barth, 1994; Dore, Doris, & Wright, 1995; for further discussion, see Feig, Chapter 3 in this volume). In a court sample of maltreated children, 50% of their parents had an alleged substance abuse problem (Murphy et al., 1991). A review of maltreatment records in Boston revealed that two thirds of the cases involved parental substance abuse (Famularo, Kinscherff, & Fenton, 1992). In a study of cocaine exposed children, the cocaine exposed children were more likely than a socioeconomically matched comparison group to be referred to state authorities due to child maltreatment, specifically regarding physical and medical neglect (Kelley, 1992).

Child neglect has been documented disproportionately among drug using families (Wasserman & Leventhal, 1991), often due to inadequate feeding and clothing of children as a result of the use of financial resources for drug purchase. Kelley, Walsh, and Thompson (1991) reported that physical and medical neglect were found in disproportionate rates among a drug using sample when compared with socioeconomically matched controls. Hawley, Halle, Drasin, and Thomas (1995) conducted a qualitative investigation of the caregiving environments of drug exposed children and found a preponderance of emotional and physical neglect due to the mother's psychological unavailability.

A State of Massachusetts study (Famularo et al., 1992) indicated that more than one third of the cases involving a cocaine using parent was reported due to child neglect. In this same study, sexual maltreatment of children by one of the parents emerged in disproportionate rates among the drug using sample. The empirical literature does not address the relationship between the incidence of child sexual maltreatment with the increased rates of maternal childhood experience of sexual maltreatment found among drug using women (cf. Boyd, 1993).

In some cases, new mothers become disinterested in their children and rarely visit them while they are hospitalized as neonates (Howard et al., 1989; Hurt, Salvador, & Brodsky, 1989). Disproportionate numbers of these mothers abandon their children in the hospital immediately after birth or in the community at a later point (Davis, 1990; U.S. Government Accounting Office [USGAO], 1990). The costs to hospitals for these abandoned drug exposed infants are estimated to be four times higher than for non-drug exposed infants (USGAO, 1990). The psychological costs to infants left in hospitals are devastating as well (Munns, 1989). The lack of immediate availability of foster homes have caused healthy infants to be "boarded" in hospitals for extended periods—thus the problem of "boarder babies" in many urban areas.

Familial Context

The larger familial and home environments also affect the experiences of the drug exposed child. There is limited research evidence in this area; however, available studies do point to compromised environments. The homes of cocaine involved families have been found to be deficient regarding maternal involvement with children (Free et al., 1990; Rodning et al., 1991). Similarly, Hawley, Halle, Drasin, and Thomas (1995) noted that children of addicted mothers live in more chaotic environments, characterized by frequent change of residence, minimal contact with the father, increased foster care placement rates, fewer concrete resources, and less real income. Alternatively, there is some evidence that the chaotic environments found in these families are similar to those found in the overall impoverished populations (Free et al., 1990).

An investigation of the home environments of biological and foster parents suggested that foster parents provided more stimulation and play materials than biological parents (Rodning et al.,

1991). In a similar study, Jones (1995) found the homes of foster parents were superior to those of biological parents regarding maternal responsivity, avoidance of restriction, organization, maternal involvement, and stimulation.

Lower levels of social support have been associated with parents of drug exposed children (Burns & Burns, 1988; OSAP, 1992), primarily due to the disorganization and instability that are often found in the extended families of these women (Regan et al., 1987). Relatives of substance abusers are more likely to abuse substances, particularly relatives of cocaine abusers (Luthar et al., 1993). In one study, it was found that addicted mothers did not differ from nonaddicted mothers in the amount of social support present, but in the source of the support. Addicted mothers received more support from institutional sources, whereas nonaddicted mothers received more familial support (Hawley et al., 1995). Drug using women tend to receive less support from spouses than nonaddicted women, because their spouses or partners are more likely to use drugs themselves (Amaro et al., 1989). Children of drug using women are less likely to have contact with their fathers (Hawley et al., 1995; Kelley et al., 1991). In addition, elevated rates of family violence (particularly interspousal violence) have been reported among drug addicted women (Amaro, Zuckerman, & Cabral, 1989; Hyser, Anglin, & McGlothlin, 1987; Regan et al., 1987).

Despite many reports of these familial stressors, there is description in the literature of a positive familial factor that often characterizes drug using families. The involvement of a relative (e.g., grandmother, aunt, etc.) in the care of high-risk children has been reported widely in the literature (cf. Chase-Lansdale, Brooks-Gunn, & Zamsky, 1994). Extended family supports have created a stabilizing force in the lives of children growing up in families with adolescent parents (Chase-Lansdale et al., 1994), intrafamilial violence (Gelles & Straus, 1988), and marital conflict and divorce (Wallerstein, 1984). Many of these familial factors characterize the drug using family as well. Preliminary research has documented improved outcome for children growing up in drug-abusing families in which there is a stable, nurturing relative available (Jones, 1995). Clinical and qualitative reports have highlighted that grandmothers and aunts often become the primary caretakers of children whose parents are unavailable due to drug use (e.g., D.C. Department of Human Services, 1994).

The Context of Poverty

The rate of child poverty in the U.S. has increased dramatically over the past decade. Currently, approximately one fourth of American children (one half of African American children) are reared in poverty (U.S. Bureau of the Census, 1992). It has been predicted that even more children will be subjected to poverty in the wake of Welfare Reform (Collins, Jones, & Bloom, 1995). Poverty places children at risk for a variety of experiences that hinder development, including drug exposure. Although maternal substance use is found across social class (Feig, Chapter 3 in this volume; Chasnoff, Landress, & Barrett, 1990), a higher *proportion* of the impoverished population abuses illicit drugs than middle- and upper-class populations (Office of Substance Abuse Prevention, 1991). The extreme poverty that some families experience may exacerbate the impact of drug exposure on children's development (Parker et al., 1988; USGAO, 1990).

It is well established that poverty alone has a deleterious impact on child development (Huston, Garcia-Coll, & McLoyd, 1994; McLoyd & Flanagan, 1990). Children born into poverty are at increased risk for a variety of poor health outcomes, including mortality in infancy and childhood, prematurity, infectious diseases, and intentional and accidental injuries (cf. Klerman, 1991). Psychological deficits are overrepresented among poor children, such as lower IQ scores, academic underachievement, psychopathology, and behavioral difficulties (cf. McLoyd & Wilson, 1991; White, 1982; Zill & Schoenborn, 1990).

Poverty is a major aspect of the social ecologies of drug involved families. Preliminary evidence from available studies of drug exposed children has delineated similar developmental outcomes for these children when compared with their nonexposed counterparts who are impoverished. As such, some scholars and practitioners have postulated that poverty is a more exacting risk factor than substance exposure, since exposed children do not deviate substantially from nonexposed children from similar backgrounds (Parker et al., 1988; Powell, 1991; Storkamp, McCluskey-Fawcett, &

Meck, 1993). The specific stressors associated with poverty shape the experiences of the children reared in these families. Among these stressors are housing instability, community violence, inadequate nutrition, and poor health care (Huston et al., 1994).

The past decade has witnessed dramatic shifts in the availability of housing for the poor. Poor young families now make up 75% of the homeless population (Bassuk, Rubin, & Lauriat, 1986; Dail, 1990). Drug involved families experience severe housing difficulties, including homelessness, overcrowded housing, and multiple moves in a short period of time (Hawley & Disney, 1992; Kelley et al., 1991). In a profile of women enrolled in a methadone maintenance program (Kaltenbach, 1994), up to 50% were homeless.

Violence has reached epidemic proportions in poor communities. The increase in violence, particularly homicide, has been directly linked to the increase in the use of crack cocaine in poor communities (*Uniform Crime Statistics, 1993*). Thus, children growing up in these drug involved neighborhoods are disproportionately exposed to violence and display increased psychological difficulties in reaction to the violence (Osofsky & Fenichel, 1994; Reiss, Richters, Radke-Yarrow, & Scharff, 1993). In addition, children in these neighborhoods spend much of their leisure hours restricted to their homes instead of outside, due to parental fears that they will be victimized by violence (Osofsky & Fenichel, 1994).

The nutrition of poor women and children has improved due to federal programs such as WIC, food stamps, and school lunch and breakfast, but chronic hunger and anemia are still found among poor children (Klerman, 1991). Inadequate nutrition has been associated with drug abuse (Keith, MacGregor, & Sciarra, 1988), which suggests that children reared in these environments may be subjected to poor nutrient intake as well. In addition, maternal use of financial resources for food to purchase drugs has implications for the nutrition of these children.

Similarly, poor women and children do not receive appropriate health care services, such as prenatal care, immunizations, and well-child visits. Kelley (1992) found that drug exposed children were less likely to have adequate immunizations and well-child visits. Drug-abusing women have also been found to underutilize the health care system, due to lack of insurance or financial resources, avoidance of public service systems, or lack of motivation to seek services (Keith et al., 1988).

It is difficult to disentangle the effects of poverty and the drug using lifestyle. Class comparison studies, which may investigate the effects of drug use on middle- and upper-class samples, are not generally conducted. Given that impoverished samples are most convenient, they are the more often studied (Chasnoff et al., 1990; Klindworth, Baumeister, & Kupstas, 1990). The synergistic effect of poverty and drug usage on developmental outcome has yet to receive full consideration in the research literature.

The Child Welfare Environment

A social cost incurred with the increase in the numbers of drug exposed children is the additional financial and personnel burden on the beleaguered child welfare system. The increasing number of drug exposed children has led to an exponential rise in the number of child abuse and neglect referrals, and to a compounded need for foster care placements across the nation (USGAO, 1990; see Feig, Chapter 3 in this volume, for further discussion).

The caregiving capacity of the child welfare system is another contextual issue that has implications for the development of drug involved children. The public child welfare system has been criticized for its maltreatment of the children brought into the system to "rescue" them from parental maltreatment. Neglect of foster children's medical, educational, and mental health needs has been documented in many child welfare systems across the country (Minuchin, 1991; National Commission on Children, 1991; Pelton, 1991). Moreover, reports of foster children being abused in foster family and group home settings suggest that some alternative caregivers may not be better at meeting the needs of high-risk children (Daly & Dowd, 1992; Solnit, 1980). The increasing numbers of drug exposed children entering the system are straining already grossly inadequate resources. Thus, the potential for these children to experience more exacting systemic maltreatment is great.

There is a paucity of empirical literature on the experiences of drug exposed children in the child welfare system. Out-of-home caretaking environments, which drug exposed children disproportionately experience (Besharov, 1990), have been explored to a minimal extent. An early study of children of drug-abusing mothers in New York (Fanshel, 1975) indicated that these children were more likely to remain in foster care longer and experience more turnover in care than children entering care for other reasons. Thus, the children of drug-abusing mothers were more financially costly to the child welfare system than others. Currently, evidence from several states has suggested that drug exposed children are more costly to the social service system due to longer hospital stays, foster care placements, and the need for specialized services (Phibbs, 1991).

Some studies have documented the influence of placement (e.g., biological parent, relative, foster parent, adoptive parent) on the lives of drug exposed children. In a study by Storkamp and colleagues (1993) comparing two groups of foster children, one with prenatal exposure and one without, there were no differences between the two groups on developmental outcome. Similarly, a Canadian research group compared prenatally exposed adopted children and nonexposed adopted children (Nulman et al., 1994). They found no cognitive differences between the two groups but did detect language differences. These studies suggest that exposure to a better caretaking environment (i.e., foster or adoptive family care) may attenuate the negative outcomes for drug affected children.

Although the samples in the various child-rearing environments were small, a UCLA research team (Howard et al., 1989; Rodning et al., 1991) found that prenatally cocaine exposed children reared by biological mothers were more likely to have insecure attachments than prenatally exposed children living with relatives or foster parents. The cocaine exposed children as a whole showed higher rates of insecure attachment than a comparison group of socioeconomically matched preterm children, despite the more sensitive caretaking provided by foster parents of some of the drug exposed children. A similar study by Jones (1995) found no differences in outcome for drug exposed children reared by foster parents and biological parents. This lack of difference was attributed to the large number of foster parents in the study who were related to the child and who were potentially more vulnerable than traditional foster parents.

The capacity of foster parents to care for drug exposed children is another area of concern that has limited data. In a study comparing biological and foster family environments, Kelley (1992) found that drug exposed foster children had better health outcomes (e.g., had well-child care visits) than their counterparts living with their biological parents. She also compared biologic and foster mothers of drug exposed children, and found increased child-related stress among the biological mothers. Soliday and Schaffer (1993) found increased child-related stress levels among foster parents of drug exposed children, particularly when the children were beyond the infancy period. In a comparison of the resources of biological and foster families of drug exposed children, it was documented that foster parents reported less depression, more concrete resources, increased social support, and more family cohesion than biological parents (Jones, 1995).

A more recent practice response to the dilemma of dwindling placement options for drug exposed infants has been the use of group care facilities. There is a dearth of evidence in this area. One recent study (Jones, 1995) compared drug exposed toddlers in congregate care facilities and foster family contexts using the Bayley Scales. The Mental Development Indices were lower in the group care sample. On the Behavioral Rating Scale, children in congregate care showed deficits in emotion regulation. However, they displayed increased interpersonal engagement, which was postulated to be due to the larger number of adults and children with whom they interacted.

Classic studies examining the developmental outcome of children reared in institutional settings have documented that these children were more likely to have developmental delays and impaired socioemotional functioning, specifically in the area of attachment (Dennis, 1973; Freud & Burlingham, 1973; Provence & Lipton, 1962; Skeels, 1966; Spitz, 1945; Tizard & Hodges, 1978). Despite these findings, it has been suggested that institutional rearing for young children represents an improvement over the too commonplace practice of multiple foster care placements (Provence, 1989).

Program Implications

Interventions for drug exposed children and their caregivers have proliferated in the past decade due to a focus on the consequences of the crack epidemic. Program developers have emphasized the need for a "continuum of care" for drug involved families that includes comprehensive, collaborative services ranging from drug treatment to child care, and from preventive to treatment approaches (Child Welfare League of America, 1992). Following is an exploration of program initiatives geared ultimately to foster the development and functioning of the drug involved child.

Child-Directed Interventions

Child-specific programs that address children's individual needs are vital for counteracting the effects of prenatal drug exposure. These interventions must be developmentally appropriate and be offered in tandem with other services in the caregiving system. Making caregivers full partners in this process not only fosters better child outcomes, but has the potential to facilitate improved parental functioning (cf. Kaplan-Sanoff & Rice, 1992).

Neonatal Period. During the neonatal period, when the direct consequences of drug exposure are salient, it is important to assess the neonate's need for medical services within and out of the hospital. For example, infants with neonatal abstinence syndrome require specific interventions. Pharmacologic treatment (e.g., paregoric, phenobarbital) is indicated to ease the physiological effects of withdrawal from opiates and other central nervous system depressants (Kaltenbach & Finnegan, 1989). Additional medical treatments may be necessary if the children are born physiologically compromised (e.g., referral for immunology follow-up if child is HIV infected, referral for genetic follow-up if child has congenital abnormalities).

Other interventions to support the functioning of drug exposed young infants are similar to those used with other high-risk newborns (cf. Als, 1995). Minimizing environmental stimulation serves to facilitate the regulatory capacities of these neonates. Excess light, noise, temperature fluctuations, and handling should be avoided. Swaddling is also a strategy that has been used to help calm hyperaroused infants, and to contain their extremities. Gentle rocking and other proprioceptive techniques can support the neonate's adjustment to life outside the womb. Infant massage has been found to be an important way of soothing dysregulated infants, helping them to relax to go to sleep, and of facilitating infant growth and development (Field, 1995). Making adjustments regarding feeding (i.e., smaller nipples, smaller amounts of formula at one feeding) may also be useful for infants who have difficulty with sucking, swallowing, or other gastrointestinal processes (Poulsen, 1995).

Infancy/Toddlerhood. During and after the neonatal period, it is important to assess the developmental status of the infant. Monitoring of the infant's progress can lead to early detection of developmental delays (Poulsen, 1995). Early intervention programs can provide infants and toddlers with practical activities that foster development across domains. Such programs are federally mandated for children with identified developmental delays. Special therapeutic services, such as physical, occupational, and speech therapy, must also be provided to these children (cf. Schutter & Brinker, 1992; Williams & Howard, 1993).

Therapeutic nurseries, targeting young children with behavioral problems, meet an important need for drug exposed children—a structured environment that will support their capacity to regulate their affect and behavior (Hodgkinson & Outtz, 1993). Child care services can serve as respite for the mother, but can also provide the children with the stable, predictable environment that is so crucial for the development of trust in the first years of life (Barton & Williams, 1993).

Preschool Years. When children enter the preschool period (ages 3 to 5), new developmental demands face them that are challenging to the nonexposed child. Drug exposed children, in particular, need interventions that are responsive, accepting, considerate of children's varying developmental needs, and focused on the whole child and family. Head Start and similar early intervention preschool programs have such a philosophy as central to their approach (cf. Zigler & Berman, 1983). Preschool programs such as Washington, D.C.'s DAISY program mainstream drug exposed children into regular classrooms, with a focus on ameliorating the effects of poverty and other global characteristics common to drug exposed and nonexposed children (Powell, 1991). These programs should be expanded to absorb many of the prenatally drug exposed children in preschool. These programs could be bolstered by funding streams specifically geared for drug exposed children, as well as resource reservoirs that support programs for high-risk children generally.

In addition, it has been documented that behavior problems tend to surface during the preschool period in the general population (cf. Campbell, 1995). Drug exposed children may be overrepresented in the behaviorally disordered group, given their susceptibility to regulatory difficulties stemming from a compromised central nervous system and environmental disorganization (Frick et al., 1992; Mayes, 1994). Thus, nursery school programs that utilize extensive structure in the classroom, behavioral management approaches, and mental health services are important interventions for preschool drug exposed children (Hodgkinson & Outtz, 1993).

Middle Childhood. Many public school systems have implemented special programs for drug involved children once they enter elementary school. These programs are often preventive in orientation, with a goal of preventing substance use in the children (cf. Gross & McCaul, 1992). Some programs provide more direct therapeutic services to children, such as play, art, and verbal therapies (Brooks et al., 1994; Kaplan-Sanoff & Rice, 1992). Interventions to address the factors that impinge upon children's academic functioning (e.g., persistence, attention, containment, etc.) have been initiated (Smith, 1995). It has been suggested that classrooms for drug exposed children be consistent, predictable, and structured, with routines, rituals, and planning (Smith, 1995).

Other programs for school-age children are provided in the communities and are designed to address the needs of the child as well as the social environment in which the child lives (e.g., Schinke, Botvin, & Orlandi, 1991). Educational supports such as tutoring and educational advocacy are offered in the context of these programs. Psychosocial interventions such as social skills training, counseling, and psychotherapeutic services are also offered as a means of assisting drug exposed children with the behavioral problems they present, such as impulsivity and aggression.

Adolescence. The literature on child-directed interventions during adolescence is primarily focused on children of alcoholic parents. Given the data that adolescents with substance-abusing parents are at increased risk for becoming substance abusers, the goal of many interventions is to prevent adolescent initiation into use of alcohol and other drugs (Botvin, Baker, Dusenbury, Tortu, & Botvin, 1990). Adolescents at risk for substance use are also more likely to exhibit other at-risk behaviors, such as poor academic achievement, school drop-out, early sexual activity, and delinquency (Dryfoos, 1990).

Interventions to address these behaviors may be school- or community-based, may be comprehensive or target specific behaviors, and may have a primary, secondary, or tertiary preventive orientation (Allen, Philliber, & Hoggson, 1990; Smith, 1995). Program models have emphasized positive decision making, self-esteem enhancement, building of social competence, and peer support (Schinke et al., 1991; Weissberg, Caplan, & Harwood, 1991). For example, school-based peer support groups modeled after the Adult Children of Alcoholics or Alcoholics Anonymous groups have been found to be effective (Smith, 1995).

Due to the multiple physical and emotional transitions occurring during adolescence, the emergence of specific emotional disorders in adolescence (e.g., depression, eating disorders, schizophrenia), and the increased likelihood of clinical dysfunction in children of substance-abusing parents, substance involved adolescents seem particularly vulnerable to mental health difficulties (Kazdin, 1993). Thus, the provision of psychotherapeutic services is an important intervention strategy. Psychotherapy can be offered on an individual, family, or group basis, in school or in the community, and be short term or long term in duration. Although the evidence is scant in this area, psychotherapy has been documented as effective for the treatment of a variety of adolescent mental health issues associated with substance use (Szapocznik, Kurtines, Santisteban, & Rio, 1990).

Summary. The programs delineated above hold great promise for addressing the psychological needs of substance exposed children. However, evaluation of the effectiveness of such approaches is still in the infancy stage (Lorion & Ross, 1992). In addition, because it is still unclear whether drug exposed children display characteristics distinct from other high-risk children, many of the interventions have been designed to facilitate the healthy development and functioning of all high-risk children (Williams & Howard, 1993). What is clear is that child-directed approaches must be accompanied by interventions that address the needs of the substance involved caregiving environments in which children have to develop (Brooks et al., 1994).

Environmental Interventions

To counteract the potential adverse effects of prenatal substance exposure on the developing child, a variety of environmental interventions are possible. Services to address the individual needs of the caregiver are discussed elsewhere in this volume (see McMahon & Luthar, Chapter 6, for further discussion). An integrated approach, which encompasses caregiver and child services, has been found to be effective with drug involved families (cf. Brooks et al., 1994; Howard & Kropenske, 1991; Kaplan-Sanoff & Rice, 1992). The following paragraphs discuss environmental interventions that have a goal of enhanced child outcome.

The sine qua non intervention for drug using parents is treatment that supports their abstention from illicit drug use (Brooks et al., 1994; Kumpfer, 1991). Outpatient and inpatient drug treatment programs that have a child component are essential for the children of drug users, and arguably may contribute to the success of the drug treatment. Some drug treatment programs have ancillary services, such as child care, therapeutic nurseries, counseling for children, parenting education, and parent-child activities (cf. Kaplan-Sanoff & Rice, 1992). Child-centered inpatient programs allow children to live with their mothers while in treatment, have flexible visitation policies for mothers and children, or work collaboratively with placement agencies to ensure quality care for the children (Child Welfare League of America, 1992; Kumpfer, 1991).

Family Preservation, Support, and Counseling

Interventions targeted at enhancing family functioning are equally important. For example, parent training on an individual and group basis that focuses on child development issues has been found to result in better outcomes for children of high-risk parents (Field, Widmayer, Stringer, Ignatoff, 1980; Meisels & Shonkoff, 1990; Powell, 1988). Parent education that focuses on the unique needs of the drug involved dyad has been found to produce positive outcomes for parents and children (Brooks et al., 1994; Kumpfer & DeMarsh, 1985).

Another treatment modality that focuses on the family unit is parent-infant psychotherapy. This type of therapy has been found to improve the parenting skills of drug using women and thus enhance the relationship they have with their children (Pawl, 1992). Family counseling can be used to address the systemic issues in a family that promote an individual's drug use and prevent positive family relations and child rearing (Kumpfer, 1991). This is particularly germane given the impact of other drug-using family members on children (e.g., fathers whose presence may lead to increased maternal drug usage and interspousal violence).

Family support programs, offering such services as parent problem-solving sessions, parent-child activities, and social and concrete support, have been initiated for drug involved populations (Ruch-Ross, 1992). Specific interventions within family support programs include male involvement and self-sufficiency initiatives. Home visitation programs have met with some success (e.g., Black et al., 1994), but clearly have to be viewed as but one component of a system of services that have to be provided to this very complex population.

Due to the extreme psychosocial difficulties inherent in these families, services are often required that allow for more intensive intervention, such as family preservation programs (Barth, 1994; Blau, Whewell, Gullotta, & Bloom, 1994; McCullough, 1991; Tracy, 1994). These programs generally are characterized by low caseloads for social workers (e.g., two families), more flexible definition of casework (e.g., transporting a family to the clinic), and 24-hour access to the worker. Family preservation strategies that increase the rate of success with drug involved families include immediate access to drug treatment, relocating the family out of drug infested neighborhoods, and the availability of funds to be used in flexible ways to support the family. Securing services for the child such as child care, educational supports, and psychological intervention is key for the efficacy of such programs.

Addressing the immediate concrete needs of drug involved families is essential (Howard & Kropenske, 1991). Housing difficulties, income deficits, lack of medical care and proper nutrition, and educational and employment needs are among the challenges that these families face. Relief from concrete difficulties has been found to enhance the psychological well-being of caregivers, and thus their interaction with their children (McLoyd, 1983). Programs designed to ameliorate poverty and its associated conditions have been found to improve developmental outcome for children (Huston, 1991; Schorr, 1991).

Assistance and training for caregivers, be they biological, foster, or adoptive, regarding the unique needs of drug exposed children are also paramount (Howard & Kropenske, 1991; White, 1992). For example, caregivers can receive information on the care of neurobehaviorally impaired infants or impulsive, labile older children who are drug exposed (cf. Villareal, McKinney, & Quackenbush, 1992). Given the recent trend toward "kinship" placement, where family members assume care of the child informally or formally (Johnson, 1994; Thornton, 1990), more intensive assistance to caregivers may be warranted. These grandmothers, aunts, and other relatives are devoid of the income, child care, legal, and emotional supports that would assist them to care for these children. The Center for the Vulnerable Child Foster Care Program in Oakland, California provides supportive services to foster parents and relatives caring for drug exposed children (Klee, Kronstadt, & Zlotnick, in press). Similarly, adoptive parents should be provided with supports as a means of facilitating their permanent care of these children.

Alternative Placements

Because of the acute nature of child-welfare decision making around children who are drug exposed, long-term planning for the best placement option is not always possible. As such, emergency and group care have become modalities that are more commonly used (Poulsen, 1995). Emergency shelters should be very time limited (e.g., overnight stays), should be used only as a last resort, should be used only for a specific population of children (e.g., children who have a higher probability of reunification with their biological families), and should provide children with a large measure of support to assist them through the transition. Quality group home placements should as much as possible imitate a home environment, should provide children with a primary caregiver, should be small relative to the age of the child (i.e., no more than four infants), and should marshall all the resources possible to develop an "emotional care plan" for the child (Poulsen, 1995).

Finally, children whose parents' drug-abuse has rendered them totally incapable of caring for them should be freed for adoption in an expeditious manner (Child Welfare League of America, 1992), abiding by a "child's sense of time" (Goldstein et al., 1986). Concomitantly, there must be an expanded recruitment effort to secure alternative family placements for these children—foster and adoptive parents who are willing to expend the energy to parent children who may present numerous challenges to their caregivers.

Conclusion

Child development is embedded in a complex interplay of biological, interpersonal, and environmental factors. The transactional approach to the phenomenon of prenatally drug exposed children allows for consideration of the synergistic effects on the developing child of the physical properties of the drug, of the familial context, and of macrosystemic factors such as poverty. There is compelling evidence that suggests that, except in the most extreme cases, environmental effects may override the biological impact of prenatal drug exposure along the developmental trajectory.

Prenatal substance exposure represents a biologic vulnerability for affected children. The postnatal environment, including the psychological functioning, parenting capacity, and lifestyle of the caregiver—particularly regarding continued substance use—has a major impact on developmental outcome. A positive caregiving context has the potential to attenuate the negative effects of prenatal substance exposure.

Programs to support the functioning of drug-involved families and alternative caregivers, as well as the affected children, hold promise for optimizing child development. The design of child welfare policies and programs should be premised on the lessons garnered from effective interventions with this population—most important is the provision of integrated, intergenerational services for drug involved families that address the concrete and emotional needs of all members. With such comprehensive and intensive supports, sturdy bridges can be constructed that will help drug exposed children transcend their developmental vulnerability to reach a destination of developmental resilience.

References

Ahl, V. (1993). *Classification by infants prenatally exposed to cocaine.* Poster presented at Meeting of the Society for Research in Child Development, New Orleans.

Alessandri, S., Sullivan, M., Imaizumi, S., & Lewis, M. (1993). Learning and emotional responsivity in cocaine-exposed infants. *Developmental Psychology, 29*, 989-997.

Allen, J., Philliber, S., & Hoggson, N. (1990). School-based prevention of teen-age pregnancy and school dropout: Process evaluation of the national replication of the Teen Outreach Program. *American Journal of Community Psychology, 18*, 505-524.

Als, H. (1995). The preterm infant: A model for the study of fetal brain expectation. In J. Lecanuet, W. Fifer, N. Krasnegor, & W. Smotherman (Eds.), *Fetal development: A psychobiological perspective.* Hillsdale, NJ: Lawrence Erlbaum.

Amaro, H., Fried, L., Cabral, H., & Zuckerman, B. (1990). Violence during pregnancy and substance use. *American Journal of Public Health, 80*, 575-579.

Amaro, H., Zuckerman, B., & Cabral, H. (1989). Drug use among adolescent mothers: Profile of risk. *Pediatrics, 84*(1), 144-151.

Azuma, S., & Chasnoff, I. (1993). Outcome of children prenatally exposed to cocaine and other drugs: A path analysis of three year data. *Pediatrics, 92*, 396-402.

Barth, R. (1991). Educational implications of prenatally drug-exposed children. *Social Work in Education, 13*, 130-136.

Barth, R. (1994). Long-term in-home services. In D. Besharov (Ed.), *When drug addicts have children.* Washington, DC: Child Welfare League of America.

Barton, M., & Williams, M. (1993). Infant day care. In C. Zeanah (Ed.), *Handbook of infant mental health.* New York: Guilford.

Bassuk, E., Rubin, L., & Lauriat, A. (1986). Characteristics of sheltered homeless families. *American Journal of Public Health, 78*, 783-788.

Bauman, P., & Dougherty, F. (1983). Drug-addicted mothers' parenting and their children's development. *International Journal of the Addictions, 18*, 291-302.

Bays, J. (1990). Substance abuse and child abuse: The impact of addiction on the child. *Pediatric Clinics of North America, 37*(4), 881-904.

Beckwith, L., Rodning, C., Norris, D., Phillipsen, L., Khandabi, P., & Howard, J. (1994). Spontaneous play in two-year olds born to substance-abusing mothers. *Infant Mental Health Journal, 15*(2), 189-201.

Beeghly, M., Brilliant, G., Cabral, H., Tronick, E., & Frank, P. (1996). *Object play as a window on the cognitive competence of low-income, prenatally substance-exposed and unexposed toddlers.* Poster presented at the Head Start Third National Research Conference, Washington, D.C.

Beeghly, M., & Tronick, E. (1994). Effects of prenatal exposure to cocaine in early infancy: Toxic effects on the process of mutual regulation. *Infant Mental Health Journal, 15*(2), 158-175.

Behnke, M., & Eyler, F. (1993). The consequences of prenatal substance use for the developing fetus, newborn, and young child. *International Journal of the Addictions, 28*(13), 1341-1391.

Bennett, L., Wolin, S., & Reiss, D. (1988). Cognitive, behavioral, and emotional problems among school-age children of alcoholic parents. *American Journal of Psychiatry, 145,* 185-190.

Bergman, A., & Weisner, L. (1976). Relationship of passive cigarette smoking to sudden infant death syndrome. *Pediatrics, 58,* 665.

Besharov, D. (1990). Crack children in foster care: Reexamining the balance between children's rights and parents' rights. *Children Today, 19*(4), 21-25.

Black, M., Nair, P., Kight, C., Wachtel, R., Roby, P., & Schuler, M. (1994). Parenting and early development among children of drug-using women: Effects of home visitation. *Pediatrics, 94*(4), 440-448.

Blau, G., Whewell, M., Gullotta, T., & Bloom, M. (1994). The prevention and treatment of child abuse in households of substance abusers: A research demonstration progress report. *Child Welfare, 73*(1), 83-94.

Botvin, G., Baker, E., Dusenbury, L., Tortu, S., & Botvin, E. (1990). Preventing adolescent drug use through a multimodal cognitive-behavioral approach: Results of a 3 year study. *Journal of Consulting and Clinical Psychology, 58,* 437-446.

Boyd, C. (1993). The antecedents of women's crack cocaine abuse: Family substance abuse, sexual abuse, depression and illicit drug use. *Journal of Substance Abuse Treatment, 10,* 433-438.

Boyd, C., & Mieczkowski, T. (1990). Drug use, health, family and social support in "crack" cocaine users. *Addictive Behaviors, 15,* 481-485.

Bresnahan, K., Brooks, C., & Zuckerman, B. (1991). Prenatal cocaine use: Impact on infants and mothers. *Pediatric Nursing, 17*(2), 123-129.

Bronfenbrenner, U. (1979). *The ecology of human development.* Cambridge, MA: Harvard University Press.

Brook, J., Brook, D., Gordon, A., Whiteman, M., & Dohen, P. (1990). The psychosocial etiology of adolescent drug use: A family interactional approach. *Genetic, Social, and General Psychology Monographs, 116*(Whole No. 2).

Brook, J., Tseng, L., & Cohen, P. (1996). Toddler adjustment: Impact of parents' drug use, personality, and parent-child relations. *Journal of Genetic Psychology, 157*(3), 281-295.

Brooks, C., Zuckerman, B., Bamforth, A., Cole, J., & Kaplan-Sanoff, M. (1994). Clinical issues related to substance involved mothers and their infants. *Infant Mental Health Journal, 15*(2), 202-217.

Burns, K., Chethick, L., Burns, W., & Clark, R. (1991). Dyadic disturbances in cocaine-abusing mothers and their infants. *Journal of Clinical Psychology, 47*(2), 316-319.

Burns, W., & Burns, K. (1988). Parenting dysfunction in chemically dependent women. In I. J. Chasnoff (Ed.), *Drugs, alcohol, pregnancy, and parenting.* Boston: Kluwer.

Campbell, S. (1995). Behavior problems in preschool children: A review of recent research. *Journal of Child Psychology and Psychiatry, 36*(1), 113-149.

Chase-Lansdale, P., Brooks-Gunn, J., & Zamsky, E. (1994). Young African-American multigenerational families in poverty: Quality of mothering and grandmothering. *Child Development, 65*(2), 373-393.

Chasnoff, I. J., Griffith, D., Freier, C., & Murray, J. (1992). Cocaine/polydrug use in pregnancy: Two-year follow-up. *Pediatrics, 89,* 284-289.

Chasnoff, I. J., Griffith, D., MacGregor, S., Dirkes, K., & Burns, K. (1989). Temporal patterns of cocaine use during pregnancy. *Journal of the American Medical Association, 261*(12), 1741-1744.

Chasnoff, I. J., Landress, H., & Barrett, M. (1990). The prevalence of illicit drug or alcohol use during pregnancy and discrepancies in mandatory reporting in Pinellas County, Florida. *New England Journal of Medicine, 322,* 1202-1206.

Chavkin, W., Paone, D., Friedmann, P., & Wilets, I. (1993). Psychiatric histories of drug using mothers: Treatment implications. *Journal of Substance Abuse Treatment, 10,* 445-448.

Chethick, L., Burns, K., Burns, W., et al. (1990). The assessment of early relationship dysfunction in cocaine-abusing mothers and their infants. *Infant Behavior and Development, 13.*

Child Welfare League of America, North American Commission on Chemical Dependency. (1992). *Children at the front: A different view of the war on alcohol and drugs.* Washington, DC: Child Welfare League of America.

Coles, C. (1993). Impact of prenatal alcohol exposure on the newborn and the child. *Clinical Obstetrics and Gynecology, 36*(2), 255-266.

Coles, C., & Platzman, K. (1993). Behavioral development in children prenatally exposed to drugs and alcohol. *The International Journal of the Addictions, 28*(13), 1393-1433.

Collins, A., Jones, S., & Bloom, H. (1995). *Children and welfare reform: Highlights from recent research.* New York: National Center for Children in Poverty.

Daghestani, A. (1988). Psychosocial characteristics of pregnant women addicts in treatment. In I. J. Chasnoff (Ed.), *Drugs, alcohol, pregnancy, and parenting.* Boston: Kluwer.

Dail, P. (1990). A profile of homeless families. *Child Welfare, 49*(4), 473-477.

Daly, D., & Dowd, T. (1992). Characteristics of effective, harm-free environments for children in out-of-home care. *Child Welfare, 71*(6), 487-496.

Davidson, C. (1991). Attachment issues and the cocaine-exposed dyad. *Child and Adolescent Social Work, 8*(4), 269-284.

Davis, S. (1990). Chemical dependency in women: A description of its effects and outcome on adequate parenting. *Journal of Substance Abuse Treatment, 7,* 225-232.

D.C. Department of Human Services. (1994). *Kinship care report.* Washington, DC: Author.

Dennis, W. (1973). *Children of the creche.* New York: Appleton-Century-Crofts.

Dore, M., Doris, J., & Wright, P. (1995). Identifying substance abuse in maltreating families: A child welfare challenge. *Child Abuse & Neglect, 19*(5), 531-543.

Downey, G., & Coyne, J. (1990). Children of depressed parents: An integrative review. *Psychological Bulletin, 108*(1), 50-76.

Dryfoos, J. (1990). *Adolescents at risk: Prevalence and prevention.* New York: Oxford University Press.

Earls, F., Reich, W., Jung, K. G., & Cloninger, R. (1988). Psychopathology in children of alcoholic and antisocial parents. *Alcoholism, 12*(4), 481-487.

Escalona, S. (1982). Babies at double hazard: Early development of infants at biologic and social risk. *Pediatrics, 70,* 670-675.

Famularo, R., Kinscherff, R., & Fenton, T. (1992). Parental substance abuse and the nature of child maltreatment. *Child Abuse & Neglect, 16,* 475-483.

Fanshel, D. (1975). Parental failure and consequences for children: The drug abusing mother whose children are in foster care. *American Journal of Public Health, 65,* 604-612.

Field, T. (1992). Infants of depressed mothers. *Development and Psychopathology, 4,* 49-66.

Field, T. (1995). Cocaine exposure and intervention in early development. In M. Lewis & M. Bendersky (Eds.), *Mothers, babies, and cocaine.* Hillsdale, NJ: Lawrence Erlbaum.

Field, T., Widmayer, S., Stringer, S., & Ignatoff, E. (1980). Teenage, lower-class, black mothers and their preterm infants: An intervention and developmental follow-up. *Child Development, 51,* 426-436.

Finnegan, L. (1988). Drug addiction and pregnancy: The newborn. In I. J. Chasnoff (Ed.), *Drugs, alcohol, pregnancy, and parenting.* Boston: Kluwer.

Fitzgerald, H. E., Kaltenbach, K. A., & Finnegan, L. P. (1990). Patterns of interaction among drug-dependent women and their infants. *Pediatric Research Abstract, 27,* 44A.

Frank, D., Zuckerman, B., Amaro, H., Aobagye, K., Bauchner, H., Cabral, H., Fried, L., Hingson, R., Kayne, H., Levenson, S., Parker, S., Reece, H., & Vinci, R. (1988). Cocaine use during pregnancy: Prevalence and correlates. *Pediatrics, 82,* 888-895.

Free, T., Russell, F., Mills, B., & Hathaway, D. (1990). A descriptive study of infants and toddlers exposed prenatally to substance abuse. *Maternal and Child Nursing, 15,* 245-249.

Freier, M., Griffith, D., & Chasnoff, I. J. (1991). In utero drug exposure: Developmental follow-up and maternal-infant interaction. *Seminars in Perinatology, 15*(4), 310-316.

Freud, A., & Burlingham, D. (1973). *Infants without families.* New York: International Universities Press.

Frick, P., Lahey, B., Loeber, R., Stouthamer-Loeber, M., Christ, M., & Hanson, K. (1992). Familial risk factors to oppositional defiant disorder and conduct disorder: Parental psychopathology and maternal parenting. *Journal of Consulting and Clinical Psychology, 60*(1), 49-55.

Fried, P. (1980). Marijuana use by pregnant women: Neurobehavioral effects in neonates. *Drug and Alcohol Dependence, 6,* 415-424.

Fried, P., & Watkinson, B. (1990). 36- and 48-month neurobehavioral follow-up of children exposed to marijuana, cigarettes, and alcohol. *Developmental Behavioral Pediatrics, 11*(2), 49-58.

Fried, P., Watkinson, B., & Gray, R. (1992). A follow-up study of attentional behavior in 6-year old children exposed prenatally to marijuana, cigarettes, and alcohol. *Neurotoxicology and Teratology, 14,* 299-311.

Gawin, F., & Kleber, H. (1988). Evolving conceptualizations of cocaine dependence. *Yale Journal of Biology and Medicine, 61,* 123-136.

Gelles, R., & Straus, M. (1988). *Intimate violence.* New York: Simon & Schuster.

Goldstein, J., Freud, A., Solnit, A., & Goldstein, S. (1986). *In the best interests of the child.* New York: Free Press.

Griffith, D., Zauma, S., & Chasnoff, I. J. (1994). Three year outcome of children exposed prenatally to drugs. *Journal of the American Academy of Child and Adolescent Psychiatry, 33,* 1.

Griffith, D., Chasnoff, I. J., & Freier, C. (1989). Effects of maternal psychopathology on the neurobehavioral development of cocaine exposed infants. *Pediatric
Research, 25,* 64.

Gross, J., & McCaul, M. (1992). An evaluation of a psychoeducational and substance abuse risk reduction intervention for children of substance abusers.
In R. Lorion & J. Ross (Eds.), Programs for change: Office of Substance Abuse
Prevention demonstration models [Special issue]. *Journal of Community Psychology,* 75-87.

Hans, S., Bernstein, V., & Henson, L. (1990). *Interaction between drug-using
mothers and their toddlers.* Paper presented at the Seventh International Conference on Infant Studies, Montreal, Canada.

Hawley, T., & Disney, E. (1992). Crack's children: The consequences of maternal
cocaine abuse. *Social Policy Report, Society for Research in Child Development,*
6(4).

Hawley, T., Halle, T., Drasin, R., & Thomas, N. (1995). Children of addicted
mothers: Effects of the "crack" epidemic on the caregiving environment and the
development of preschoolers. *American Journal of Orthopsychiatry, 65*(3), 364-
379.

Hodgkinson, H., & Outtz, J. (1993). *Against their wills: Children born affected by
drugs.* Washington, DC: Institute for Educational Leadership, Inc.

Howard, J., & Kropenske, V. (1991). A prevention/intervention model for chemi-
cally dependent parents and their offspring. In S. Goldston, C. Heinicke, R.
Pynoos, & J. Yager (Eds.), *Preventing mental health disturbances in childhood.*
Washington, DC: American Psychiatric Press.

Howard, J., Beckwith, L., Rodning, C., & Kropenske, V. (1989). The development
of young children of substance abusing parents: Insights from seven years of
intervention and research. *Zero to Three, 9*(5), 8-12.

Hurt, H., Salvador, A., & Brodsky, N. (1989). Infants of cocaine abusers have fewer
parent contacts during hospitalization than controls [Abstract]. *Pediatric Research, 25,* 254A.

Huston, A. (Ed.). (1991). *Children in poverty: Child development and public policy.*
New York: Cambridge University Press.

Huston, A., Garcia-Coll, C., & McLoyd, V. (1994). Children in poverty [Special
issue]. *Child Development, 65*(2).

Hyser, Y., Anglin, M., & McGlothlin, W. (1987). Sex differences in initiation of use.
American Journal of Drug and Alcohol Abuse, 13, 33-57.

Jacobson, S., Fein, G., Jacobson, J., Schwartz, P., & Dowles, J. (1984). Neonatal
correlates and prenatal exposure to smoking, caffeine and alcohol. *Infant Behavior and Development, 7,* 253-265.

Johnson, H., & Rosen, T. (1990). *Interaction between drug-using mothers and their
toddlers.* Paper presented at the Seventh International Conference on Infant
Studies, Montreal, Canada.

Johnson, I. (1994). Kinship care. In D. Besharov (Ed.), *When drug addicts have
children.* Washington, DC: Child Welfare League of America.

Jones, B. (1995). *Caregiving contexts and drug-exposed children.* Unpublished doctoral dissertation, Yale University.

Kaltenbach, K. (1994). Effects of in-utero opiate exposure: New paradigms for old
questions. *Drug and Alcohol Dependence, 36,* 83-87.

Kaltenbach, K., & Finnegan, L. (1988). The influence of the neonatal abstinence syndrome on mother-infant interaction. In E. J. Anthony & C. Chiland (Eds.), *The child in his family: Perilous development: Child raising and identity formation under stress* (pp. 223-230). New York: John Wiley.

Kaltenbach, K., & Finnegan, L. (1989). Prenatal narcotic exposure: Perinatal and developmental effects. *Neurotoxicology, 10,* 597-604.

Kandel, D. (1990). Parenting styles, drug use, and children's adjustment in families of young adults. *Journal of Marriage and the Family, 52,* 183-196.

Kaplan-Sanoff, M., & Rice, K. (1992). Working with addicted women in recovery and their children: Lessons learned in Boston City Hospital's Women and Infants Clinic. *Zero to Three, 13*(1), 17-22.

Kazdin, A. (1993). Adolescent mental health. *American Psychologist, 48*(2), 127-141.

Keith, L., MacGregor, S., & Sciarra, J. (1988). Drug abuse in pregnancy. In I. J. Chasnoff (Ed.), *Drugs, alcohol, pregnancy, and parenting.* Boston: Kluwer.

Kelley, S. (1992). Parenting stress and child maltreatment in drug-exposed children. *Child Abuse & Neglect, 16,* 317-328.

Kelley, S., Walsh, J., & Thompson, K. (1991). Prenatal exposure to cocaine: Birth outcomes, health problems, and child neglect. *Pediatric Nursing, 17*(2), 130-136.

Khantzian, E. (1985). The self-medication hypothesis of addictive disorders: Focus on heroin and cocaine dependence. *The American Journal of Psychiatry, 142,* 1259-1264.

Klee, L., Kronstadt, D., & Zlotnick, C. (in press). Foster care's youngest: A preliminary report. *American Journal of Orthopsychiatry.*

Klerman, L. (1991). The health of poor children: Problems and programs. In A. Huston (Ed.), *Children in poverty.* New York: Cambridge University Press.

Klindworth, L., Baumeister, A., & Kupstas, F. (1990). *Cocaine review.* Unpublished manuscript, Vanderbilt University.

Kumpfer, K. (1991). Treatment programs for drug-abusing women. *The Future of Children (Drug Exposed Infants), 1*(1), 50-60.

Kumpfer, K., & DeMarsh, J. (1985). Genetic and family environmental influences on children of drug abusers. *Journal of Children in Contemporary Society, 3/4,* 49-91.

Ladwig, G., & Anderson, M. (1989). Substance abuse in women: Relationship between chemical dependency of women and past reports of physical and/or sexual abuse. *International Journal of the Addictions, 24,* 655-673.

Lester, B. (1992). Infants and their families at risk: Assessment and intervention. *Infant Mental Health Journal, 15,* 54-66.

Lester, B., Corwin, M., Sepkoski, C., Seifer, R., et al. (1991). Neurobehavioral syndromes in cocaine exposed newborn infants. *Child Development, 62,* 694-705.

Lester, B., & Tronick, E. (1994). The effects of prenatal cocaine exposure and child outcome. *Infant Mental Health Journal, 15*(2), 107-120.

Lindenberg, C., Alexander, E., Gendrop, S., Nencioloi, M., & Williams, D. (1991). A review of the literature on cocaine abuse in pregnancy. *Nursing Research, 40*(2), 69-75.

56   SUBSTANCE ABUSE, FAMILY VIOLENCE & CHILD WELFARE

Lorion, R., & Ross, J. (Eds.). (1992). Programs for change: Office for Substance Abuse Prevention demonstration models [Special issue]. *Journal of Community Psychology.*

Luthar, S., Merikangas, K., & Rounsaville, B. (1993). Parental psychopathology and disorders of offspring. *Journal of Nervous and Mental Disease, 181*(6), 351-357.

Mayes, L. (1994). Neurobiology of prenatal cocaine exposure: Effect on developing monoamine systems. *Infant Mental Health Journal, 15*(2), 121-133.

Mayes, L., Granger, R., Bornstein, M., & Zuckerman, B. (1992). The problem of prenatal cocaine exposure: A rush to judgement. *Journal of the American Medical Association, 267*(3), 406-408.

McCance-Katz, E. (1991). The consequences of maternal substance abuse for the child exposed in utero. *Psychosomatics, 32*(3), 268-273.

McCullough, C. (1991). The child welfare response. In Center for the Future of Children, *The future of children: Drug exposed infants, 1*(1), 61-70.

McLoyd, V. (1983). Early intervention and its effects on maternal and child development. *Monographs of the Society for Research in Child Development, 48*(4, Serial 202).

McLoyd, V., & Flanagan, C. (Eds.). (1990). *New directions for child development: Vol. 46. Economic stress: Effects on family life and child development.* San Francisco: Jossey-Bass.

McLoyd, V., & Wilson, L. (1991). The strain of living poor: Parenting, social support, and child mental health. In A. Huston (Ed.), *Children in poverty.* Cambridge, UK: Cambridge University Press.

Meisels, S., & Shonkoff, J. (Eds.). (1990). *Handbook of early childhood intervention.* New York: Cambridge University Press.

Minuchin, S. (1991, Spring). Family abuse and neglect: Child welfare system indicted. *The Prevention Report,* pp. 7-8.

Munns, J. (1989). *The youngest of the homeless: Characteristics of hospital boarder babies in five cities.* Washington, DC: Child Welfare League of America.

Murphy, J., Jellinek, M., Quinn, D., Smith, G., Poitrast, F., & Goshko, M. (1991). Substance abuse and serious child mistreatment: Prevalence, risk, and outcome in a court sample. *Child Abuse & Neglect, 15,* 197-211.

Myers, B., Olson, H., & Kaltenbach, K. (1992). Cocaine-exposed infants: Myths and misunderstandings. *Zero to Three, 13*(1), 1-5.

National Commission on Children. (1991). *Beyond rhetoric.* Washington, DC: Author.

National Committee for the Prevention of Child Abuse. (1989). *Substance abuse and child abuse fact sheet.* Washington, DC: Author.

Neuspiel, D., & Hamel, S. (1991). Cocaine and infant behavior. *Journal of Developmental and Behavioral Pediatrics, 12,* 55-64.

Nulman, I., Rovet, J., Altmann, D., Bradley, C., Einarson, T., & Koren, G. (1994). Neurodevelopment of adopted children exposed in utero to cocaine. *Canadian Medical Association Journal, 151*(11), 1591-1597.

Nunes, E., Quitkin, F., & Klein, D. (1989). Psychiatric diagnosis in cocaine abuse. *Psychiatry Research, 28*(1), 105-114.

Odom, L., Lampkin, B., Tannuous, R., Buckley, J., & Hammond, G. (1990). Acute monoblastic leukemia: A unique subtype: A review from the Children's Cancer Study Group. *Leukemia Research 14,* 1-10.

Office of Substance Abuse Prevention. (1991). Crack cocaine: A challenge for prevention. *OSAP Prevention Monograph No. 9*. Rockville, MD: USDHHS.

Office of Substance Abuse Prevention. (Ed.). (1992). Identifying the needs of drug-affected children: Public policy issues. *OSAP Prevention Monograph No. 11* (DHHS Publication No. ADM 92-1814). Rockville, MD: Office of Substance Abuse Prevention.

Oro, A., & Dixon, S. (1987). Perinatal cocaine and methamphetamine exposure: Maternal and neonatal correlates. *Journal of Pediatrics, 111*, 571-578.

Osofsky, J., & Fenichel, E. (Eds.). (1994). *Hurt, healing, hope: Caring for infants and toddlers in violent environments*. Arlington, VA: Zero to Three.

Overpeck, M., & Moss, A. (1991). *Children's exposure to environmental cigarette smoke before and after birth*. Hyattsville, MD: U.S. Department of Health and Human Services.

Parker, S., Greer, S., & Zuckerman, B. (1988). Double jeopardy: The impact of poverty on early child development. In B. Zuckerman, M. Weitzman, & J. Albert (Eds.), Children at risk [Special issue]. *Pediatric Clinics of North America, 35*, 1227-1240.

Patterson, G. (1982). *Coercive family processes*. Eugene, OR: Castalia.

Pawl, J. (1992). Interventions to strengthen relationships between infants and drug-abusing or recovering parents. *Zero to Three, 13*(1), 6-10.

Pelton, L. (1991). Beyond permanency planning: Restructuring the public child welfare system. *Social Work, 36*(4), 337-343.

Phibbs, C. (1991). The economic implications of substance exposure. *The Future of Children. Drug Exposed Infants, 1*(1), 113-120.

Picone, T., Allen, L., Olsen, P., & Ferris, M. (1982). Pregnancy outcome in North American women: II. Effects of diet, cigarette smoking, stress, and weight gain on placentas, and on neonatal physical and behavioral characteristics. *American Journal of Clinical Nutrition, 36*, 1214.

Poulsen, M. (1995). Children at risk in out-of-home placement. In G. Smith, C. Coles, M. Poulsen, & C. Cole (Eds.), *Children, families, and substance abuse*. Baltimore, MD: Brooks.

Powell, D. (1991, Spring). Family-based intervention with prekindergarten children prenatally exposed to drugs. *The Prevention Report*, pp. 1-3.

Powell, D. (Ed.). (1988). *Parent education as early childhood intervention*. Norwood, NJ: Ablex.

Provence, S. (1989). Infants in institutions revisited. *Zero to Three, 9*(4), 1-4.

Provence, S., & Lipton, R. (1962). *Infants in institutions*. New York: International Universities Press.

Radke-Yarrow, M., Cummings, E. M., Kulzynski, L., & Chapman, M. (1985). Patterns of attachment in two- and three-year olds in normal families and families with parental depression. *Child Development, 56*, 884-893.

Regan, D., Ehrlich, S., & Finnegan, L. (1987). Infants of drug addicts at risk for child abuse, neglect, and placement in foster care. *Neurotoxicology and Teratology, 9*, 315-319.

Regier, D., Farmer, M., Rae, D., Locke, B., Keith, S., Judd, L., & Goodwin, F. (1990). Comorbidity of mental disorders with alcohol and other drug abuse. *Journal of the American Medical Association, 264*, 2511-2518.

Reiss, D., Richters, J., Radke-Yarrow, M., & Scharff, D. (Eds). (1993). *Violence and children*. Hillsdale, NJ: Lawrence Erlbaum.

Rivers, P. (1989). Substance abuse and psychopathology: The special population of the dual-diagnosis patient. In G. Lawson & A. Lawson (Eds.), *Alcoholism and substance abuse in special populations*. Rockville, MD: Aspen Publishers.

Robison, L. L., Buckley, J. D., Daigle, A. E., Wells, R., Benjamin, D., Arthur, D. C., & Hammond, G. D. (1989). Maternal drug use and risk of childhood nonlymphoblastic leukemia among offspring. An epidemiologic investigation implicating marijuana. *Cancer, 63*, 1904-1911.

Rodning, C., Beckwith, L., & Howard, J. (1989a). Characteristics of attachment organization and play organization in prenatally drug exposed toddlers. *Development and Psychopathology, 1*, 277-289.

Rodning, C., Beckwith, L., & Howard, J. (1989b). Prenatal exposure to drugs: Behavioral distortions reflecting CNS impairment? *Neurotoxicology, 10*, 629-634.

Rodning, C., Beckwith, L., & Howard, J. (1991). Quality of attachment and home environments in children prenatally exposed to PCP and cocaine. *Development and Psychopathology, 3*, 351-366.

Rohsenow, D., Corbett, R., & Devine, D. (1988). Molested as children: A hidden contribution to substance abuse? *Journal of Substance Abuse Treatment, 5*, 13-18.

Root, M. (1989). Treatment failures: The role of sexual victimization in women's addictive behavior. *American Journal of Orthopsychiatry, 59*, 542-549.

Rosen, R. S., & Johnson, H. L. (1982). Children of methadone maintained mothers: Follow-up to 18 months of age. *Journal of Pediatrics, 101*, 192-196.

Rosett, H. (1980). A clinical perspective on the fetal alcohol syndrome. *Alcoholism Clinical and Experimental Research, 4*, 119-122.

Rosett, H., & Weiner, L. (1984). *Alcohol and the fetus: A clinical perspective*. New York: Oxford University Press.

Rounsaville, B., & Luthar, S. (1994). Family/genetic studies of cocaine abusers and opioid addicts. In T. Kosten & H. Kleber (Eds.), *Clinician's guide to cocaine addiction*. New York: Guilford.

Ruch-Ross, H. (1992). The Child and Family Options Program: Primary drug and alcohol prevention for young children. In R. Lorion & J. Ross (Eds.), Programs for change: Office of Substance Abuse Prevention demonstration models [Special issue]. *Journal of Community Psychology*, pp. 39-54.

Sameroff, A. (1986). Environmental context of child development. *Journal of Pediatrics, 109*, 192-200.

Sameroff, A., & Fiese, B. (1990). Transactional regulation and early intervention. In S. Meisels & J. Shonkoff (Eds.), *Handbook of early childhood intervention*. Cambridge, UK: Cambridge University Press.

Samet, J., Lewit, E., & Warner, K. (1994). Involuntary smoking and children's health. *The Future of Children, 4*(3), 94-114.

Schinke, S., Botvin, G., & Orlandi, M. (1991). *Substance abuse in children and adolescents: Evaluation and intervention*. Newbury Park, CA: Sage.

Schorr, L. (1991). *Within our reach*. Garden City, NY: Anchor.

Schuckit, M., & Sweeney, S. (1987). Substance use and mental health problems among sons of alcoholics and controls. *Journal of the Study of Alcoholism, 48*, 528-534.

Schutter, L., & Brinker, R. (1992). Conjuring a new category of disability from prenatal cocaine exposure: Are the infants unique biological or caretaking casualties? *Topics in Early Childhood Education, 11*(4), 84-111.

Sexton, M., Fox, N., & Hebel, J. (1990). Prenatal exposure to tobacco: II. Effects of cognitive functioning at age three. *International Journal of Epidemiology, 19,* 17-77.

Singer, L., Farkas, K., & Kleigman, R. (1992). Childhood medical and behavioral consequences of maternal cocaine use. *Journal of Pediatric Psychology, 17*(4), 389-406.

Skeels, H. (1966). Adult status of children with contrasting early life experience: A follow-up study. *Monographs of the Society for Research in Child Development, 31*(3).

Smith, G. (1995). Classroom strategies for children and adolescents. In G. Smith, C. Coles, M. Poulsen, & C. Cole (Eds.), *Children, families, & substance abuse.* Baltimore, MD: Brooks.

Soliday, E., & Schaffer, J. (1993). *Developmental status of drug-exposed children in foster care.* Paper presented at the Biennial Meeting of the Society for Research in Child Development, New Orleans.

Solnit, A. (1980). Too much reporting, too little service: Roots and prevention of child abuse. In G. Gerber, C. Ross, & E. Zigler (Eds.), *Child abuse: An agenda for action.* New York: Oxford University Press.

Spitz, R. (1945). Hospitalism: An inquiry into the genesis of psychiatric conditions in early childhood. *The Psychoanalytic Study of the Child, 1,* 53-74.

Storkamp, B., McCluskey-Fawcett, K., & Meck, N. (1993). *The effects of prenatal drug-exposure on toddlers' temperament, development, and play behavior.* Paper presented at the meeting of the Society for Research in Child Development, New Orleans.

Strauss, M., Lesson-Firestone, J., Chavez, C., & Stryker, J. (1979). Children of methadone treated women at five years of age. *Pharmacology Biochemical and Behavioral Supplement, 11,* 3-6.

Streissguth, A. P. (1986). The behavioral teratology of alcohol: Performance, behavioral and intellectual deficits in prenatally exposed children. In J. West (Ed.), *Alcohol and brain development.* New York: Oxford University Press.

Streissguth, A. P., Martin, D. C., Barr, H. M., & Sandman, B. (1984). Intrauterine alcohol and nicotine exposure: Attention and reaction time in 4-year old children. *Developmental Psychology, 20,* 533-541.

Streissguth, A., & Randels, S. (1989). Long term effects of fetal alcohol syndrome. In G. Robinson (Ed.), *Alcohol and child/family health.* Vancouver: University of British Columbia Press.

Szapocznik, J., Kurtines, W., Santisteban, D., & Rio, A. (1990). Interplay of advances between theory, research, and application in treatment interventions aimed at behavior problem children and adolescents. *Journal of Consulting and Clinical Psychology, 58,* 696-703.

Tarter, R., Blackson, T., Martin, C., Loeber, R., & Moss, H. (1993). Characteristics and correlates of child discipline practices in substance abuse and normal families. *American Journal on Addictions, 2,* 18-25.

Thornton, J. (1990). Permanency planning for children in kinship foster homes. *Child Welfare, 70*(5), 593-600.

Tizard, B., & Hodges, J. (1978). The effect of early institutional rearing on the development of eight year old children. *Journal of Child Psychology and Psychiatry, 16*, 99-118.

Tracy, E. (1994). Maternal substance abuse: Protecting the child, preserving the family. *Social Work, 39*(5), 534-546.

Tubman, J. (1993). A pilot study of school age children of men with moderate to severe alcohol dependence: Maternal distress and child outcome. *Journal of Child Psychology and Psychiatry, 34*(5), 729-741.

U.S. Bureau of the Census. (1992). Poverty in the United States: 1988 and 1989. *Current Population Reports* (Series P-60, No. 171). Washington, DC: Government Printing Office, June 1991.

U.S. Department of Health and Human Services. (1992). *Maternal drug abuse and drug exposed children: Understanding the problem* (DHHS Publication No. [ADM] 92-1949). Washington, DC: Government Printing Office.

U.S. Department of Health and Human Services. (1994). *Substance abuse among women and parents*. Washington, DC: HHS Office of the Assistant Secretary for Planning and Evaluation.

U.S. Department of Health and Human Services. (1995). *Preliminary estimates from the 1994 National Household Survey on Drug Abuse*. Washington, DC: DHHS Substance Abuse and National Health Services Administration.

U.S. General Accounting Office. (1990). *Drug exposed infants: A generation at risk* (HRD 90-138). Washington, DC: General Accounting Office.

Uniform Crime Statistics Report. (1993). Federal Bureau of Investigation. Washington, DC.

Van Baar, A., Fleury, P., Soepatmi, S., Ultee, C., & Wesselman, P. (1989). Behavior in the first year after drug dependent pregnancy. *Archives of Diseases in Children, 64*, 241-245.

Villareal, S., McKinney, L., & Quackenbush, M. (1992). *Handle with care: Helping children prenatally exposed to drugs and alcohol*. Santa Cruz, CA: ETR Associates.

Wallerstein, J. (1984). Children of divorce: Preliminary report of a ten-year follow-up of young children. *American Journal of Orthopsychiatry, 54*(3), 444-498.

Wasserman, D., & Leventhal, J. (1991). Maltreatment of children born to cocaine dependent mothers. *American Journal of Diseases of Children, 145*, 410-411.

Weiner, L., & Morse, B. (1988). FAS: Clinical perspectives and prevention. In I. J. Chasnoff (Ed.), *Drugs, alcohol, pregnancy, and parenting*. Boston: Kluwer.

Weissberg, R., Caplan, M., & Harwood, R. (1991). Promoting competent young people in competence-enhancing environments: A systems-based perspective on primary prevention. *Journal of Consulting and Clinical Psychology, 59*, 830-841.

Wen, S., Goldenberg, R., Cutter, G., et al. (1990). Smoking, maternal age, fetal growth and gestational age at delivery. *American Journal of Obstetrics and Gynecology, 162*, 53-58.

Weston, D., Ivins, B., Zuckerman, B., Jones, C., & Lopez, R. (1989). Drug exposed babies: Research and clinical issues. *Zero to Three, 9*(5), 1-7.

White, E. (1992). Foster parenting the drug-affected baby. *Zero to Three, 13*(1), 13-17.

White, K. (1982). The relations between socioeconomic status and academic achievement. *Psychological Bulletin, 91*, 46-48.

Williams, B., & Howard, V. (1993). Children exposed to cocaine: Characteristics and implications for research and intervention. *Journal of Early Intervention*, *17*(1), 61-72.

Wilson, G. (1989). Clinical studies of infants and children exposed prenatally to heroin. *Annals of New York Academy of Science* (Prenatal Abuse of Licit and Illicit Drugs), *562*, 183-194.

Wilson, G., McCreary, R., Kean, J., & Baxter, C. (1979). The development of preschool children of heroin-addicted mothers: A controlled study. *Pediatrics*, *63*, 135-141.

Woods, N., Eyler, F., Behnke, M., & Conlon, M. (1993). Cocaine use during pregnancy: Maternal depressive symptoms and infant neurobehavior over the first month. *Infant Behavior and Development*, *16*(1), 83-98.

Zigler, E., & Berman, W. (1983). Discerning the future of early childhood intervention. *American Psychologist*, *38*, 894-906.

Zill, N., & Schoenborn, C. (1990). *Health of our nation's children: Developmental, learning, and emotional problems. United States, 1988. Advance data* (Number 190). Hyattsville, MD: National Center for Health Statistics.

Zuckerman, B. (1988). Marijuana and cigarette smoking during pregnancy: Neonatal effects. In I. J. Chasnoff (Ed.), *Drugs, alcohol, pregnancy, and parenting*. Boston: Kluwer.

Zuckerman, B., Amaro, H., & Beardslee, W. (1987). Mental health of adolescent mothers: The implications of depression and drug use. *Journal of Developmental and Behavioral Pediatrics*, *8*, 11-116.

Zuckerman, B., & Bresnahan, K. (1991). Developmental and behavioral consequences of prenatal drug and alcohol exposure. *Pediatric Clinics of North America*, *38*(6), 1387-1406.

CHAPTER 3

Understanding the Problem: The Gap Between Substance Abuse Programs and Child Welfare Services

LAURA FEIG

Substance abuse, by definition, impairs an individual's decision-making abilities. An individual who is abusing or addicted to alcohol or other drugs is not making rational choices about the substance and its effect on his or her life. The behaviors surrounding the acquisition and use of the drug have at least begun to crowd out other important aspects of the abuser's daily activities. When the substance abuser is a parent, it is likely that the chemical dependence has led to parenting styles that are detrimental to his or her children.

Child welfare agencies, charged with protecting children from abuse and neglect, have long recognized that substance abuse is highly prevalent among the families who come to their attention (Fanshel, 1975). While families' drugs of choice have changed over the years, the fact that alcohol and other drug abuse affects many dysfunctional families has not. Studies have shown both that substance abusers are more likely than other parents to abuse and neglect their children (Kelley, 1992) and that maltreating parents are more likely than other parents to abuse alcohol or other drugs

AUTHOR'S NOTE: The views expressed here are those of the author and do not necessarily reflect positions of the Office of the Assistant Secretary for Planning and Evaluation or the U.S. Department of Health and Human Services.

(Famularo, Stone, Barnum, & Wharton, 1986; Jaudes, Ekwo, & Van Voorhis, 1995; Kelleher, Chaffin, Hollenberg, & Fischer, 1994). These problems co-occur quite frequently, but even when the substance-abusing parent seeks help, or is the target of a community service agency's outreach activity, rarely are both the parent's substance abuse treatment needs and the family functioning issues related to child safety addressed simultaneously (Child Welfare League of America, 1992; McCullough, 1991).

In a parent, most often a mother, who both is abusing alcohol or drugs and is neglectful or abusive toward her children, the substance abuse and the child neglect/abuse are not separate issues, but rather are both aspects of the same intertwined problem. Unless both pieces are addressed, a healthy, functioning family is unlikely to result. It is rare, however, for substance abuse treatment programs and child welfare programs to work together in a truly collaborative manner.

Substance abuse treatment counselors and child protective services staff both work with many substance-abusing parents, but generally approach the addict and her family from quite different perspectives. There are often misunderstandings and even mutual distrust between professionals in the different fields that may prevent constructive collaborations. The lack of close cooperation between agencies that each have as their goal positive outcomes for the family being served may actually impede both agencies' progress with the family and disserve clients.

At the heart of conflict between child welfare and substance abuse treatment agencies is the conflict generally about the nature of substance abuse. Is substance abuse primarily a health problem, a social problem, or a criminal problem? Is addiction a disease, characterized by an inability to control one's use of the substance, or is it simply intentional misconduct by the substance abuser? Should our reaction to substance abuse be treatment or punishment? While the health and substance abuse treatment community generally views substance abuse and addiction as a chronic, progressive disease, much of the rest of society, often including child welfare agencies, views substance abuse as an irresponsible choice that should be punished. It is this division that lays the groundwork for a lack of understanding and cooperation between these two fields and others that produces ineffective interventions, unreasonable expectations, and poor outcomes that serve neither the families' needs nor the needs of the agencies with which the families interact.

The remainder of this chapter discusses the phenomenon of substance abuse among parents, illustrates the different perspectives of child welfare and substance abuse agencies, discusses in more detail the legislative and policy context in which potential collaborations are being developed or abandoned, and suggests several directions both fields might consider in seeking to better address the needs of these families, together.

Substance Abuse Among Parents

Substance abuse is not a yes/no, clear-cut, or black-and-white phenomenon; rather, it is a continuum of shades of gray. There are no clear lines between where, clinically, the use of alcohol or other drugs becomes abuse of them, or where abuse becomes dependency. Clinicians use a list of primarily behavioral symptoms to diagnose substance abuse; the more symptoms an individual displays, the farther along the spectrum he or she is likely to be diagnosed. Clinical professionals, however, may disagree about where on the spectrum an individual is at any given time. The terms *substance abuse, addiction,* and *chemical dependence* are used interchangeably in this volume. Families served by substance abuse and child protective service agencies may be anywhere along the continuum of substance abuse and addiction when they come to the attention of service providers.

The *Diagnostic and Statistical Manual of Mental Disorders, Fourth Edition* (or *DSM-IV* as it is commonly called) contains the standard diagnostic criteria used by professionals to diagnose substance abuse and addiction (American Psychiatric Association, 1994). The *DSM-IV* defines substance abuse as "a maladaptive pattern of substance use leading to clinically significant impairment or distress, as manifested" by one (or more) of several symptoms during the course of a year, including (the following are paraphrased)

- failure to fulfill major role obligations at work, school, or home
- use of the substance in hazardous situations
- legal problems related to the use of the substance
- continued use despite the social and interpersonal problems it has caused

Similarly, symptoms of substance dependence include (again, paraphrased)

- tolerance (needing increased quantities of the substance for the same effect)
- withdrawal (adverse physical symptoms when use is curtailed)
- use in larger amounts or over a longer period than was intended
- a persistent desire or unsuccessful efforts to cut down or control substance use
- a great deal of time spent to obtain, use, or recover from effects of the substance
- important activities given up or reduced because of substance use
- use continued despite problems caused or exacerbated by the substance

Among parents, particularly mothers, the neglect of child-rearing activities is one of the most common symptoms of substance abuse and dependence.

Substance abuse does not usually occur by itself, but is usually accompanied by a host of other physical and social problems that either may be the consequences of the abuse or may have preceded and precipitated the abuse. Among women particularly, clinical depression and other psychiatric disorders are present in many of those with substance abuse problems. Indeed, 79% of all mental health disorders (including substance abuse) occur in individuals who have had at least two such disorders in their lifetimes (Kessler et al., 1994). For some, the use of alcohol or other drugs may be self-medication, that is, the woman is using the drugs to relieve the psychiatric symptoms. Many women in treatment also have long histories of trauma such as rape and childhood abuse. Studies have found that between 40% and 85% of women in substance abuse treatment report either physical or sexual abuse as children, depending on the population studied and the types of abuse included in the inquiry (Black & Mayer, 1980; Boyd, 1993; Cohen & Densen-Gerber, 1982).

The Effects of Substance Abuse on Parenting

For proper social and emotional development, children need consistent caregiving. They need consistent rules and routines, and to understand what is expected of them. Households characterized by substance abuse, however, tend to be extremely disorganized and chaotic. A parent may react to his or her child's behaviors in one way when sober and in another when intoxicated. Rules don't exist or are applied inconsistently, and there is little supervision. Without such consistency, children may not develop a sense of cause and effect, may fail to establish appropriate patterns of behavior, and may not learn to recognize how their own behaviors affect others' behaviors toward them. They may not develop the internal sense of control important to regulating their behavior. Seilhamer (1991) reports a mother's observations about her children's relationship with their alcoholic father: "He yells a lot of the time at them; other times he lets them get away with things he punishes another time. . . . My children never know how to act toward him" (p. 181).

Among the characteristics of substance abuse is that the abuser becomes focused on the acquisition and use of the substance and on recuperating from its after effects. Increasing amounts of time and energy are spent on activities relating to the use, leaving little time or energy for parenting. As a result, children may be neglected or underparented. Virtually every child welfare agency in the nation has received reports of young children left alone or abandoned at a neighbor's home while the parent seeks drugs. In fact, in substance-abusing families neglect is much more likely than physical abuse to be the reason a family is reported to child protective services. One study, for instance, found that of children in foster care for whom parental alcohol or drug use was a factor in their placement, nearly 70% were neglect or abandonment cases versus 15% physical abuse cases. For children in foster care from families in which alcohol and drugs were not a factor, 37% were neglect or abandonment cases and 33% had been physically abused (Walker, Zangrillo, & Smith, 1991, 1994). Because women tend to be the primary caregivers for their children, such neglect cases almost always involve mothers rather than fathers.

A substance-abusing individual tends to be very focused on himor herself and his or her own emotional and physical needs. Within a family, household members tend to concentrate their attentions on satisfying the desires of the substance abuser in order to avoid his or her rages or other inappropriate reactions. In addition, a child will often take over the parent's roles and responsibilities, including caring for younger children, cooking, and cleaning. It is not unusual to find "parentified" children as young as 6 or 7 trying to take on major household responsibilities.

An addicted mother's unavailability (whether physical, emotional, or both) and inconsistent reactions to her child may also disrupt the attachment between mother and child. Children who are insecurely attached are at increased risk of a variety of behavioral problems and difficulties maintaining interpersonal relationships. Studies estimate that 70% to 80% of maltreated children show evidence of anxious attachment to their primary caregiver (Colin, 1991).

The Developmental Effects of Substance
Abuse and Child Abuse on Children

Early literature on children prenatally exposed to drugs painted a bleak picture of potential outcomes for these children (Chasnoff, 1985; Chasnoff, Burns, & Schnoll, 1983). More recent studies have found that although certain medical risks to the infant are clear, particularly the risk of premature birth and low birth weight, it is less certain that prenatal drug exposure per se (as separate from other factors such as the postnatal caregiving environment) routinely causes long-term developmental problems (Robins & Mills, 1993; Zuckerman, Frank, & Brown, 1995). Research has clearly documented, however, that child maltreatment has developmental, behavioral, and emotional consequences that persist into adolescence and adulthood. For instance, some children become defiant and distrustful of adults, while others become withdrawn and distracted. Many are described as having poor impulse control (National Research Council, 1993). Children of substance abusers are subject to a variety of challenges to healthy development both prenatally and postnatally, and many of them will ultimately show deficits. Brenda Jones Harden (see Chapter 2 in this volume) thoroughly reviews the literature about the effects of substance abuse on child development.

How Many Substance-Abusing Parents Are There?

National estimates reveal that in 1991 there were 3.4 million parents, about equally divided between fathers and mothers, who reported having used an illicit drug in the past month (U.S. Department of Health and Human Services, 1994). These parents (5.3% of all parents in 1991) had approximately 6 million children under age 18 living in their households. These figures do not include children who have been removed because of abuse or neglect and do not include absentee parents. Table 3.1 shows parents' drug use patterns by substance and by frequency of use. More recent figures show the rate of illicit drug use among parents has remained virtually unchanged (5.2% among all parents in 1994; 5.5% among women with children under 2 years of age in 1995), but detailed breakouts of recent data are not available (U.S. Department of Health and Human Services, 1995b, 1996b).

Of the parents who are current users of illicit drugs, three quarters have incomes above the poverty line, and one quarter have incomes above 300% of the poverty line. Those parents are 64% white, 21% non-Hispanic black, and 10% Hispanic. There are also several million alcoholic parents.

These figures may be somewhat misleading, since not all those who are currently using illicit drugs are using them to the point of abuse or addiction. Even severely limiting the population, however, there are about 158,000 parents, with roughly 300,000 to 400,000 children, who have used cocaine at least weekly in the past year, and there are 879,000 parents, with 1 to 2 million children, who report having used marijuana daily or almost daily for the past year. These figures may be compared with 445,000 children nationally who resided in foster care in 1993 (Curtis, Boyd, Leopold, & Petit, 1995).

The figures presented so far have included children at all ages, but the media and the child protection field have most often concentrated on drug exposed infants. The best figures available on prenatal drug use find that of the 4 million women who gave birth in 1992, 5.5% (or nearly 221,000 women) used illicit drugs during

Table 3.1 Prevalence of Drug and Alcohol Use by Parents According to Sex and Pattern of Use: 1991

Substance and Pattern of Use	Mothers		Fathers		All Parents	
	Number	Rate (%)	Number	Rate %	Number	Rate %
Alcohol						
Weekly or almost weekly for past year	4,522,634	12.7	8,524,823	30.5	13,047,457	20.5
Daily or almost daily for past year	1,371,515	3.8	3,875,465	13.9	5,246,980	8.2
Five or more drinks one or more times in past month	2,945,829	8.3	6,914,180	24.7	9,860,009	15.5
Five or more drinks three or more times in past month	1,440,943	4.0	3,739,628	13.4	5,180,572	8.1
Marijuana						
Past year	2,663,960	7.5	2,688,163	9.6	5,352,122	8.4
Past month	1,274,327	3.6	1,324,467	4.7	2,598,794	4.1
Weekly for past year	606,639	1.7	750,498	2.7	1,357,137	2.1
Daily or almost daily for past year	379,244	1.1	498,709	1.8	877,953	1.4

(continued)

69

Table 3.1 Continued

Substance and Pattern of Use	Mothers		Fathers		All Parents	
	Number	Rate (%)	Number	Rate %	Number	Rate %
Cocaine						
Past year	746,943	2.1	1,079,235	3.9	1,826,178	2.9
Past month	263,677	0.7	361,113	1.3	624,790	1.0
Weekly for past year	110,666	0.3	58,356	0.2	169,023	0.3
Nonmedical use of psychotherapeutic drugs						
Past year	1,509,049	4.2	1,117,026	4.0	2,626,075	4.1
Past month	529,920	1.5	457,337	1.6	987,257	1.6
Any illicit drug use						
Past year	3,809,906	10.7	3,399,779	12.2	7,209,685	11.3
Past month	1,804,046	5.1	1,588,250	5.7	3,392,296	5.3
Total population[a]	35,655,842	100.0	27,972,406	100.0	63,628,248	100.0

SOURCE: U.S. Department of Health and Human Services (1994). *Substance abuse among women and parents* (p. 26). Washington, DC: HHS Office of the Assistant Secretary for Planning and Evaluation.

NOTE: The category of illicit drug use includes nonmedical use of marijuana or hashish, cocaine (including crack), inhalants, hallucinogens (including PCP), heroin, or psychotherapeutic drugs. Numbers and percentages may not sum to totals because of rounding. Past year use includes use in the past month. Persons are counted as parents if they are 15 years of age or older and have their biological children under age 18 living with them or any stepchildren or adopted children living with them.

a. Totals represent the total numbers of mothers, fathers, and all parents in the population, and are given for purposes of comparison.

pregnancy. This included nearly 119,000 who used marijuana, 45,000 who used cocaine, 12,000 who used inhalants, and 3,600 who used heroin (National Institute on Drug Abuse, 1996). It is clear that far more children are affected by parents' substance abuse during childhood than are actually exposed prenatally.

Child Abuse and Neglect as a Precursor to Substance Abuse

Child abuse or neglect has often been cited as a consequence of substance abuse. Less often is child abuse and neglect considered as a cause of substance abuse. Childhood trauma may be a key predictor of substance abuse, however. Although methodological problems have limited thorough investigation of these issues to date, researchers are now examining alcohol and drug abuse as potential problems resulting from abuse and neglect. It has been hypothesized that alcohol and drugs may provide psychological escape for abuse victims, may serve to enhance the adolescent's self-esteem, or may reduce isolation by providing a peer group (National Research Council, 1993).

Differing Professional Perspectives

Substance abuse treatment agencies and child welfare agencies bring different professional missions, approaches, and biases to their interactions with substance-abusing families that influence their responses to these clients. Understanding these approaches and reactions may help bridge the gaps between them.

How Substance Abuse Agencies Typically Address Child Protection

Substance abuse treatment is not a monolithic intervention. There are many models and philosophies of alcohol and drug treatment interventions. Among the main types, or "modalities," are the following (adapted from Marion & Coleman, 1991):

- *Detoxification* is a short-term, medically supervised procedure to facilitate the individual's safe withdrawal from the substance. It usually involves a hospital stay of several days. Detoxification is usually viewed as a first step toward recovery, but is not a full treatment regime.

- *Outpatient Treatment Programs* are services provided on an individual or group basis for several hours each week. Programs usually include counseling and education about addiction and its progressive effects on clients' lives, and teach skills for leading drug-free lives.

- *Intensive Outpatient Programs* meet for more extended periods, generally several hours per day, 4 to 6 days per week. Such treatment is designed for clients who need more structure and rehabilitation than is available in standard outpatient programs.

- *Inpatient or Residential Treatment Programs* may be provided either in a hospital or in a nonmedical rehabilitation setting where patients reside 24 hours a day for extended periods. Most residential treatment programs last several weeks, although some are structured to provide several months of services to clients. Residential programs are appropriate for more severely addicted clients.

- *Therapeutic Communities and Halfway Houses* are structured, long-term drug-free living arrangements established to support recovery while gradually promoting the client's reintegration into the community.

- *Self-Help Groups* such as Alcoholics Anonymous and Narcotics Anonymous provide a forum within which the substance abuser can examine the effects of alcohol and drug use on his or her life and take steps to recover. Such groups are not considered formal treatment, although most treatment programs support their use in conjunction with treatment and as aftercare. There are no professionals or fees involved. These groups are based on the premise that addicts and alcoholics can help each other recover.

About 75% of clients in substance abuse treatment in 1992 were patients of outpatient treatment facilities, and 11% participated in residential programs. Among those abusing both alcohol and other drugs the use of residential programs was somewhat higher (18%; U.S. Department of Health and Human Services, 1995a).

Most substance abuse treatment programs were designed to treat men, and most substance abuse treatment clients are single men with no children in their households. In the publicly funded substance abuse treatment system, just under a third of clients are females, about 500,000 nationally in 1994 (National Association of State Alcohol and Drug Abuse Directors, 1996). While these figures do not include private treatment facilities receiving no public funding, figures are similar in samples including private providers (U.S. Department of Health and Human Services, 1995a). Few clients are mothers with children in their care. In a representative sample of clients receiving publicly funded substance abuse treatment in California in 1991-1992, 18% were women with children in their households (Gerstein, Johnson, Larison, Harwood, & Fountain, 1997).

Given that mothers are a relatively small segment of their client population, it is no wonder that treatment agencies often overlook child and family issues in their programs. Evaluations of treatment programs rarely even ask whether a client has children; rarely are improved family functioning, child protection, or custody issues examined as desirable outcomes of substance abuse treatment. Yet when clients are women, children are often important factors in the clients' interest in treatment and ability to participate actively. Women in treatment are much more likely than men to have children in their care and are three times as likely as men to report that parenting concerns are an important reason for their decision to enter treatment (Gerstein et al., 1997).

When treatment programs do consider clients as parents, it is usually around the need for child care. Many female substance abuse treatment clients are single parents and need child care if they are to attend treatment consistently. Yet few substance abuse treatment programs either provide or arrange for child care for their clients. The lack of child care may contribute to shorter average lengths of stay in treatment programs for clients with children in their care.

Many treatment programs will acknowledge potential child safety issues in some client families and the need to report serious child safety concerns to child protection authorities when they are aware of them. Because most programs rarely observe parents and children together, however, they are unlikely to detect safety concerns, nor do they view it as their responsibility to watch for potentially dangerous conditions or behaviors of clients toward their children. In fact, because building trust between their staff and clients is a high priority, treatment programs are often reluctant to maintain ongoing relationships with child protective service agencies because clients are likely to view such contacts negatively.

Substance abuse treatment programs typically view "success" in terms that do not include improved family functioning. Evaluations generally measure frequency of drug use as their principal outcome measure. Cost savings are measured most often in reduced criminal activity and incarceration and in lowered health care costs for the client. Some programs have also looked toward improved employment outcomes and decreased public welfare dependence as outcome measures. Only very rarely have programs examined family functioning, avoidance of foster care, and avoidance of health and social problems in clients' children as potential positive outcomes of substance abuse treatment.

How Child Welfare Agencies
Typically Address Substance Abuse

Each state has a system in place designed to investigate reports of child abuse or neglect and to intervene if a child is being endangered by a parent or other person. Collectively known as the child welfare system, the agencies performing these functions may be state or locally based and are generally either public or private, nonprofit agencies. The child welfare system is organized to investigate reports of child abuse or neglect, determine whether children who are the victims of abuse or neglect are safe in their homes, remove to alternative living arrangements (e.g., foster care) those children for whom it is unsafe to remain with their families, and provide services to alleviate the child safety problems. If a child is removed from his or her parents' care, the agency must develop a "permanency plan" for the child, designed to ensure a swift resolution of the situation for the child and family so that the child is not left in limbo. Child safety and permanency planning are the central concepts in child welfare service delivery. The permanency plan and progress toward it are reviewed periodically by the court. Services (often referred to as "reasonable efforts," reflecting federal statutory language that provides a framework for the child welfare system) must be provided to achieve the plan, which is usually to reunite the family while keeping the child safe. Other possible plans include adoption, guardianship, or independent living (for some older children).

The variety of reunification services that might be provided varies considerably from community to community, but among the most common are parenting training, individual or group counseling, and homemaker aides who teach basic household skills. Substance abuse and mental health treatment are usually provided through referral to local providers.

Many of the clients reported to and served by child welfare agencies have substance abuse problems. Indeed, professionals in child welfare agencies often feel as though all the families they serve have substance abuse issues, and as though they see all families with substance abuse problems. In fact, however, neither is true. Very few of the total number of substance-abusing families are ever reported to child protective services; and even of those reported, fairly few become the subject of open child welfare cases, and even fewer ever have children removed from the household. In 1994, children in approximately one million families nationally had open child welfare cases, and child welfare caseworkers were aware of substance abuse by the primary caretaker in 26% of these families. In cases where the primary caretaker was known to have a substance abuse problem, half received substance abuse treatment services, 23% were offered services that were not delivered (most likely because they were refused), and 23% were not offered services (Westat, 1997).

Most of the women who use drugs during pregnancy will never come to the attention of child protective services, even with mandatory reporting laws. In one study of the Medicaid expenditures for substance exposed infants, it was found that even when there was an alcohol or drug abuse diagnosis on the mother during or around the time of pregnancy, rarely was there a drug related diagnosis on the child (Ellwood, Adams, Crown, & Dodds, 1993). Because hospitals' child abuse reporting of infants is most often based on a positive drug test on the child at birth, if no such information is in the child's medical file it is unlikely a child protection report was filed. While 25% of the children identified as drug exposed in this study resided in foster care for most of the first 2 years of life, 75% of the children did not. Substance abuse is more likely to be a factor in the cases of infants reported to child protective services than for older children (Herskowitz, Seck, & Fogg, 1989).

In substance-abusing families, the overwhelming reason for the substantiation and for removal of the child from the household is neglect rather than abuse (Walker et al., 1991, 1994). Most often, in the midst of her addiction the mother fails to provide minimally adequate care to her children, prompting child protective service workers to make alternative arrangements for the children. Neglect cases reported to child protective services most often involve single mothers who are the primary (or sole) caretakers for their children. Where it is a father who is the substance abuser, neglect is less often the issue because the mother is usually present to care for the children. Child protective services is likely to become involved only if the father is physically abusive. Even in families where the father may be abusive toward the mother, if child protective services becomes involved, the case may be substantiated as the mother's neglect in failing to protect the child from the father's inappropriate behavior rather than as abuse by the father (Aron & Olson, 1997).

A frequently cited problem in the child welfare system is that children remain in foster care too long before decisions are made about their lives and permanent living arrangements. One reason for such delays is that services to address parents' problems (like substance abuse treatment) are often unavailable in a timely fashion. Until adequate treatment is provided, the agency can neither ensure a child's safety at home, nor can it demonstrate to a judge's satisfaction that the problem cannot be resolved in a satisfactory manner. Therefore the child waits in limbo. Such situations are a constant frustration to child welfare agencies that are accountable for the well-being of the children but do not control access to the services necessary to resolve the situation (Child Welfare League of America, 1992).

Manifestations of These Different Perspectives

The different perspectives of child welfare and substance abuse treatment programs become evident as they work together. While the differences can be overcome (or at least accommodated), if not addressed, they can prevent effective collaborations. The issues below illustrate several of these differences.

Who Is My Client?

For the child welfare agency, the child at risk is the client, first and foremost. While the child's needs cannot be considered outside the context of the family, the parents' needs are secondary. Child safety is the principal concern, though social workers prefer to ensure the child's safety within the family if possible. When the child's safety is in doubt, however, the child's needs must come first. Parents, particularly mothers, are often the focus of attention in trying to change the family environment to assure child safety.

The substance abuse treatment program views the substance-abusing parent as the principal client, and the child rarely enters into decision making about services. The parent's relationship with the drug is the focus of intervention. If the treatment program is aware of an abusive or neglectful parenting situation, staff may report it to child protective services, but most often an ongoing collaborative relationship with the child welfare agency is viewed as undermining the process of building trust with the parent client. The presence of children may be the reason a client is referred to an outpatient program rather than a more intensive, residential program, if no one would be available to care for the children while a mother is in residential treatment. Some programs offer parenting classes, but in very few are there extensive therapeutic activities involving both parent and child.

What Are My Goals?

Both agencies would prefer a healthy, functioning, drug-free family as the outcome of their interventions, but the alcohol and drug agency is principally interested in decreasing alcohol and drug use and decreasing the personal consequences of drug use, whereas the child welfare agency is concerned with ensuring the child's safety. For the child welfare agency that goal may best be achieved by separating the parent and child, sometimes permanently. Although not ideal, that may be a good outcome. For the treatment program, reduced use may be achieved regardless of child placement decisions. The goals are not mutually exclusive, but may at times conflict. For instance, a decision to remove a child to foster care may precipitate the parent's dropping out of drug treatment. Then, if the child is not in the household (and particularly if the case goal is something other than reunification), there is little immediate reason for the child welfare caseworker to care whether or not the parent continues treatment. In fact, it is easier for the caseworker if the parent drops out of treatment and thus can be shown uncooperative with the case plan. The situation is further complicated if Medicaid is the payment source for a mother's treatment. If the child is placed in foster care, the mother may lose eligibility for both welfare and Medicaid, eligibility for which is generally predicated on having a child in the household.

Is Addiction a Disease or Voluntary Behavior?

Substance abuse treatment professionals and the medical community consider addiction a disease, with diagnosable symptoms, identifiable stages, and a predictable course. Like many other diseases, it can be treated but not cured. Also like many other diseases, patients may not always adhere to the treatment regimen. For instance, rates of compliance with treatments for diabetes, high blood pressure, and other conditions are less than 50% (National Association of State Alcohol and Drug Abuse Directors, 1996). While the disease concept of addiction has become accepted in the medical community, many others continue to believe substance abuse is a behavioral choice and that alcohol or other drug abuse is simply "willful misconduct."

Child welfare professionals often consider substance abuse as bad behavior rather than as a disease needing treatment. Noncompliance may be viewed as evidence that a parent does not love his or her child or is unwilling to care for the child adequately. The ongoing abuse of alcohol or other drugs is seen as a choice. This difference in perspectives comes down to whether the professional believes the parent *can't* stop using, or *won't* stop using.

How Should I Respond to Relapse?

In a substance abuse treatment program, relapse prevention is an important part of therapy, but relapse is also an expected part of the recovery process. In fact, some professionals see certain relapses as therapeutic because they may teach a client he or she cannot somehow return to manageable levels of use. For the treatment professional, relapse signals the need for a more intensive or structured treatment regime and may trigger the revocation of privileges earned. The expectation is that many or most clients can be reengaged in treatment following a relapse.

Child welfare staff and judges are understandably frustrated by the slow, "two steps forward one step back" pace of recovery and seek to make a permanent placement for a child as soon as possible.

A relapse, particularly in a woman with an extensive history with the agency, is likely to be viewed as proof that the client cannot be trusted with custody of her child.

How Should I Guard My Client's Confidentiality?

Both child welfare agencies and substance abuse treatment programs operate under strict confidentiality standards that govern to whom they can release information. Designed to protect the parent's rights and the child's privacy, these standards may at times interfere with interagency cooperation. Except for the purpose of a child abuse or neglect report, substance abuse treatment programs cannot release information to a child welfare agency without the client's consent. Similarly, child welfare agencies cannot release information about the families they serve except to facilitate services for the benefit of the child. While the confidentiality rules both agencies operate under provide for working relationships on behalf of the client, the exchange of information is not automatic. Further, the inclination on both sides to keep information close may work against collaborative efforts.

Are My Client's Children Better Off With the Child Welfare (or Substance Abuse Treatment) Agency Involved?

From the substance abuse treatment agency's perspective, collaborating with the child welfare agency may come at the price of some measure of client trust. To make the cost worthwhile, the treatment agency must believe that working with the child welfare agency brings some benefit to their families. Where the child welfare agencies are overloaded and not operating well, however, the substance abuse treatment program may not see such a benefit. If the experience of the substance abuse treatment program is that child abuse reports do not result in services on behalf of the family, or that sharing of information about clients' progress does not result in favorable reunification decisions when the client does well, the treatment program may be reluctant to collaborate in the future. Similarly, if the experience of child welfare caseworkers is that treatment does not result in sufficient change to parents' behavior to resolve child safety issues, caseworkers may see little reason to expend effort on collaboration.

How Does the Time Frame of Recovery Relate to the Child's Need for Permanence?

Substance abuse is a chronic, relapsing condition that has generally taken years to develop and, even in successful clients, will take years to resolve (although progress may be seen more quickly). Childhood is short, however, and child welfare agencies are charged with assuring permanent safe living arrangements for children in their care relatively quickly, usually within 18 months. These conflicting time lines may cause tension between substance abuse treatment and child welfare agencies. Child welfare agencies will want to know quickly whether or not a parent will recover, and may be exasperated by setbacks in a parent's performance in treatment. Social workers, from the treatment agency's perspective, either may push to declare defeat too soon, or may try to reunify a family too quickly, when a parent begins recovery but may not yet be ready for the stress of parenting responsibilities. The prospect that a parent may express a desire for treatment and begin attending a treatment program and then relapse is vexing for child welfare workers and creates more work for them. Because they find it easier and may consider it better for the child if the parent does not try in the first place, they may undermine treatment efforts.

Is Addiction to Crack Different From Addiction to Other Drugs and Alcohol?

Most substance abuse treatment agencies view a client's addiction to crack cocaine as being little different from alcoholism or heroin addiction. The principles of treatment and expectations for recovery are similar. The disease of addiction is the same. In fact, polydrug abuse (the abuse of multiple drugs and alcohol rather than a primary substance) is the norm among substance abuse treatment clients.

Most child welfare professionals, however, view crack as being more ominous and more dangerous to children living in the household than alcohol or other substances: "More than alcohol, and more than heroin, crack cocaine threatens the well-being of hundreds of thousands of children" (Besharov & Baehler, 1994). Case-workers who do not view as significant a parent's years' long history of alcohol abuse may seek to place a child in foster care if a parent reports a single incident of crack use or, alternatively, may be willing to reunify a family where a parent with a long substance abuse history stops using an illegal drug but continues to drink heavily.

Child welfare workers cite social factors of crack addiction as reasons why crack is more dangerous to children of substance abusers. These include that cocaine is expensive and harder to acquire than alcohol, taking the parent's time, attention, and re-sources away from child rearing. Women are reported to be more inclined to use crack rather than heroin, in part because it is smoked rather than injected, and the criminal activity that often accompanies the drug trade adds a danger factor to children that is not generally present with alcohol abuse.

At least some major treatment outcome studies show similar rates and patterns of recovery for a variety of drugs including cocaine and alcohol (Gerstein et al., 1994). These different perceptions by staff in the two fields may promote misunderstanding and conflict as the workers view the same phenomenon differently.

Together We're Stronger

The previous sections of this chapter have described how and why the differing professional perspectives of substance abuse treatment and child welfare agencies often impede effective collaboration. In this section I will argue that while our differences are real and rational, to the extent we let them get in the way of collaboration we both disserve our mutual clients and sabotage the goals both of our clients and of both agencies. Working together, not despite our differences but because our differing perspectives make us stronger united, we can improve our work with and outcomes for our clients, both parents and children.

As described above, treatment providers and child welfare pro-fessionals differ in their priorities and approaches to substance-abusing families. These differences are rooted in their different missions, each of which is important for the parents and children involved and for communities and society as a whole. Improving these agencies' working relationships does not require that either lessen their commitments to their core missions, only that they recognize that both sets of goals are compatible and can best be achieved by joint efforts.

Understanding the Policy and Legislative Context

At the Federal and State Levels: Welfare Reform

Welfare reform, however it plays out in the states and at the federal level, is likely over the next several years to define the context of policies and programs regarding substance-abusing parents with children, particularly those involved with the child welfare system. Because so many of these families are welfare recipients, and are among those least likely to be immediately employable, they are likely to face increased stresses under the time limits, sanctions, personal responsibility agreements, and other policy features being debated as states transform their welfare systems.

Welfare reform is likely to present both challenges and opportunities to states seeking to deal with the problems of substance abuse and child protection. Some would argue that the welfare system has prolonged the addictions of some recipients by eliminating negative economic consequences of substance abuse. Others argue that restricting cash assistance will harm children because their parents (particularly those abusing substances) will not or cannot respond to incentives for self-sufficiency, at least not within tight time frames. Both may be true to some extent, but it seems clear that significant changes in welfare will have important consequences for these families. It may be possible to steer some toward treatment, recovery, and self-sufficiency. In other cases, increased child protection may be necessary.

At the State and Local Levels:
Support for Collaborative Efforts

Collaborations require support from all levels of an agency. Management must recognize and value the time staff spend to develop and maintain relationships with their counterparts in other agencies. Similarly, staff must understand and respect the value of their counterparts' efforts in other agencies. Unless both management and line workers are committed to a collaboration, and value the outcomes sought, change will not be achieved. Further, effective collaborations are most likely to be established when each agency involved brings resources, be they funding, facilities, or services, to the joint activities. Unless an agency approaches potential collaborators with ideas about what it can offer to a partnership and not just what it wants, collaborations will be difficult to establish. Establishing and maintaining collaborative efforts is difficult. At many points along the way it seems easier to give up and go back to old ways of doing business. There are good reasons to push forward with collaborative efforts, however. Without them, service systems tend to become fragmented and duplicative, as agencies each try to create services their clients need and don't build on each others' strengths. In addition, unless they work together and take joint responsibility for client outcomes, each agency sees its role as limited, and no agency is responsible for the totality of the service plan and assuring it is carried out. Families get lost in between.

Directions for the Future

Through positive relationships with child welfare services, substance abuse treatment agencies can build records showing that families that stick with treatment can regain or maintain custody of their children. Similarly, by working with substance abuse treatment agencies, child welfare agencies can assure appropriate substance abuse treatment services are available to meet their clients' needs. Yet in building such relationships professionals in both fields will need to consider some new directions. Later chapters in this volume will provide detail about considerations in building new relationships between agencies and about the lessons learned by agencies that have already begun to make changes. Here I begin a discussion of new directions by suggesting several steps and concepts that should be explored as we endeavor to build a bridge between our fields. It should be noted that few reliable data are available to show effectiveness for the approaches suggested; such research simply does not currently exist. The notions described below, therefore, are instead informed speculations about what steps could be tried and tested where we know that current standard practice is not producing the outcomes we desire. These potential directions are divided into four groups: (a) collaborations regarding the planning and administration of programs; (b) collaborations around case monitoring and ongoing activities; (c) joint treatment concepts; and (d) prevention for the next generation.

New Directions: Program Planning and Administration

In treatment programs serving a population of women with children, significant numbers of clients will at some point be involved with the child welfare system. While relatively few children will actually be placed in foster care, many are likely at some point to be the subject of child protective services reports (Goerge, Van Voorhis, & Sanfilippo, 1996). Planning ahead for the interactions between agencies will avoid problems that might otherwise arise and will make it less contentious to resolve issues that will arise even with efforts to work together. Several steps might be taken:

• *Provide joint training for social services and substance abuse treatment staff*
If staff are to work together, it is helpful that they first understand their respective roles and each others' missions and programs. Until child welfare staff understand the black box of substance abuse treatment and substance abuse treatment staff understand the bottom lines for child protection, misunderstandings are inevitable. Preservice training in each profession rarely includes much information on the other (Dore, Doris, & Wright, 1995). It is therefore likely that in-service training opportunities organized by each agency will be the most convenient opportunity to introduce this material. Opportunities for staff to share their expectations for and experiences with treating joint clients are particularly useful. Several curricula for joint training are available and may be adapted to individual communities' needs. Because frequent staff turnover is a problem in both the substance abuse treatment and child welfare fields, training opportunities should be available at frequent intervals.

- *Develop team staffing approaches*

It is unrealistic to expect that all substance abuse treatment staff will become child protection experts and vice versa. Although staff should have a basic familiarity with both sets of issues, they don't need to do each others' jobs. In fact, recognizing that they don't need to be experts in each others' fields to work together may go a long way toward easing workers' fears that collaboration will mean another set of activities to master in addition to those for which they are already responsible. Team staffing arrangements may allow workers to collaborate on behalf of clients without needing to impinge on each others' responsibilities. For instance, a substance abuse treatment staff person may be stationed on site part-time at the social service agency to do substance abuse assessments, and child services staff could spend time at the substance abuse treatment agency to work with parents and children together. Involving child welfare staff in planning substance abuse treatment discharge and aftercare (and substance abuse treatment staff in foster care discharge planning) may also be helpful.

- *Provide joint funding for services*

As agencies begin to discuss collaborative efforts, the issue of financing quickly arises. Too often joint efforts are pitched as why your agency should do more for (and pay for) my clients. Less often are collaborations proposed as joint efforts, jointly funded. Yet unless both agencies are financially committed to the endeavor, they will not place equal value on the outcomes of the effort and staff will not "own it" as theirs. Further, an agency director is likely to view a request rooted in arguments about what his (or her) agency should do for yours as a grab for his budget rather than a sincere proposal for a mutually beneficial arrangement. Both substance abuse treatment and child welfare agencies are perpetually underfunded; neither can be viewed as a deep pocket. In proposing a collaboration, bring something to the table; don't just come with a list of what the other agency can do for you.

- *Conduct joint goal-setting for programs*

Speaking with local staff, one often realizes that talking to each other as services are designed and implemented would likely improve agencies' ability to meet client needs. Regularly staff tell stories about how "they" don't do well on behalf of "my" clients.

Airing both agencies' goals and expectations and trying to match those up with respect to joint clients would help diffuse such tension. Typically, stories from child welfare staff involve the delays in the availability of a treatment program, that the treatment program is not providing services tailored for women and families, or that treatment usually fails to achieve the outcomes child welfare staff seek from it. Substance abuse treatment staff in turn talk about how child welfare staff make capricious placement decisions or are not supportive enough of treatment progress.

By talking through these problems on a systematic rather than case by case basis can assure agencies that their concerns are understood and steps to address them can be agreed upon up front.

New Directions: Case Monitoring and Ongoing Activities

Ongoing collaborations must involve more than planning and administration. The true test of collaborations is in the ongoing, day-to-day interactions between agencies regarding joint clients. If systems are to work together well, staff must be comfortable sharing information that advances the client's treatment plan and must understand one another's decision making sufficiently to come together around the client's needs, prognosis, and what consequences are to result from clients' progress or lack thereof. Possibilities include the following:

- *Develop jointly sought treatment milestones*
Recovery may be a lifelong process, but it should be possible to measure progress in the near term. Child protection agencies must make decisions about children's well-being on an ongoing basis. For children in foster care, decisions about placements must be reviewed every 6 months, and decisions about permanency must usually be made within 12 to 18 months. Guidance from the treatment agency about the parent's prognosis and expected progress is helpful in this decision making, but treatment agencies often do not or cannot provide guidance that child welfare agencies find useful. Joining together to discuss what treatment outcomes each agency is expecting and what progress can be viewed along the way would be useful. Expecting complete abstinence immediately and forever is unrealistic, but if treatment is accomplishing useful

outcomes for child welfare purposes, then positive progress should be seen over a period of months. Similarly, if progress is being made on both substance abuse and other child safety issues, clients should be able to expect positive feedback from child welfare agencies, including increased access to their children and ultimately favorable custody recommendations.

• *Improve family risk assessments as they relate to substance abuse*
Many risk assessments used by child welfare professionals barely mention substance abuse, although the behaviors associated with substance abuse may underlie symptoms observed (Dore et al., 1995). As was discussed earlier in this chapter, substance abuse is a continuum of symptoms and impairment rather than a yes/no phenomenon. It would be useful to have tools that better enable child welfare staff to differentiate between severe and milder impairment, and to allow for a better recognition of when substance abuse in conjunction with other factors about the parent's social environment is likely to represent a significant child safety problem. Similarly, being able to recognize the signs of relapse would assist staff in assessing ongoing safety. Substance abuse professionals recognize that relapse is a process rather than an event, and that warning signs are visible well before the individual resumes use. These signals may be observed by members of the family's social network or by professionals in regular contact with the family.

• *Adapt and test TASC (Treatment Alternatives to Street Crime) and RMA (Referral and Monitoring Agency) concepts for social service clients*
Unless both agencies find ways of building relationships with families and by doing so continue to work with clients over time, success rates will be low. In the substance abuse treatment field, a client's length of stay in care is a key predictor of success. Similarly, those child welfare clients who maintain regular contact with the agency and follow through with their treatment plans are more likely to provide safe environments for their children and are more likely to retain or regain custody. Cooperatively, child welfare and substance abuse treatment agencies can assist one another to retain clients. In the treatment field, many providers have found that another agency's monitoring of its clients helps to maintain clients' resolve toward recovery. For instance, many programs prefer clients

who are referred through the criminal justice system because the clients are motivated to participate—they realize that dropping out means revocation of parole or other serious consequences. Clients referred through and monitored by law enforcement agencies have been found to have lower drop-out rates and longer lengths of stay (in some studies, much longer) than other clients (Collins & Allison, 1983; Haller, Elswick, Dawson, Knisely, & Schnoll, 1993). In the criminal justice community such efforts are often referred to as Treatment Alternatives to Street Crime (or TASC) programs. Similar concepts showed promise in monitoring treatment for disabled addicts and alcoholics in the Supplemental Security Income and Social Security Disability Insurance programs operated by the Social Security Administration before they were eliminated by Congress in 1996. In the Social Security context they were referred to as Referral and Monitoring Agencies, or RMAs.

Child welfare agencies may be able to perform a similar function working cooperatively with treatment agencies around a client's recovery and to assure the safety of the client's children. A client who continues with treatment can earn or retain significant responsibilities with respect to her children; clients who drop out or otherwise fail to maintain satisfactory participation in treatment must be more closely monitored. Close communication between child welfare and substance abuse treatment agencies around the needs of their mutual clients and progress (or lack of it) toward goals is essential in such efforts.

New Directions: Joint Treatment Concepts

Working together cannot stop at monitoring and case management. If both agencies are to be responsible for client outcomes, both must also participate in the intervention. For a population of parents whose children have suffered or are at risk of neglect and abuse, both the substance abuse and the parenting issues must be addressed. Rather than sending clients all over town for disparate interventions, we are likely to be more successful if we deliver our services as a single package, in a single program. Even those substance-abusing parents who are not the subject of official child protective service cases are likely to benefit from both types of interventions. Delivering them together will ensure the same messages are being delivered by both agencies, that parents' concerns for their children are addressed in treatment, and that clients are less likely to play one agency against the other. Joint treatment concepts might include the following:

- *Use a parenting focus as a treatment "hook"*
Professionals in substance abuse treatment agencies and child protection agencies speak of similar issues as they discuss the problems they face in assisting clients to recover and strengthen their families and their interactions with their children. In particular, service providers working with substance-abusing families routinely find it difficult to attract clients to their programs and to maintain families' commitment to recovery once they have begun. Collaborations may improve recruitment and retention by better addressing clients needs and concerns. For instance, female substance abuse treatment clients with children in their care often report that parenting or child custody concerns are an important reason for their participation in treatment (Gerstein et al., 1997; U.S. Department of Health and Human Services 1996a). By providing services closely tied to parenting issues, agencies may be better able to attract these clients and retain them in care. Child welfare agencies may be able to provide parenting classes in substance abuse treatment settings, or may otherwise be helpful in funding or designing such services. Assistance with child care, early intervention services, or other child-related services may also be available through child welfare agencies.

- *Integrate child development services with substance abuse treatment*
Readers of this volume are no doubt well aware that substance abuse is a multigenerational problem. A parent's substance use affects his or her child in profound ways. Providers of programs that treat parents, particularly those whose families are involved with child protective services, know that the children in these families will have significant developmental needs apart from their parents. Addressing these child development issues in conjunction with the parent's treatment needs is likely to be cost-effective. Thomas McMahon and Suniya Luthar (see Chapter 6 in this vol-

ume) detail the advantages of adding child development staff to treatment programs.

• *Provide long-term services*
Child welfare and substance abuse treatment professionals accept in principle that treatment efforts will not be effective for all clients. For an individual client, however, it is often difficult to decide that the client is unreceptive and unlikely to make significant changes in her life in the near future. But it is precisely the near-term decision making about recovery prospects that allow child welfare agencies to make permanency decisions for children. A child should not need to wait through six treatment attempts over 3 years for an agency to figure out that this particular mother isn't able to make the changes necessary for her to care for her children. Programmatic and research attention to developing early indicators and predictors of successful treatment would be helpful to both fields.

We need to recognize that short-term programs produce short-term results, and that is not what we seek for these clients. The problems that bring them to our agencies' doorsteps are years in the making and are not likely to be solved with a few weeks of intervention. While services may become less intensive over time and may change form as clients progress, clients' families are likely to require support in one form or another over a period of years if they are to endure day-to-day life and extraordinary crises without losing their social equilibrium. We must be prepared to develop long-term supports for some families if there is to be long-term recovery. Concentrating on the development of new social networks that support sobriety and child development is one strategy for assuring long-term support as program interventions become less intensive.

• *Experiment with joint mother-child placements*
As was mentioned earlier, addicted women often have long histories of trauma, beginning in childhood. They may need not rehabilitation, but the initial development of life and social skills. It has often been observed that drug users' emotional development stops at the point the drug use was initiated. Although adults in body, emotionally many of these women are children and are not initially capable of putting their children's needs above their own. A number of communities are now developing or considering

multigenerational child welfare placements in which both parent and child live with a family that will work with the dyad around parenting skills and will model appropriate parent-child behaviors. While no data exist to date regarding the effectiveness of such approaches, the approaches offer a possible way to provide intensive work with mother and child without separating the two.

- *Involve kin who may be caring for clients' children*
  Increasingly, grandparents and other relatives are providing care to children whose parents cannot care for them (Wulczyn, 1994). These may be informal arrangements in which a relative has stepped in to care for the child, or they may be formal foster care placements. Regardless of whether the relative has formal custody, these kin are important parts of the family's social network. They may assist the children and agencies by providing safe alternative care for children without breaking bonds between parent and child. On the other hand, relatives may also undermine treatment attempts because a parent's recovery may upset long-established family structures. Either way, involving these kin in treatment planning can help assure that those with influence over the parent are working toward the same goals.

New Directions: Prevention

Children of substance abusers generally, and particularly children who are in foster care or who are the subjects of open child welfare cases, have endured great stress and trauma. They are at extremely high risk of a great many social problems, among them substance abuse. If we are to avoid these children becoming the next generation's substance-abusing parents, prevention activities are vital. Child welfare agencies and substance abuse treatment programs that are treating parents see these children on a regular basis. Services designed to foster resilience and to help these children find a safe, drug-free path to adulthood are sorely needed.

Mutual Responsibilities

Parents and families must take the first steps toward recovery and must become committed to sober lifestyles and must provide safe home environments for their children, but the government and

92   SUBSTANCE ABUSE, FAMILY VIOLENCE & CHILD WELFARE

private sectors also have a responsibility to provide the tools
families need to make the journey—appropriate substance abuse
treatment, including aftercare; child welfare services that assure
child safety; and social supports that encourage continued sobriety.
These supports are central to all our goals in any of our agencies.
They are most effectively delivered collaboratively. To the extent
we fail to work together and instead undermine each other's efforts,
we and our clients lose.

The remaining chapters in this volume will expand upon these
themes and suggest specific ways in which child welfare and substance abuse treatment agencies may work together in order to
assist clients more efficiently and effectively to achieve healthy,
drug-free lives and safe, functional families.

References

American Psychiatric Association. (1994). *Diagnostic and statistical manual of mental disorders* (4th ed.). Washington, DC: American Psychiatric Association.

Aron, L. Y., & Olson, K. K. (1997). *Efforts by child welfare agencies to address domestic violence: The experiences of five communities.* Washington, DC: HHS Office of the Assistant Secretary for Planning and Evaluation.

Besharov, D. J., & Baehler, K. (1994). Introduction. In D. Besharov (Ed.), *When drug addicts have children* (pp. ix-xxvi). Washington, DC: Child Welfare League of America and American Enterprise Institute.

Black, R., & Mayer, J. (1980). Parents with special problems: Alcoholism and opiate addiction. *Child Abuse & Neglect, 4,* 45-54.

Boyd, C. J. (1993). The antecedents of women's crack cocaine abuse: Family substance abuse, sexual abuse, depression and illicit drug use. *Journal of Substance Abuse Treatment, 10,* 433-438.

Chasnoff, I. J. (1985). Effects of maternal narcotic vs. nonnarcotic addiction on neonatal behavior and infant development. In T. M. Pinkert (Ed.), *Current research on the consequences of maternal drug abuse* (NIDA Research Monograph No. 59). Rockville, MD: National Institute on Drug Abuse.

Chasnoff, I. J., Burns, W. J., & Schnoll, S. H. (1983). Perinatal addiction: The effects of maternal narcotic and nonnarcotic substance abuse on the fetus and neonate. In *Problems of drug dependence, 1983: Proceedings of the 45th annual scientific meeting, The Committee on Problems of Drug Dependence, Inc.* (NIDA Research Monograph No. 49). Rockville, MD: National Institute on Drug Abuse.

Child Welfare League of America, North American Commission on Chemical Dependency. (1992). *Children at the front: A different view of the war on alcohol and drugs.* Washington, DC: Child Welfare League of America.

Cohen, F. S., & Densen-Gerber, J. (1982). A study of the relationship between child abuse and drug addiction in 178 patients. *Child Abuse & Neglect, 6*(4), 383-387.

Colin, V. L. (1991). *Human attachment—What we know now.* Washington, DC: HHS Office of the Assistant Secretary for Planning and Evaluation.

Collins, J. J., & Allison, M. (1983). Legal coercion and retention in drug abuse treatment. *Hospital and Community Psychiatry, 34*(12), 1145-1149.

Curtis, P. A., Boyd, J. D., Leopold, M., & Petit, M. (1995). *Child abuse and neglect: A look at the states.* Washington, DC: Child Welfare League of America Press.

Dore, M. M., Doris, J., & Wright, P. (1995). Identifying substance abuse in maltreating families: A child welfare challenge. *Child Abuse & Neglect, 19*(5), 531-543.

Ellwood, M. R., Adams, E. K., Crown, W. H., & Dodds, S. (1993). *An exploratory analysis of the Medicaid expenditures of substance exposed children under 2 years of age in California.* Washington, DC: U.S. Department of Health and Human Services, Office of the Assistant Secretary for Planning and Evaluation.

Famularo, R., Stone, K., Barnum, R., & Wharton, R. (1986). Alcoholism and severe child maltreatment. *American Journal of Orthopsychiatry, 56*(3), 482-485.

Fanshel, D. (1975). Parental failure and consequences for children: The drug abusing mother whose children are in foster care. *American Journal of Public Health, 65*(6), 604-612.

Gerstein, D. R., Johnson, R. A., Harwood, H., Fountain, D., Suter, N., & Malloy, K. (1994). *Evaluating recovery services: The California drug and alcohol treatment assessment.* Sacramento: California Department of Alcohol and Drug Programs.

Gerstein, D. R., Johnson, R. A., Larison, C. L., Harwood, H. J., & Fountain, D. (1997). *Alcohol and drug abuse treatment for parents and welfare recipients: Outcomes, benefits and costs.* Washington, DC: HHS Office of the Assistant Secretary for Planning and Evaluation.

Goerge, R., Van Voorhis, J., & Sanfilippo, L. (1996). *Final report of the Core Dataset Project—Child welfare service histories.* Washington, DC: U.S. Department of Health and Human Services, Office of the Assistant Secretary for Planning and Evaluation.

Haller, D. L., Elswick, R. K., Dawson, K. S., Knisely, J. S., & Schnoll, S. H. (1993). Retention in treatment of perinatal substance abusers. In L. Harris (Ed.), *Problems of drug dependence, 1992: Proceedings of the 54th annual scientific meeting, The College on Problems of Drug Dependence, Inc.* (NIDA Research Monograph No. 132). Washington, DC: National Institute on Drug Abuse.

Herskowitz, J., Seck, M., & Fogg, C. (1989). *Substance abuse and family violence.* Boston: Massachusetts Department of Social Services, Research, Evaluation and Planning Unit.

Jaudes, P. K., Ekwo, E., & Van Voorhis, J. (1995). Association of drug abuse and child abuse. *Child Abuse & Neglect, 19*(9), 1065-1075.

Kelleher, K., Chaffin, M., Hollenberg, J., & Fischer, E. (1994). Alcohol and drug disorders among physically abusive and neglectful parents in a community-based sample. *American Journal of Public Health, 84*(10), 1586-1590.

Kelley, S. J. (1992). Parenting stress and child maltreatment in drug-exposed children. *Child Abuse & Neglect, 16,* 317-328.

Kessler, R. C., McGonagle, K. A., Zhao, S., Nelson, C. B., Hughes, M., Eshleman, S., Wittchen, H., & Kendler, K. S. (1994). Lifetime and 12-month prevalence of DSM-III-R psychiatric disorders in the United States: Results from the National Comorbidity Survey. *Archives of General Psychiatry, 5,* 8-19.

Marion, T. R., & Coleman, K. (1991). Recovery issues and treatment resources. *Treating the chemically dependent and their families* (pp. 100-127). Newbury Park, CA: Sage.

McCullough, C. (1991). The child welfare response. *The Future of Children: Drug Exposed Infants, 1,* 61-71.

National Association of State Alcohol and Drug Abuse Directors. (1996). *State resources and services relating to alcohol and other drug problems for fiscal year 1994.* Washington, DC: Author.

National Institute on Drug Abuse. (1996). *National Pregnancy and Health Survey.* Washington, DC: U.S. Department of Health and Human Services, National Institutes of Health.

National Research Council. (1993). *Understanding child abuse and neglect.* Washington, DC: National Academy Press.

Robins, L. N., & Mills, J. L. (1993, December). Effects of in utero exposure to street drugs. *American Journal of Public Health, 83*(Suppl.).

Seilhamer, R. A. (1991). Effects of addiction on the family. In D. C. Daley & M. S. Raskin (Eds.), *Treating the chemically dependent and their families* (pp. 172-194). Newbury Park, CA: Sage.

U.S. Department of Health and Human Services. (1994). *Substance abuse among women and parents.* Washington, DC: HHS Office of the Assistant Secretary for Planning and Evaluation.

U.S. Department of Health and Human Services. (1995a). *Overview of the National Drug and Alcoholism Treatment Unit Survey (NDATUS): 1992 and 1980-1992.* Washington, DC: HHS Substance Abuse and Mental Health Services Administration.

U.S. Department of Health and Human Services. (1995b). *Preliminary estimates from the 1994 National Household Survey on Drug Abuse.* Washington, DC: HHS Substance Abuse and Mental Health Services Administration.

U.S. Department of Health and Human Services. (1996a). *The National Treatment Improvement Evaluation Study.* Washington, DC: HHS Substance Abuse and Mental Health Services Administration.

U.S. Department of Health and Human Services. (1996b). *Preliminary estimates from the 1995 National Household Survey on Drug Abuse.* Washington, DC: HHS Substance Abuse and Mental Health Services Administration.

Walker, C. D., Zangrillo, P., & Smith, J. M. (1991). *Parental drug abuse and African American children in foster care: Issues and study findings.* Washington, DC: U.S. Department of Health and Human Services, Office of the Assistant Secretary for Planning and Evaluation.

Walker, C. D., Zangrillo, P., & Smith, J. M. (1994). Parental drug abuse and African American children in foster care. In R. Barth, J. D. Berrick, & N. Gilbert (Eds.), *Child welfare research review* (pp. 109-122). New York: Columbia University Press.

Westat. (1997). *National study of preventive, protective, and reunification services delivered to children and their families.* Washington, DC: U.S. Department of Health and Human Services, Children's Bureau.

Wulczyn, F. (1994). Status at birth and infant foster care placement in New York City. In R. Barth, J. D. Berrick, & N. Gilbert (Eds.), *Child welfare research review* (pp. 146-184). New York: Columbia University Press.

Zuckerman, B., Frank, D., & Brown, E. (1995). Overview of the effects of abuse and drugs on pregnancy and offspring. In C. N. Chiang & L. P. Finnegan (Eds.), *Medications development for the treatment of pregnant addicts and their infants* (NIDA Research Monograph No. 149, pp. 16-38). Rockville, MD: National Institute on Drug Abuse.

• *CHAPTER 4* •

Child Welfare and Substance Abuse: Premises, Programs, and Policies

HANK RESNIK

STEPHEN E. GARDNER

CARL M. ROGERS

Increasingly, professionals and researchers in a variety of fields are exploring the links between child welfare and substance abuse. The damaging effects of parental and family substance abuse, the primary focus of this chapter, contribute to a host of child welfare problems including child abuse and neglect, juvenile delinquency, runaways, youth homelessness, and substance use among youth themselves.

Services and programs to address these interrelated problems at all levels of society—federal, state, county, and local—are scattered across a huge and poorly coordinated array of governmental, non-profit, and private sector agencies and initiatives. In a landmark report titled *Children at the Front: A Different View of the War on Alcohol and Drugs* (1992), the Child Welfare League of America documented at the federal level alone eight major agencies with responsibilities for addressing chemical dependency in families and 37 diverse programs and initiatives totaling billions of dollars. Our society is still far from having a coherent, unified theoretical and research-based approach to the prevention and treatment of substance abuse-related child welfare problems.

Although focusing primarily on child welfare and substance abuse within the family context, this chapter examines several aspects of the relationship of substance abuse and child welfare and the implications for effective programs and policies. These include

- The effects of parental substance abuse on children
- Challenges to social service providers
- Promising approaches that address substance abuse from a child welfare perspective
- Substance abuse programs that have an impact on child welfare
- Implications for program development and improvement

Parental/Family Substance Abuse and Related Problems

In the past two decades some patterns of adult substance abuse have shifted in ways that are having a significant impact on adults and children alike. Specifically, many more women are substance abusers today when compared to previous periods (CASA, 1996; U.S. General Accounting Office [USGAO], 1990). Much of the increase in female drug abusers has been attributable to the accessibility and low cost of crack cocaine. According to the National Household Survey (Substance Abuse and Mental Health Services Administration, 1995), use of crack cocaine declined from 1991 to 1992 but then rose to exceed 1991 levels. In 1994, about 4 million people had used crack cocaine at least once in their lives, and about 1.2 million people had used it within the past year.

The problem of substance abuse among women is particularly important in the following discussion because the vast majority of families involved in child welfare systems are headed by females, and substance abuse among women has increased at alarming rates. This is not to say that women are "to blame" for substance abuse-related child welfare problems or that men and fathers are never involved. On the contrary, substance abuse among males often exceeds that among females; according to the National Crime Victimization Survey done by the Bureau of Justice Statistics, 2.5 million women a year are victims of violence in the United States; and alcohol and drugs are associated with up to 50% of all spousal abuse cases (Join Together, 1996).

Substance-abusing men play a critically important, often highly negative role in troubled families. Nevertheless, most families that become closely involved with child welfare systems are poor (wealthy families are better able to pay for services that provide privacy and protection). Because of welfare eligibility requirements, cultural predilections, and other factors, low-income women often are left to shoulder the responsibility for children's welfare when substance abuse is a family problem. As a result, programs and services that address the interrelated issues of child welfare and substance abuse have tended to focus on the female parent, because female-headed families in which the parent has a substance abuse problem are usually the ones at greatest risk.

The National Institute on Drug Abuse (NIDA; 1996) has noted that when a woman uses drugs like cocaine, she and her unborn child are exposed to significant health risks. During pregnancy, almost all drugs cross the placenta and enter the bloodstream of the developing baby. The most serious possible adverse effects on the unborn child's health are premature delivery and low birth weight. Other possible problems include ectopic pregnancy, stillbirth, sudden infant death syndrome, and small gestational size. The woman who uses drugs is herself at increased risk of hemorrhage, spontaneous abortion, toxicity, sexually transmitted diseases, and nutritional deficiencies. In addition, injection drug use by women puts women and their children at risk for HIV/AIDS.

Increases in heroin use are also a cause for concern. A 1995 NIDA review (National Institute on Drug Abuse, 1995) noted that although crack cocaine use has commanded more attention, heroin use remains a serious problem in the United States. The number of hospital emergency department visits related to the use of heroin rose from 38,100 in 1988 to 63,000 in 1993, an increase of 65%. In addition, some researchers have noted that snorting and smoking heroin may be growing in popularity as alternatives to injecting the drug.

Although illicit drug use among parents is a major factor in the incidence of child abuse and neglect, legal substances are at least as destructive, if not more so. Chomitz, Cheung, and Lieberman (1995) note that cigarette smoking is the largest known risk factor for low birth weight and that approximately 20% of all low birth weight could be avoided if women did not smoke during pregnancy.

Alcohol abuse among parents occurs in as much as 10% of the population. Psychosocial maladaptation among children of alcoholics can affect both their cognitive and emotional development. Parental alcoholism, moreover, is often accompanied by domestic conflict and violence and a host of related problems (Johnson & Rolf, 1990). Alcohol use during pregnancy accounts for 10% of all mental retardation. An estimated 12,000 babies each year are born with fetal alcohol syndrome (FAS), which is associated with behavioral abnormalities, physical deformities, and mental retardation (CASA, 1996, p. 8).

The National Center on Child Abuse and Neglect, in their 1991 study of the relationship between alcohol abuse and child maltreatment (National Center on Child Abuse and Neglect, 1993b), found that the incidence of maltreatment among children in alcohol-abusing families was 3.6 times higher than for children in families without alcohol abuse. The same study found that in 78% of child maltreatment cases with substance-abusing perpetrators, caseworkers reported that the substance abuse directly led to or contributed to the maltreatment, and that 65% of these children were maltreated while the perpetrator was under the influence of alcohol or illicit drugs.

Even if not exposed to alcohol or drugs during the prenatal period, children may experience other difficulties related to their parents' substance abuse. Infants and children of substance abusers tend to live in chaotic and often dangerous home environments that are not conducive to their overall physical, social, and psychological development. It is extremely difficult for parents who are abusing substances to fulfill their parenting roles and responsibilities. The need for drugs and/or alcohol usually takes precedence over providing food and other necessities for children (Feig, 1990).

Parental substance abuse also increases a child's risk of becoming a victim of physical abuse, sexual abuse, or neglect. Substance abuse clouds perception and impairs parental judgment. Parents may not comprehend that their children are not being well fed, adequately clothed, or sufficiently supervised. Also, drugs such as alcohol and crack cocaine (in contrast to some others like tobacco and marijuana) tend to be associated with increased violent behavior. In 1993, 1,018,692 cases of child abuse and neglect were confirmed by state child protective services agencies (National Center on

Child Abuse and Neglect, 1993a). Estimates vary regarding what percentage of these cases involved parental or caretaker alcohol or drug abuse. Some studies say it is as low as 40% (Daro & McCurdy, 1991), others that it is as high as 80% (Child Welfare League of America, 1989).

In short, parental substance abuse is closely associated with child abuse and neglect. It is also linked with a variety of problems affecting children ranging from low birth weight to difficulties with cognitive and emotional development, school failure, dropout, delinquency, and alcohol and drug use in adolescence. Not all children of substance abusers experience such problems; many demonstrate great resilience and a capacity for adaptation. Nevertheless, parental substance abuse is one of the strongest indicators for developing a host of problems among children and youth.

The Effects on Families

As a result of parental substance abuse, infants and children of substance-abusing parents are at an increased risk of out-of-home placement, either through foster care with strangers or formal or informal placement with relatives. Maltreated children in alcohol-abusing families are more likely to be removed from the home (30%) when compared to other maltreated children (National Center on Child Abuse and Neglect, 1993b). Substance abuse alone is now cited as one of the three primary causes of out-of-home placement of children, in addition to child abuse or neglect (which may also reflect substance abuse) and economic stress (Children's Defense Fund, 1992). In New York City's Harlem, of the 1,900 drug-exposed children born between 1986 and 1990, only 25% were receiving primary care from their biological mothers. In most cases a grandmother or a foster mother was the primary caregiver. An Illinois study of 385 children placed in foster care in 1986 found that one half had come from families with substance abuse problems (Bays, 1990).

Although most studies focus on the effects of parental substance abuse on younger children, this often results in chaotic and dysfunctional family environments for adolescents as well. While younger children in substance-abusing and maltreating families may come to the attention of child welfare agencies, many adolescents simply leave home, and others are pushed out or abandoned by their parents. In a review of existing programs and services, the Southeastern Network of Runaway and Homeless Youth Services (1989) found that 20% of youth reported that their parents had substance abuse problems.

Challenges to Social Service Providers

The impact of substance abuse-related maltreatment, neglect, and abandonment cases on child protection systems is considerable. Estimates of the number of children living with chemically dependent parents vary, ranging from 675,000 (Bays, 1990) to as many as 9 to 10 million (National Committee for the Prevention of Child Abuse, 1989). In Wyoming, where only 23% of child protective services reports involve parental substance abuse, such cases account for more than half of the state's child abuse fatalities. In Boston, researchers found that 64% of substantiated child abuse and neglect involved parental alcohol abuse (McCullough, 1991).

Nationally, substance abuse has become the dominant characteristic in the child maltreatment and neglect caseloads of 22 states and the District of Columbia. Local estimates of the proportion of child welfare cases involving substance abuse are 50% in Illinois; 80% in Washington, D.C.; 76% in San Francisco; 64% in Boston; and 70% in Philadelphia (Feig, 1990). In many of these cases the children have suffered extreme neglect, and in some cases they have been completely abandoned.

In combination with the above, other challenges to service providers include the following.

- Comprehensive approaches are needed to address the problems of substance-abusing families and their children in a systematic way because a particular family or child may present a problem to more than one system. Yet family-serving systems are often characterized by lack of coordination and communication.
- The rise in the use of highly addictive drugs such as crack cocaine and heroin has placed significant stresses on already overloaded child welfare service providers.

- The growth in absolute numbers of substance-related child welfare cases has been accompanied by an increase in the difficulty of investigating and providing services to these cases. The Child Welfare League reported that 83% of child protective services providers interviewed believed that problems associated with substance abuse increased the time they spent investigating a case. In addition, 93% of the respondents said that substance abuse was increasingly a factor in initial investigations. Despite this, only 65.9% said that their agency provided training associated with the problem of family substance abuse (Curtis & McCullough, 1993).

Ensuring the safety of children who are exposed to parental substance abuse in their homes often involves extensive monitoring and in-home services, yet child protective services systems often lack the staff and financial resources to meet the needs of these families. As a result, caseload sizes are increasing beyond what workers can be expected to handle. Referrals of substance-abusing families have resulted in caseloads as high as 60 to 70 children (Walker & Zangrillo, 1991).

Although parental substance abuse may place children at increased risk for abuse or neglect, it may not be well documented enough to warrant a report to child protective services. Many children, therefore, may receive no outside assistance or intervention despite the fact that their parents are abusing alcohol, drugs, or both. Similarly, the role and authority of child welfare systems to intervene in cases of prenatal exposure to drugs and alcohol remains unclear, and action in response to a positive drug-exposure report varies considerably according to state and local agency practice.

Gregoire (1994) reports that in spite of the significance of the problem of parental substance abuse, many social workers know little about the role or impact of addictions in child abuse and neglect. In this study, social workers failed to identify and respond to a client's alcohol problem in 83% of the cases they handled. The study concluded that most social workers receive little or no formal training in substance abuse-related behavior and may avoid dealing with clients' drug problems. Similarly, Tracy's (1994) study found that child welfare workers generally had limited training in alcohol and drug abuse treatment issues and were poorly prepared to assess the level of risk or to develop appropriate case plans for families with substance abuse problems.

Family Maintenance, Foster Care, and Adoption When Substance Abuse Is a Problem

Although maintaining families is usually the first priority in the child welfare field, when the safety of the child cannot be ensured, the child must be removed from the home. Finding appropriate out-of-home placements for children while working toward a permanent plan for the child (whether family reunification or termination of parental rights and adoption) is the primary responsibility of the foster care system. Because of the close relationship between child protective and foster care services, there is a clear "trickle down" effect of family substance abuse on foster care.

Between 1985 and 1996, the number of children requiring foster care placements rose from 245,000 to more than 500,000 (Kilborn, 1997). During the same period, because of a shortage of available foster parents, the number of foster families decreased from 137,000 to 100,000 (U.S. Advisory Board on Child Abuse and Neglect, 1993). In addition, although foster care was initially conceived as a temporary response, children are now staying in foster care longer than they did 10 years ago. In New York City in 1986, 60% of the babies discharged from hospitals to foster care—mostly babies exposed to crack cocaine—were still in foster care 3 years later. Of those in foster care, 56% had been in two or more foster homes, and 20% had been in three or more homes. Several children under age 5 had been in more than five homes (Besharov, 1990).

The Child Welfare League of America found that 87.1% of those providing foster care services reported that children prenatally exposed to alcohol or drugs were more likely to require multiple foster care placements than other children, although the same was reported to be true for nonexposed children whose parents abuse substances. In addition, these children tended to remain in foster care for longer periods than other children (Curtis & McCullough, 1993).

Increased parental substance abuse and associated HIV infection also contribute to the problem of so-called boarder babies. These are babies who remain in the hospital due to parental abandonment and/or the lack of an available appropriate foster care placement, rather than for medical reasons. Some states require hospitals to refer every infant with a positive toxicology to child welfare authorities. The number of babies boarding in hospitals is highest in areas where the law requires a child protective services referral for all drug-exposed newborns. Shortly after such a law was passed in Florida, for example, it was not uncommon to find between 20 and 30 babies in need of foster care boarding in a Miami hospital at any one time (McCullough, 1991).

Nationally, the average amount paid to foster care parents per child ranges from $1,000 to $4,000 (Besharov, 1990; McCullough, 1991). However, specialized foster care, such as the kind boarder babies and other substance-exposed children often require, may cost as much as $36,000 annually.

Although broadening the conditions for terminating parental rights may release children for adoption at younger ages, there is still a question of whether adoptive homes will be waiting for many of these children (Anderson, 1990). Many of the children of substance-abusing parents need years of extensive services that prospective adoptive parents may be unable to afford or reluctant to provide. In fact, 83.5% of adoption workers who have placed prenatally exposed children in adoptive homes claim it is more difficult to place these children than other children (Curtis & McCullough, 1993).

Just as the focus of foster care and adoption agencies is changing in response to substance use problems, runaway and homeless youth programs are finding that reunifying adolescents with their families may not be in the youths' best interest. As the number of children with substance-abusing parents who seek shelter and services has increased, so has the need for shifting priorities and alternative living arrangements. This has created a serious problem for shelter providers, most of whom are limited to sheltering youth for no more than 2 weeks except in special circumstances. Although child welfare placements in foster care (including group homes) may offer temporary respite, the resources are insufficient to meet the demand. For youth aged 16 and older, alternative long-term placements may be virtually nonexistent.

Addressing Substance Abuse From
a Child Welfare Perspective

Policy and Legal Approaches

The most widespread prevention strategies linking child welfare and substance abuse are policy related. In addition to statutes requiring child welfare workers, educators, and others who regularly have contact with children to report indicated cases of child abuse and neglect, states are increasingly relying on statutes to provide for the healthy development of the fetus by criminalizing the prenatal transmission of drugs. Laws incorporating either prenatal drug exposure or prenatal drug use into child abuse and neglect statutes have been passed in several states, including Florida, Hawaii, Illinois, Massachusetts, Minnesota, Oklahoma, New York, Nevada, and Rhode Island (Feig, 1990). California, New York, and Illinois require hospitals to report all cases in which infants are born exposed to drugs. Minnesota has gone even farther, requiring all mandated reporters to notify local child welfare agencies of pregnant women suspected of, or known to be, using controlled substances (USGAO, 1990).

In contrast, many other states require hospitals to report substance exposure to child welfare agencies only when the infant is actually physically drug dependent and must undergo withdrawal. In one state, hospitals have been instructed by child welfare agency personnel to report drug-exposed infant cases only when the mother cannot care for her child (USGAO, 1990). Indeed, when the question of prosecuting pregnant women has reached the courts, judges have tended to view cases individually, and women generally have not been prosecuted (Madden, 1993).

Inevitably, questions arise about the efficacy and fairness of legal approaches to prevention. There is a lack of consensus on the desirability and value of court-ordered treatment. Such approaches also raise serious ethical and philosophical issues. Child welfare workers and social workers tend to view themselves as advocates of their clients and may therefore be reluctant to enforce what they regard as punitive legal mandates. As one recent essay on the subject observed, "The essential social work values dilemma is the conflict between respect for a woman's liberty and duty to aid vulnerable persons, in this case the child-to-be and the woman who may have impaired competence to make voluntary decisions because of an addictive disease" (Andrews & Patterson, 1995). Although most studies show little or no difference in the rates of drug abuse during pregnancy across racial groups, women of color are disproportionately tested and are more likely to be subject to child protective services intervention (Goldberg, 1995). Middle- and upper-class substance abusers may be just as likely to harm their children, but they are less likely to be identified or, if identified, subjected to formal interventions (Kropenske & Howard, 1994).

Those opposed to criminal prosecution of substance-abusing women argue that the data do not support incarceration as an effective impetus to accepting help for a drug problem (Hutchins & Alexander, 1990). They emphasize that even if criminalization were an effective approach, few drug treatment facilities accept pregnant women. Critics of legal approaches also believe women fearing punitive actions against them will not seek medical attention during pregnancy, placing fetuses at increased risk of complications resulting from prenatal drug exposure.

Prevention and Treatment Approaches

According to leading child welfare advocates throughout the country, legal approaches need to be balanced by policies and programs that provide a wide range of prevention and treatment services to families with substance abuse problems. In recent years, a variety of child welfare agencies and advocacy groups have developed programs and initiatives that bridge the gap between child welfare and substance abuse from a child welfare perspective, that is, in settings and through programs and procedures that are familiar to child welfare professionals.

Substance Abuse-Specific Assistance and Support to Foster Parents. The primary approach to addressing the impact of family substance abuse on foster care has been, first, to focus on services that make initial entry of the child into foster care less likely and, second, to promote family reunification through provision of supportive services. One approach increasingly being used is the formation of multidisciplinary teams to coordinate services to assist families. In Chicago, the major hospitals use such teams to conduct health and safety needs assessments for drug-exposed infants. Workers then use these assessments to determine the type of placement required (Ahart, Rutsch, Morgan Holmes, & Kotler, 1991). In 1988, to meet the needs of boarder babies, Congress passed legislation to establish the Abandoned Infants Assistance Demonstration Grants Program. The intent of the program is to provide needed social services to families of abandoned infants; to recruit, train, and retrain foster parents; and to operate residential programs for drug-exposed children and children with AIDS. In addition, respite care programs have been established, and health and social service personnel have been recruited and trained to work with families, foster families, and residential care staff. Program components include home visits, developmental child care, parenting education for mothers during and after pregnancy, and drug and alcohol treatment (Feig, 1990).

The National Advisory Board on Child Abuse and Neglect has recommended even more sweeping measures to address the complex needs of children removed from the home. The Board suggests that foster care be made part of a constellation of neighborhood-based supports for children and families. Ensuring the protection of children would be at the heart of local responses. This would mean developing such programs as open or partial foster care in which children would go to a second home after school but still live with their parents, and whole-family foster care in which the entire family participates in the foster care experience (U.S. Advisory Board on Child Abuse and Neglect, 1993).

One way in which adoption agencies are attempting to ensure permanency for children removed because their parents abuse alcohol and drugs is through a process known as "fast-tracking" adoptions. Children removed from particularly dangerous situations may be placed into "pre-adoptive" homes while they wait for the termination of parental rights process to be completed (U.S. Department of Health and Human Services [DHHS], 1992). Many states are also moving to speed up the termination process in cases of abandonment, from an average of 1 to 2 years to an average of 6 months (DHHS, 1992).

Another response being used by adoption agencies incorporates "Fost-Adopt" programs. These are programs in which foster parents plan to adopt the child for which they are caring. More and more states are accepting these programs as legitimate avenues for ensuring permanent homes for children (DHHS, 1992).

Comprehensive Services to Families With Substance-Abusing Parents. In many cases, removal from the home may be the only acceptable option for child welfare programs and professionals addressing the needs of abused or neglected children of substance abusers. More difficult and challenging, yet in the view of child and family advocates more desirable, are family maintenance programs that keep troubled families together, strengthen those families, and at the same time address parental substance abuse through effective treatment and prevention strategies. A growing number of social welfare programs and initiatives across the country have taken this approach.

In order to help serve families affected by substance abuse, in 1991 the National Center for Child Abuse and Neglect (NCCAN) began funding the Emergency Child Abuse and Neglect Prevention Grant Program. This program makes funds competitively available to improve the delivery of services to children whose parents are substance abusers. Such services may include the hiring of additional personnel, training for personnel to improve their ability to provide emergency child abuse prevention services, expanding services to deal with family crises created by substance abuse, and establishing or improving interagency coordination.

NCCAN has also recommended that specialized child protective services units be established to work with chemically dependent families. Programs of this type address the needs of substance-abusing families by keeping worker caseloads low; providing intensive training in alcohol- and drug-related topics; and through "vertical case management," allowing a single caseworker to handle emergencies, family maintenance, family reunification, and permanency planning services for the family (National Center on Child Abuse and Neglect, 1994).

Head Start/Early Childhood Programming. Head Start has also played a leadership role in aiding families affected by substance abuse. Toward this end, the Head Start Bureau initiated Family Service Centers (FSC) demonstration projects. The purpose of these projects is to strengthen Head Start's capacity to build on existing program features and develop effective strategies for collaboration among Head Start programs and community agencies in order to address three main problems faced by many Head Start families: substance abuse, illiteracy, and unemployment.

Since 1990, the Children's Bureau has encouraged Head Start agencies to develop and implement FSC demonstration projects (Administration for Children and Families, 1994). In 1994, Head Start and the Robert Wood Johnson Foundation initiated a collaborative effort to help local Head Start programs develop and implement model substance abuse prevention projects. The goal is to reduce children's vulnerability to a range of high-risk behaviors, particularly substance abuse, as they grow older. This initiative funds specific projects focusing on substance abuse prevention at six Head Start sites. The projects link families with human service, substance abuse treatment, and health organizations that can work with them well beyond a child's Head Start years.

Community-Based Programs With Documented Positive Outcomes. Responding to the need for comprehensive, community-based programs that assist substance-abusing parents while at the same time preserving and strengthening families, many localities across the country have initiated a variety of treatment and prevention efforts. Although there is a paucity of studies evaluating the outcomes of these programs, evidence of their effectiveness is accumulating in response to the need for accountability and documented results.

New York City's Family Rehabilitation Program, for example, targets families that have been reported to child protective services with allegations of parental substance abuse. Priority is given to families in which newborns show a positive toxicology for drugs, and cases are considered suitable for referral if the safety of the children would not be compromised by remaining at home. Families in the program are assigned a team of supervisors, a caseworker, and a home aide, and caseload ratios are limited to 1:6. According to one study, this program has had a high degree of success, with all the study participants ($N = 20$) successfully completing the program, undergoing drug treatment, and increasing their sense of self-worth and control over their lives (Carten, 1996).

The Epiphany Infant Program, based in San Francisco's Mt. St. Joseph-St. Elizabeth community-based child and family service agency, focuses exclusively on newborn infants of substance-abusing parents. Each infant is placed in a residential family grouping of four and provided with intensive health, nutritional, physiological, and emotional support. The parents, in turn, are enrolled in the center's drug treatment program. A study of the program found that all the infants in the program made consistent developmental gains and that support for each mother's interest in her child helped to keep mothers in drug treatment (Perez, 1996).

Another noteworthy child welfare program focusing on substance abuse is Project Connect, a multiagency collaborative effort based in Providence, Rhode Island. Families eligible for participation in the program have been identified for child abuse or neglect by the child welfare system and also have an identified problem of substance abuse. Most are headed by young single mothers. Services and support include an in-depth assessment of the family, development and monitoring of a service plan, home-based substance abuse assessment and counseling, individual and family counseling, parent education, pediatric nursing services, and linkages with local substance abuse treatment programs and other resources. An evaluation of the program's impact on 66 parents with 176 children found that the majority of parents made steady progress on service plan goals related to substance abuse and in substance abuse treatment. Significant improvements were also found in the risks associated with the habitability of the family's housing, the parent's mental health, and her knowledge of child care (Olsen, 1995).

Addressing Child Welfare From a Substance Abuse Perspective

One of the most important distinctions between child welfare programs that address the problem of parental substance abuse and substance abuse programs that address issues of child abuse and neglect is their point of view. The staff of child welfare programs tend to view the parent(s), the child(ren), and the family system as the client. The identified problem is a need for better individual and family system functioning in relation to social contexts such as agencies, institutions, and systems. Although substance abuse prevention and treatment programs also include a range of personal and social problems, they tend to focus on alcohol and drug use and addiction as health issues, with the solution found in healthier individual choices and personal functioning. Nevertheless, increasingly the two fields—child welfare and substance abuse—are finding common ground as they attempt to resolve the complex and interrelated problems associated with substance abuse. One reason for this is that, increasingly, both fields have adopted a broader view of the treatment of health and social problems that encompasses diverse, complex, and interrelated factors.

As is often the case in an evolving field or discipline, for substance abuse prevention and treatment programs addressing the specific needs of women, infants, children, and families, rigorous research on program impact and effectiveness has often lagged behind the development of new theories and strategies. Nevertheless, as Finkelstein (1993) notes in a detailed review of existing substance abuse programs for pregnant and parenting women, the field is sufficiently well established to identify a set of clear guiding principles.

A Framework for Substance
Abuse Prevention and Treatment

Substance abuse experts have proposed a variety of strategies that, taken together, offer a framework for conceptualizing comprehensive prevention and treatment efforts. Key aspects of such a framework include the following:

- *The importance of reducing risk factors, enhancing protective factors, and increasing resilience in children.* Risk-focused prevention strategies are associated with improved outcomes such as reduced substance use and decreases in related behavior, for example, school failure and violence among youth. Among the most important risk factors for substance use among youth are parental substance use, parental attitudes favorable to substance use, and family management problems. Another key risk factor often associated with children involved in the child protective system is school failure. Protective factors include positive bonding to family and school, disapproval of drug use, and involvement with positive peers.

- *The need to base prevention efforts on a comprehensive, coordinated, communitywide approach.* In recent years, substance abuse prevention initiatives have increasingly sought the involvement and cooperation of a wide range of local agencies, for example, local government, schools, businesses, nonprofit organizations, the media, and others. The assumption is that change is needed in the broader environment in which the problem exists in order to lower the incidence of individual (and family) substance abuse.

In addition, Finkelstein (1993) proposes seven basic principles for substance abuse prevention and treatment targeting pregnant and parenting women identified in an extensive review of the literature. Services and programs for this population should:

- Be family-focused or "family-centered," that is, not focused solely on individuals, as in traditional substance abuse approaches
- Promote competency building and empowerment
- Be community-based
- Be multidisciplinary, comprehensive, and coordinated, working toward collaborative models
- Address the multiplicity of problems and needs of alcohol- and drug-dependent mothers and their families
- Be individually tailored and long term
- Offer a range of levels of service intensity, from outpatient to day treatment to inpatient and long-term residential care

Family-Focused Substance Abuse Treatment

Family-focused inpatient treatment programs for substance-abusing mothers have been a particularly promising model. In a series of studies, the National Institute on Drug Abuse (NIDA) has conducted research on addressing treatment of substance abuse in women of childbearing age, and preliminary results have been encouraging. Goldberg (1995), in reviewing preliminary findings from studies in Boston and Philadelphia, found that pregnancy outcomes were dramatically improved by both residential and intensive outpatient treatment programs that included children as well as their mothers with a focus, for example, on effective parenting skills.

Many observers have noted that family-focused substance abuse treatment is a relative novelty in the treatment field (Stevens & Arbiter, 1995). The majority of treatment models, such as therapeutic communities and 12-step groups, were originally developed for predominantly male populations. An emphasis on the needs of women, particularly in their role as mothers, is a much-needed innovation.

Stevens and Arbiter (1995) describe a therapeutic community (TC) drug treatment model that has successfully adapted principles of drug treatment originally developed for exclusively male populations to groups of female alcohol and drug abusers who are either pregnant or who already have children. Building on a pilot project that included women and their children in long-term residential TC treatment, the Amity Center for Women and Children studied a population of 57 women and their children over a 2-year period, with an average of 18 months in treatment. Those who completed treatment showed significantly higher rates of abstinence from alcohol and drug use when compared with a group of program dropouts. Also significantly improved were this group's rates of arrests for probation violations, employment, ability to stay off public assistance, family stability, and use of aftercare services and support.

Involvement of Parents and Family Members in Prevention Education and Training

In order truly to prevent child abuse and neglect in situations involving substance abuse, Chasnoff (1991) proposes that professionals develop a way to involve mothers in primary prevention programs. He suggests that prenatal education and training can improve the prognosis of children prenatally exposed to drugs. Home-based educational and skills training services in the perinatal and postnatal period have been found to reduce drug abuse, improve care levels, and promote an overall healthier home environment for children of substance-abusing parents (Chasnoff, 1991).

The National Association for Perinatal Addiction (NAPARE) helps to direct women into prenatal care programs through its Alcohol, Drugs, and Pregnancy Hotline (formerly the Cocaine Baby Hotline). Approximately one third of the calls to the hotline are from women seeking information about the effects of drug use on their pregnancy or on their unborn child. Services provided through the hotline include dissemination of prevention materials, phone assessment and treatment referrals, access to community resources, and referral to professional teams at NAPARE (Perinatal Addiction Research and Education, 1993).

Case Management

Increasingly, substance abuse prevention and treatment profes-sionals have found it useful to adapt case management techniques from the field of social work, and this has been particularly effective in addressing the needs of substance-abusing parents and their children. In the context of substance abuse prevention and treat-ment, approaches that incorporate case management view the cli-ent's needs in a holistic way by developing detailed profiles of regularly used services, assigning caseworkers who provide regular monitoring and follow-up to individual clients, and drawing on an array of available services as needed.

The experience of the Seattle (Washington) Birth to 3 Project, a paraprofessional case management program for substance-abusing mothers, offers an instructive example of the need for a client advocacy approach. The purpose of the project was to test "inten-sive, relational, and long-term paraprofessional advocacy with one of [the city's] most difficult populations" (Grant, Ernst, Streissguth, Phipps, & Gendler, 1996). Toward this end, the project developed a network of paraprofessional peer advocates, women who had experienced many of the same types of adverse experiences as their clients yet who were also carefully trained. Clients were recruited through local hospital and community referral; all had experienced heavy drug or alcohol use during pregnancy and had little or no successful involvement with community programs or services, in-cluding prenatal care. After a 1-year period of developing close relationships with their caseworker-advocates, the clients showed significant progress in such areas of their lives as increased involve-ment with drug and alcohol treatment agencies, decreased drug use, increased use of birth control, and increased involvement with supportive and skill-building groups such as parenting classes (Grant et al., 1996).

Another model that has attracted broad interest and support is Hawaii's "Healthy Start" program, a statewide initiative to improve family coping skills and functioning and to promote positive par-enting skills, parent-child interaction, and child development. The program begins with systematic hospital-based identification of at-risk families, then provides community-based home visiting fam-ily support services, individualized services based on family needs and levels of risk, linkages to medical services, coordination of a range of health and social services, and continuous follow-up with the family until the child reaches age 5; also included are standardized training for all staff and a special emphasis on staff recruitment and retention (Breakey & Pratt, 1991).

Community-Wide Initiatives

A wide range of community-based substance abuse prevention initiatives in recent years, such as the Robert Wood Johnson Fighting Back grants and the Center for Substance Abuse Prevention Community Partnerships, have played an important role in strengthening families and improving the welfare of children affected by substance abuse. Here the emphasis has been primarily on community and environmental issues that place stress on families and are precursors of both substance abuse and child abuse and neglect. These have included the following:

- *Alienation:* neighborhoods plagued by drug dealing, drug abuse, gangs, graffiti, and violence
- *Lack of coordination of services:* particularly among schools, families, and other community service agencies
- *Availability of substances and community norms that favor their use:* proliferation of alcohol sales outlets and widespread use of alcohol at community social or athletic events
- *Unemployment or underemployment*

Within the context of broad-based community efforts, organizing strategies are likely to include:

- *Establishing interagency councils or task forces* that focus on specific issues, for example, positive youth development, child welfare, family violence, youth violence
- *Extensive community-wide needs assessments* that focus on risk factors, protective factors, the incidence of specific types of substance abuse, and related issues
- *Development of comprehensive community-wide plans* for substance abuse prevention based on the assessed needs
- *Involvement of a broad spectrum of leaders* representing diverse segments of the community, for example, business leaders, government officials, faith leaders, school officials, and others

- *Block organizing*, often in conjunction with community policing
- *Community forums and media campaigns*

Coordination of Systems and Services

Promoting organizational changes and developing cooperative interagency relationships are commonly cited as key factors in the successful delivery of services to families in which parental substance abuse is a problem. Whatever the age of the children, such families tend to experience problems in many different dimensions of their lives and to require assistance from a wide range of community agencies. Improved delivery of services to such families often requires revisions in policies and procedures based on new knowledge, provider training, delivery of skill-building workshops to providers, cost-effective training of trainers models, and ongoing efforts to improve interagency communication and networking.

Implications for Policy and Programming

Substance abuse is one aspect of a complex web of family and community dysfunction affecting the welfare of children. It is both a symptom and a cause of the ecological, economic, and systemic factors associated with families needing child welfare services— often low-income families with single mothers as heads of household and disproportionately representing undereducated, minority populations.

One of the most important issues in addressing substance abuse in female-headed families is the need to distinguish between conventional approaches to substance abuse treatment, which tend to have a male orientation and focus, and those that target women. The problems of chemically dependent women are far more complex than those of men, primarily because women in treatment often are the sole adults responsible for their children. In contrast to men, the client becomes not just the female addict or substance abuser but her entire family—all her children, born and unborn. Other aspects of the problem associated with this include:

- *Assistance in meeting basic needs.* Female substance abusers and their children often need assistance in obtaining transportation, food, housing, and financial support.
- *Low skills levels and/or multiple problems.* Typically, clients are so lacking in basic life skills that they have a very low level of functioning. Many are overwhelmed by the day-to-day struggles of living.
- *Living with chaos.* Although often poorly prepared to have and raise children, female substance abusers are also less likely than other women to be involved in family planning. They may lead lives that are chaotic and unpredictable, drifting from one crisis and one baby to the next.
- *Limited resources.* Given the extent of clients' needs, local programs and service providers often find it difficult to offer adequate services.
- *Child care.* Obtaining treatment requires women to be available to participate, yet the first obligation of many women is child care. Male-oriented programs can assume their clients' availability; female-focused programs often need to provide child care on site, or to locate acceptable child care, just to get their clients to come to the program.
- *Family services.* Female substance abusers are often involved with child protective services and other components of the child welfare system. Their children may be in foster care or other placements on either a temporary or long-term basis. Working closely with these systems and pursuing the goal of family reunification may be demanded of program staff who may have limited experience in addressing these issues.
- *Interagency networking.* Addressing the multiple, complex needs of substance-abusing women and their families virtually requires program staff to access a wide range of community services and to work cooperatively with other agencies. In many programs and communities, however, staff have had little or no experience in fulfilling this role.
- *The need for systems coordination.* Neglected and abused children or substance-abusing parents come into contact with and are either affected or served by a range of diverse systems.

The lack of appropriate programs, especially those oriented toward females, is almost universally cited as a barrier to effective intervention. Frequently, parents are required to choose between inpatient treatment and voluntary relinquishment of their children or only outpatient treatment (Cygnus, 1995).

There is also a need to improve the assessment of current responses of service delivery systems to the needs of children and families involved with substance abuse. Little has been published documenting the successes and failures of these efforts, their strengths and deficiencies, and the factors that contribute to positive and negative outcomes. Particularly lacking is research on the effect of changes in public policies, statutes, or regulations that address or affect family substance abuse-related problems.

Similarly, the long-term consequences of public policies mandating reporting and sometimes temporary removal or accelerated termination of parental rights procedures for infants exposed to substances remain for the most part unexamined. Though criminalization of prenatal drug exposure has both its supporters and its detractors, little concrete research exists to support its efficacy.

Consistent with all these problems and challenges, recruitment and retention of clients is a major concern of programs for substance-abusing women, and it dominates the literature. One review noted that, "There is growing evidence that pregnant women dependent on alcohol and other drugs often avoid health and human services established to improve their health and the well-being of their infants" (Poland, 1993). Denial of their alcohol and drug problems often keeps women away from services that could help them and their children. On the other hand, knowledge of the effects of substance abuse on the fetus may be the key motivator in their seeking help.

Once these women enter treatment, the dropout rates are disturbingly high. "Many women experienced relapse episodes," noted one program evaluation, "and discontinued program services for a period of time" (Macro International, 1993). When women became involved with treatment because initially they sought help with their pregnancy, often they were more concerned about the pregnancy than their substance abuse.

Successes That Show the Way

Despite the numerous obstacles and the severity of the problems, new models and systems for addressing the needs of substance-abusing women and families have evolved that have achieved well-documented success. Effective treatment and prevention strategies have covered the entire range of services from outreach and recruitment to follow-up and support after clients complete the program. Key elements of successful programming have included the following:

Awareness. Raising awareness about the needs of substance-abusing women and families is critically important in developing support for programs for this population. Information may target diverse audiences for different purposes. One group is substance-abusing women themselves, who need to be aware of the consequences of substance abuse and addiction on their children, as well as the availability of services to help them. Another is substance abuse and other helping professionals, who need to know about effective methods for treating this population and ways to integrate support systems throughout the community. A third audience is the general community.

Outreach/Recruitment. Programs have reached out to and recruited substance-abusing parents in a variety of ways. Telephone hotlines, often supported by print and broadcast media campaigns, have been particularly effective for initial contacts and outreach efforts (Poland, 1993). Trained hotline personnel can act as advocates for families in need. Outreach efforts have also been successful in diverse settings where substance-abusing parents are likely to be served or housed, such as clinics, hospitals, emergency rooms, and jails.

Screening. Assessment of substance-abusing women needs to include a wide range of problems and issues ranging from physical and mental health status, including substance abuse, to family issues such as child custody and involvement with child protective services. Hamilton (1993) notes that screening mechanisms "should be *valid* (measure what the screener wants to measure) and should yield *reliable* results (results that are consistent over time and across different test raters)" (p. 135). In-depth interviews can be particularly helpful in assessing the range of clients' problems and recommending treatment. Also important are methods for assessing the health and development of neonates.

Comprehensive Treatment Programs. Broad-based, comprehensive treatment programs must address a wide range of client needs. Effective programs offer diverse drug treatment modalities from detoxification to residential treatment to relapse prevention and self-help groups, connecting clients with the appropriate treatment modalities when they are not available within the program. The client's substance abuse is only one aspect of the problem, however. Comprehensive treatment for substance-abusing parents should also include medical and perinatal services, parenting education, both individual and group counseling, and basic and vocational education.

Case Management. Case management, often in conjunction with home visits, has continually been cited as an element of effective programs (Donelly, 1992). Successful approaches to case management range from individual advocates as case managers to multidisciplinary, interagency case management teams. Case management can begin on site and continue through individual home visits. Whatever the structure, case management offers a context for assessing a broad range of problems, developing a plan for individualized treatment and care, and ensuring supervision and follow-up.

In principle, almost everyone would agree that what is needed now is comprehensive, family-focused approaches representing a continuum of care, including home-based services and family support and preservation programs, as well as appropriate and accessible residential substance abuse treatment and aftercare (Azzi-Lessing & Olsen, 1996). Before that can happen, however, there must be greater coordination and integration at all administrative levels—federal, state, and local—of substance abuse prevention and treatment programs and programs that address child welfare and family welfare. This integration and coordination must extend well beyond traditional patterns of interagency service referral systems. It requires a new kind of community-wide, integrated network of services and programs providing support to families in their child-rearing role, effectively preventing the emergence of family alcohol and substance abuse problems, and offering appropriate family-focused substance abuse treatment when substance abuse occurs.

Even more important, and perhaps more difficult to achieve, bridging the gaps between the child welfare and substance abuse fields will require a shared vocabulary and point of view; it will require agreement on basic principles, training, procedures, and effective program approaches. Such an agreement will help to break down the barriers created by two specialized professional fields that have continued to move along parallel tracks while pursuing similar goals. In the future it will be not just desirable but necessary for those parallel tracks if not to merge, at least to move closer together.

References

Administration for Children and Families. (1994). *Head Start Family Service Center Demonstration Projects, 1994*, pp. 1-5.

Ahart, A., Rutsch, C., Morgan Holmes, C., & Kotler, M. (1991). *Programs serving drug-exposed children and their families* (Unpublished report dated July 21, prepared by Macro Systems, Inc., Contract No. HHS-100-87-0039, submitted to the Assistant Secretary for Planning and Evaluation, U.S. Department of Health and Human Services).

Andrews, A. B., & Patterson, E. G. (1995). Searching for solutions to alcohol and other drug abuse during pregnancy: Ethics, values and constitutional principles. *Social Work, 40*(1), 55-64.

Azzi-Lessing, L., & Olsen, L. J. (1996). Substance abuse-affected families in the child welfare system: New challenges, new alliances. *Social Work, 41*(1), 15-23.

Bays, J. (1990). Substance abuse and child abuse: Impact of addiction on the child. *Pediatric Clinics of North America, 37*(4), 881-904.

Besharov, D. J. (1990). Crack children in foster care. *Children Today, 19*(4), 21-35.

Breakey, G., & Pratt, B. (1991). Healthy growth for Hawaii's "Healthy Start": Toward a systematic statewide approach to the prevention of child abuse and neglect. *Zero to Three, 11*(4), 16-22.

Carten, A. J. (1996). Mothers in recovery: Rebuilding families in the aftermath of addiction. *Social Work, 41*(2), 214-223.

CASA (Center on Addiction and Substance Abuse at Columbia University). (1996). *Substance abuse and the American woman*. New York: Author.

Chasnoff, I. J. (1991). Prevention and intervention: Prenatal population. Overview of the issue. In *The Wingspread Conference Proceedings, Substance Abuse and Child Abuse: Developing a Collaborative Action Plan* (pp. 5-6). Chicago: National Committee for Prevention of Child Abuse.

Child Welfare League of America. (1989). *Highlights of questions from the working paper on chemical dependency*. Washington, DC: Author.

Child Welfare League of America. (1992). *Children at the front: A different view of the war on alcohol and drugs*. Washington, DC: Author.

Children's Defense Fund. (1992). *The state of America's children: 1992*. Washington, DC: Author.

Chomitz, V. R., Cheung, L. W. Y., & Lieberman, E. (1995). The role of lifestyle in preventing low birth weight. *Future of Children, 5*(1), 121-138.

Curtis, P. A., & McCullough, C. (1993). The impact of alcohol and other drugs on the child welfare system. *Child Welfare, 72*(6), 533-542.

Cygnus Corporation. (1995). *Final report: Study of the impact on service delivery of family substance abuse* (ACYF Contract #105-91-1811). Washington, DC: Author.

Daro, D., & McCurdy, K. (1991). *Current trends in child abuse reporting and fatalities: The results of the 1989 Annual States Survey.* Chicago: National Center on Child Abuse Prevention Research.

Donelly, A. C. (1992). Healthy families America. *Children Today, 21*(2), 25-28.

Feig, L. (1990). *Drug exposed infants and children: Service needs and policy questions* (pp. 1-30). Washington, DC: U.S. Department of Health and Human Services.

Finkelstein, N. (1993). Treatment programming for alcohol and drug-dependent pregnant women. *International Journal of the Addictions, 28*(13), 1275-1309.

Goldberg, M. E. (1995). Substance-abusing women: False stereotypes and real needs. *Social Work, 40*(6), 789-798.

Grant, T. M., Ernst, C. C., Streissguth, A. P., Phipps, P., & Gendler, B. (1996). When case management isn't enough: A model of paraprofessional advocacy for drug- and alcohol-abusing mothers. *Journal of Case Management, 5*(1), 3-11.

Gregoire, T. K. (1994). Assessing the benefits and increasing the utility of addiction training for public child welfare workers: A pilot study. *Child Welfare, 73*(1), 69-81.

Hamilton, A. (1993). Screening and assessment. In *Pregnancy and exposure to alcohol and other drug use* (CSAP Tech. Rep. #7, DHHS Publication No. (SMA) 93-2040). Rockville, MD: Center for Substance Abuse Prevention.

Hutchins, E., & Alexander, G. (1990). Substance use during pregnancy and its effects on the infant: A review of issues. *Health and Human Services Region III Consortium technical report series.* Philadelphia: DHHS Region III Office.

Join Together. (1996). *Domestic violence and substance abuse fact sheet.* Boston: Author.

Johnson, J. L., & Rolf, J. E. (1990). When children change: Research perspectives on children of alcoholics. In R. L. Collins, K. E. Leonard, & J. S. Searless (Eds.), *Alcohol and the family: Research and clinical perspectives.* New York: Guilford.

Kilborn, P. T. (1997, April 29). Priority on safety is keeping more children in foster care. *New York Times,* p. 1.

Kropenske, V., & Howard, J. (1994). *Protecting children in substance-abusing families.* Washington, DC: National Center on Child Abuse and Neglect.

Macro International. (1993). *Final report: CSAP PPWI Demonstration Program findings.* Unpublished report, Macro International, Washington, D.C.

Madden, R. G. (1993). State actions to control fetal abuse: Ramifications for child welfare. *Child Welfare, 72*(2), 130-140.

McCullough, C. B. (1991). The child welfare response. *The Future of Children, 1*(1), 61-71.

National Center on Child Abuse and Neglect. (1993a). *Child maltreatment 1993. Reports from the states to the National Center on Child Abuse and Neglect.* Washington, DC: Author.

National Center on Child Abuse and Neglect. (1993b). *Study of child maltreatment in alcohol abusing families: A report to Congress, 1993.* Washington, DC: Author.

National Center on Child Abuse and Neglect. (1994). *Protecting children in substance-abusing families: The user manual series.* Washington, DC: U.S. Dept. of Health and Human Services, Administration on Children, Youth and Families.

National Committee for the Prevention of Child Abuse. (1989). *Fact sheet: Substance abuse and child abuse.* Chicago: Author.

National Institute on Drug Abuse. (1995, July/August). *NIDA Notes, 10*(4), Rockville, MD: NIDA.

National Institute on Drug Abuse. (1996). *NIDA capsule on crack/cocaine use.* Rockville, MD: Author.

Olsen, L. J. (1995). Services for substance abuse-affected families: The Project Connect experience. *Child and Adolescent Social Work Journal, 12*(3), 183-195.

Perez, L. (1996). The Epiphany Center: A family centered approach to providing early intervention services to substance exposed infants and toddlers. *The Source, 6*(1), 3-5.

Perinatal Addiction Research and Education. (1993, April). *Head Start programs address substance abuse.*

Poland, M. (1993). Practical approaches to outreach, maintenance, and followup. In *Pregnancy and exposure to alcohol and other drug use* (CSAP Tech. Rep. #7, DHHS Publication No. (SMA)93-2040). Rockville, MD: Center for Substance Abuse Prevention.

Southeastern Network of Runaway and Homeless Youth Services. (1989).

Stevens, S. J., & Arbiter, N. (1995). A therapeutic community for substance-abusing pregnant women and women with children: Process and outcome. *Journal of Psychoactive Drugs, 27*(1), 49-56.

Substance Abuse and Mental Health Services Administration (SAMHSA). (1995). *National Household Survey on Drug Abuse.* Rockville MD: Author.

Tracy, E. M. (1994). Maternal substance abuse: Protecting the child, preserving the family. *Social Work, 39*(5), 534-540.

U.S. Advisory Board on Child Abuse and Neglect. (1993). *Neighbors helping neighbors: A new national strategy for the protection of children.* Washington, DC: Government Printing Office.

U.S. Department of Health and Human Services. (1992). *Maternal drug abuse and drug-exposed children: Understanding the problem* (DHHS Publication No. [ADM]92-1949). Washington, DC: Government Printing Office.

U.S. General Accounting Office. (1990). *Drug exposed infants: A generation at risk* (GAO/HRD-90-138). Washington, DC: Author.

Walker, C., & Zangrillo, P. (1991). *Parental drug abuse and African American children in foster care.* Washington, DC: National Black Child Development Institute.

CHAPTER 5

The Bridges of Child Welfare/ Substance Abuse County

MARTIN BLOOM

The Nature of Bridges: Foundations

The visible portions of bridges are the breath-taking spans and external supports that provide the immediate passage between two opposite bodies. Hidden from view are the painstaking efforts that give bridges their foundation and stability, even in the changes of climate that put unknown stresses on the span. I begin consideration of this engineering metaphor with regard to the bridging concept between child welfare and substance abuse by inquiring about the nature of the substantive bodies being connected. What is included in the professional fields of child welfare and substance abuse? Why would anyone want to go to the other side of the bridge when there is plenty to do right here in River City?

Child Welfare

The geography of child welfare is a wide-ranging and variable domain, where the shifting sands of public opinion and policy make it difficult to build any strong central features. Among the many services under the label "child and family welfare" are protective services for abused and neglected children, aid for unwed mothers, homemaker services to certain families through difficult periods of time, day care, foster family services, adoption, various institutional and residential treatment centers, and a host of others. The professional inhabitants roam the land as apparently autonomous workers, but in reality, they are tied to the state administrative bodies by bonds of minute procedures, which are not necessarily of their own choosing. Demands made on these workers are often great, and resources often too few. This is a poor country, either economically poor in ways that limit the resources accessible to children and their families, or poor in a psychosocial way where expected human relationships and activities are often absent in families for one reason or another, in which cases children are likely to suffer. Or both.

The child welfare professionals as a group are often maligned in the mass media, by conservative government leaders, and by the public who sees part of their taxes going to "welfare cheats, ablebodied loafers, and unloved minorities or foreigners," even though the facts of the case are very different. Sixty percent of poor able-bodied people work, either full-time, part-time, seasonally, or whenever they can find odd jobs, even though their pay does not move them out of the poverty zone; the other 40% include children, aged, chronically ill and disabled persons, and single mothers with young children (Queralt, 1996, pp. 141-142). While the public is disposed to value fair play and succor for visible suffering and cases of obvious need—such as "the hundred neediest cases" listed in newspapers at Christmas time—it is unlikely to support amorphous compensatory efforts like affirmative action. Swings in public moods are fickle, making it difficult to fathom the solid depths on which to build solid social structures. Nothing seems to last forever in this land; the next legislature and executive often undo or redo the work of the prior leaders. This is a soft land, much unloved even by native inhabitants who would as soon be somewhere else than at the mercies of the welfare system—if they had opportunities and resources that those in power seem never quite ready to grant them. In fairness, it must be said that those in power often see the lack in the motivation and efforts of the natives who do not take advantage—or fair advantage—of whatever aid is provided at present. Everything depends on interpretation.

The neediest natives of this territory are in large measure young children, old people, and the chronically ill or disabled, groups that are out of the economically productive mode that society values so highly. Adults (mostly single women) are present, but often as care providers for the young, the old, or both. Mainstream society is suspicious of pure caretaking, as contrasted to "productive" (i.e., salaried) efforts. Even though everyone recognizes the importance of the younger generation as future adults, citizens, and tax payers—roles that require health, education, and well-being for their full manifestation—there is a general reservation about investing too much in the present for future predicted conditions (Schweinhart & Weikart, 1988). This reservation includes present-day investment in preventive services for young children who are at high risk for problem behavior as adolescents and adults, despite strong cost-benefit analyses favoring such investments (Barnett, 1993). There are also few funds to promote the gifted and talented among the children, especially among minority children (Renzulli, 1973), as would-be future leaders, artists, and scientists. In such ways, the shifting sands and smoky thinking surrounding the field of child welfare reduce visibility for the future.

Substance Abuse

The geography of substance abuse is rockier than child welfare; it is a more difficult terrain and harder on its inhabitants. Substance abuse is theoretically connected to the larger territory of substance use, and travelers are advised to mark the differences carefully. Some substances, such as alcohol or cigarettes, may be legal at times for people of a certain age, or illegal at other times (e.g., Prohibition, and the recent federal efforts aimed at stopping underage smoking). Other substances, such as the wide variety of drugs that staggers the imagination—literally and figuratively—have been illegal, at least in recent times. This discussion will focus largely on the latter, abuse of illicit substances.

This focal topic itself involves a fairly narrow band of illegal activities, from the production and distribution of the substances, which are often imported to the United States as contraband at great risk and coordinated through illegal bureaucratic structures, to their consumption by the direct user of mind-altering substances. Illegal and risky behavior is involved at every point of production, distribution, and consumption. To engage in this process is highly risky—but also highly lucrative, at least to the middlemen and -women. The end product of the use of substances has to be considered as an important part of the territory because it provides producers and distributors with a stable if often anonymous audience of consumers. Substances are addictive; they supply for relatively brief periods of time powerful effects that are highly desired even if not highly desirable from a societal point of view. Their effects are highly predictable and, once addiction takes hold, supply enormous motivation to reexperience the feelings. Like any controlled market, the price can vary, and as increasing need meets with increased costs, the addict or user may be driven to increasingly risky actions to obtain funds to get the drugs.

Most addicts understand on some level of thought that they are engaged in illegal actions, that they will likely become addicted, that they will be under great pressure to obtain funds to continue to buy larger quantities of drugs to satisfy their habit. These are risks that they accept, even as they come to recognize the other hidden costs and benefits of drugs. For example, they may experience the unpleasant physical and physiological effects of drugs on their bodies and minds; they may come to recognize the extent to which they sacrifice other desired life experiences, such as family and ordinary social life, to the demands of their addiction. However, they may find pleasant company in other addicts, especially if pleasurable experiences are few in their oppressive life situation. Breaking into this rough terrain is difficult. Addicts are often forced into the treatment system, to go through a very difficult detoxification process, perhaps accompanied by time in the criminal justice system. These experiences also have powerful effects on family and friends (Hairston, 1995). Whether or not treatment and criminal justice experiences have lasting effects is debatable (Howell, 1995).

Conceptual Foundations for a Bridge Between Child Welfare and Substance Abuse

Child Welfare

Given these two very different territories, we may need to build the foundations for a bridge in somewhat different ways. Child welfare may be viewed conceptually as three concentric spheres of defenses and enhancements. At the innermost sphere, and at the individual level within this sphere, is the concept of rugged individualism, or the expectation that an individual will be as self-sufficient as possible. Also in this sphere are self-help groups (a primary group-level concept that includes natural helping networks like family, and artificial ones like constructed sports teams), and universal social supports like government postal services or free schooling that exist as part of the nature of society. All of these elements of the first sphere can be seen as the natural working of a social system that expects its citizens to work and to succeed on their own, provided that the playing field is level and fair. Thus, at the individual, primary group, secondary group, and societal levels, there are "natural" systems at work to enable or support the individual to become all he or she is able to be. By "support," I refer to those services, formal or informal, given by others that enable individuals and families to achieve some basic standard beyond what they can attain on their own (Kadushin, 1980). This would address the needs of families that are basically healthy and well functioning, but limited in what they can achieve on their own. For example, a parent may be working at a minimum wage job and lack the funds to provide an adequate home, food, and clothing for his or her family without some tax credit or food stamps (Queralt, 1996).

There is much to recommend this first sphere of defense and enhancement. The only question is how to have as many people as possible (individuals, families, neighborhoods, and sociocultural groups) enjoy the benefits of these factors. The resilience literature (Werner, 1989) suggests that a significant proportion of people (about a third) will make it successfully into adulthood in spite of powerful disadvantages in their childhood. The remaining conceptual task is to identify these natural strengths and attempt to provide or to stimulate these in the others (Cowen, Wyman, Work, & Iker, 1995).

It is unfortunate that many citizens lack these "natural resources," or have limited portions of them, or suffer accidents that divert these ordinary resources and leave them bereft, making them turn to a second sphere of defense and enhancement in order to survive. This is the second conceptual nature of child welfare, and it involves both the supportive types of services of the first sphere, plus supplemental services (Kadushin, 1980). Conceptually, these services supplement parental functions in order to maintain ordinary family operations and the expected growth and development of the children. Supplemental services are generally extended to stressed and overloaded families whose functioning is compromised by multiple problems and challenges. There are varying degrees of this dysfunction, as well as different periods of time in which families remain in this mode.

The third conceptual stage of child welfare services involves substitutive services (Kadushin, 1980). This third sphere of defense and enhancement operates when the family is so dysfunctional that illegal behavior is at question—such as child abuse or neglect. At that point, the power of the state is brought to bear on the family. An investigation is legally required, with or without the family's permission, and the decisions of this elaborate investigation will determine the changes to be made in the family, including breaking up that family by transferring the child(ren) to foster or adoptive families. With adoption, all legal rights and responsibilities are transferred from the family of origin to new social contexts. This is a very powerful force, one that society uses only with great reservation.

It is also important to emphasize that these three conceptual spheres involve both defense against existing problems *and* enhancement of desired goals. For example, supportive defense might include food stamps for a poor working family, while supportive enhancement might include encouragement to join a shared recreation provided by a natural helping network. A supplemental defense might include a home aide who comes to a dysfunctional family on a temporary basis, while a supplemental enhancement might include a family life education class to aid effective discipline. A substitutive defense would include removal of a child from an abusive family situation, while a substitutive enhancement would involve placing that child in a permanent situation that provided needed love and care.

It is these three spheres that have to be considered in relationship to a bridge to substance abuse. Some of the power of the state in substitutive situations may be directly transferable to the legal territory of substance abuse, while preventive efforts may involve more of the supportive and supplemental areas.

Substance Abuse

There are a number of ways to view the substance abuse area for conceptual foundations for a bridge. Economically, substances represent a major area of employment, for farmers who produce the raw materials and to merchants who distribute them; and to consumers who use them for the reliable highs they generate. Socially, substance distribution and use often involve a number of positions and roles, along with informal norms governing behavior within drug subcultures—in contrast to the norms for behavior within the larger society of which substance agents are one part. Psychologically, substances produce effects that are so highly desired by consumers that they are willing to sacrifice their legal status, their physical health, and their psychosocial relationships in order to obtain a personal effect. Each of these—and other conceptual perspectives —offers different ways to approach the issue of substance abuse.

Economically, one might seek to change the profit:expense ratio for engaging in any of the stages of the substance process. Governmental policies of increasing (or quietly decreasing) the numbers of police, border guards, and the like modify that profit:expense ratio, as do changes of laws punishing persons caught in this process. These are essentially negative or punitive measures. It is also possible to attempt to give farmers alternative crops that are somewhat lucrative (but less risky than illegal crops). It seems unlikely that one could offer legal occupations to the distributors of drugs, but at the street level, some sort of parity might be found between income and legality in favor of lawful employment, especially among young persons who have bona fide opportunities in life.

Socially, the drug world is relatively vicious to its members. Turf becomes a major point of conflict at the street level, just as it is at the level of cartels that handle the production and distribution of drugs. Since the entire enterprise is illegal, illegal and often violent means are used to settle "border disputes" between rivals. While it is possible to display the wealth derived from drugs—the gold chains and fancy cars are just as important in this drug world as they are in any Veblanian universe—these marks of "success" also become marks for suspicion and observation by the authorities, and leave a kind of stigma on ordinary living (the "king pins" in the drug world live very well, and are often beyond local laws because of illegal payoffs).

Psychologically, the addictive nature of drugs is very powerful. The desire for substance-induced highs is not inevitable, however, and much prevention work has been directed at facilitating alternative (legal) highs, such as dance, religion, vigorous exercise, (safe) love making, food, education, and the like (Cohen, 1975). There is also a matter of burnout: that at some point, even addictive drugs fail to satisfy existential needs. Or, the contexts change, such as when many Vietnam soldiers returned home and voluntarily gave up their drug use.

Gatekeepers

Who are the stakeholders in child welfare and substance abuse? The persons involved in these domains will have much to say about whether and what kind of bridges are to be built between the territories. Child welfare workers have the longest formal history in the sense that social work effectively began as services to children and families, and has continued in these areas as the principal player (as contrasted to "guests" in other host settings, like criminal justice, medicine, or education). Theirs is a proud tradition, one that serves the weak and powerless—in a society that values strength and power. Yet it is also a strange position, between a rock and a soft place, to modify an old saying. The rock is the capitalistic society with its individualistic profit-making orientation, along with an antipathy to taxation going to welfare; the soft place is the real need of people being hurt and hurting in a society that does not supply "universal" services—health, education, and welfare—to a sufficient degree to enable people to compete on equal grounds for the available rewards of the socioeconomic system. Thus, child welfare workers and organizations find themselves at the bottom of the socioeconomic ladder on the one hand, but at or near the top of the moral ladder on the other. It is difficult to climb two ladders at the same time. Praised for helping the needy and blamed for giving too much help to "welfare cheats," child welfare workers are understandably cautious about new demands placed on their time and energy, especially when the potential new assignment has many sticky and difficult tasks. Expect sincere interest in unsolved and preventable problems, but deep suspicion by child welfare workers to any new proposals, especially those that take them away from their already overwhelming tasks within the heartland of child and family welfare.

Substance abuse workers and organizations have a well-earned reputation for being tough and aloof, which is understandable given their thankless task of dealing with a seemingly endless line of tough and aloof clients. Seeing people on the "vomit line" at detoxification places is enough to wean new workers of some of the kinder and gentler attitudes they may have had coming into this field. But beyond the individual experiences of line workers, there is a larger orientation of aloofness and isolation that pervades the substance abuse area, as if there is so much to deal with just in substance abuse that anything else would be, to twist a phrase, the straw that breaks Joe Camel's back. Ingrown and proud of it, substance abuse workers will not take kindly to invitations to join others on overlapping problems and challenges. The distinctness of boundaries perhaps helps them to define this isolation—and feelings of superiority, perhaps engendered by the legal power they can command. If we are going to build bridges with these gatekeepers, we had better have something strong to offer them to persuade them even to risk associating with us long enough to see whether what we offer has any value. The basic issue will be to convince substance abuse workers that problems do not stop at the borders of substance abuse, that there are many forms of dual diagnoses—and triple diagnoses, and quadruple diagnoses.

Anticipated Stresses on the Bridge

One principle of engineering is to build a bridge far stronger than any imaginable stress on it because there will be such an unimaginable stress—the once-a-century flood, for example. So, we can discuss the anticipated stresses on the bridge connecting child welfare and substance abuse, but it is the unanticipated stresses we have to prepare for as we begin to build these relationships.

We might anticipate the problems of dual diagnosis—such as the substance-abusing parent who also commits child abuse or neglect, possibly as part of the dynamics of the mental instability of drug use. Even when there is no direct abuse or neglect of the children, we must consider the nature of a home situation involving illegal drug use. What is the indirect price of substance abuse that takes often limited funds away from essential purchases like food, clothing, shelter, or medicine in favor of personal experiences (drug highs)? Are there real harms being done to the children, whether or not we like the associated substance abuse occurring in the household?

More problematic is the matter of jurisdiction: Is the above-mentioned family to be dealt with as an illegal substance abuser or as a suspected child neglecter or abuser? Are there adequate laws or professional expertise on the dual (or triple or more) diagnoses? How many cases slip past us unnoticed because of the legal, social, and professional unclarity on handling multiple-problem cases?

Another problematic condition involves the ambivalence of the public—strongly in favor of the defenseless child and strongly opposed to the substance abuser. But when these actors are all in the same family so that helping one helps the other, and harming the one harms the other, some people get understandably confused and irresolute. Different legislators may choose to emphasize one or the other horn of this dilemma, leaving its victims to swing in the winds of change.

But what about the unanticipated forces acting on this bridge? Let me try to project some difficulties that may be beyond the edge of current thinking. Is it not possible that a joint effort might be seen as a vehicle to reduce the funding to both parties in the name of economy of size and organization? Could not the connection between child welfare and substance abuse be expanded to include education (cf. Dryfoos, 1994)? Or medicine—or the psychologizing of medical or social problems? Does building a bridge mean the beginning of filling in the land between and making one large and unwieldy province? Maybe there is good reason for keeping the areas separate, even if some individuals fall between the cracks.

The Bridge Span

What a thing of beauty is the well-designed and engineered bridge! Sleek powerful lines jet out into open space, defying gravity by means of the slender external supports, as well as the solid foundations built into the two opposite lands. What do we conceive of as the span between child welfare and substance abuse?

In the nature of services within child welfare and substance abuse, we would anticipate a bridge to involve at least three dimensions: primary prevention, treatment, and rehabilitation. For both child welfare defenses and enhancements, and for the many substance abuse efforts, we must be able to prevent predictable problems, protect existing states of healthy functioning, and promote desired goals; we must be able to treat existing problems; and we must attempt to rehabilitate involved persons back to the highest levels of social functioning to which they are capable of returning. This classic triad of modes of helping is as necessary in child welfare and substance abuse as in any other content areas.

However, conceptually, we have to recognize that in connecting two different bodies, we may be able to move or shift from treatment in one area to prevention in another. If we can deal with the substance user's addiction (treatment), it may (or may not) be possible to prevent that adult's child from becoming a substance user (primary prevention). Or, if we can treat the child-abusing adult (treatment), we may (or may not) be able to prevent that person from becoming a substance abuser. The point is to recognize the shifts or transfers between the modes of service that will likely take place "on the bridge."

Conceptually, we have to begin to think in terms of these shifts, which is to say, we have to begin to operationalize our systems thinking. The existence of a bridge is de facto recognition that systems effects will take place and that we had better be ready to deal with them—even to instigate them for constructive purposes. For example, when we have taken the police power to institutionalize substance abusers for their "treatment," is it possible that during the successful process of their treatment we may invite them to come (voluntarily) for a family service effort? This family service intervention would represent the next step in the system of events that reconstitutes their lives so as to prevent their children from beginning drug use (or other predictor actions that might lead to antisocial activities) as well as to initiate relapse prevention efforts for the substance abusers themselves (Marlatt & George, 1984). If the legal power of substance abuse treatment works well, it may (or may not) encourage the client to take the next self-help step in his or her own health and in the health and welfare of his or her family. We have to begin thinking in configural terms to see the possibilities—and then to make the necessary legal and social changes that would enable us to test such ideas as effective or not.

In structural terms, we have been asking the question, from which side of the bridge do we begin to address dual diagnoses? Our conceptual reinterpretation changes the nature of the question and answer: There are no two sides of the problem—there are no "dual diagnoses." There is only a systemic problem that has to be addressed all at once, from both its treatment/rehabilitation aspect and its preventive aspect.

The conceptual meaning of "all at once" sends shivers of fear into the heart of the self-respecting trained professional, because he or she never learned those lessons in school, and the boundaries of agency service have managed to keep this professional as naive and parochial as possible. Problems never stop at the door of one agency, even if we do. "All at once" is a conceptual idea whose time has come. We have to begin thinking all at once. Let's try to provide a scaffolding for this new concept, and then, when (and if) it seems to be weight-bearing, we can remove the scaffolding.

Imagine a house-like building on the bridge between the child welfare and the substance abuse territories. In this house on the bridge we have a multistory building through which all traffic is to pass. Sometimes the traffic can move directly through, as if operating on the same wavelength in both territories. Perhaps this can be illustrated by a school program that engages children in social skills training, to resist blandishments by peers to engage in activities the person does not wish to do, such as taking drugs. In one program, we have the preventive efforts at improving child well-being (a child welfare issue) and reducing the likelihood of becoming a substance user (a substance abuse issue).

At other times, the traffic is on different levels, and some transfer or shift has to take place. Imagine a kind of elevator or escalator by which social services can be connected despite their differences. For example, the client comes into the house on the bridge because of being abused by a parent, and as part of the treatment for this abuse, the child is also schooled on social skills that include refusal skills (seeking to prevent a vulnerable child from being pressured by peers in yet another untoward way). This child has been taken by escalator from one level (treatment) to another (prevention) as part of the same overall service program.

What we need as a conceptual guide is a theory or model that has us look for these kinds of transfers or shifts as a matter of course. We would propose that primary prevention become a first line of consideration when possible because of its characteristics of influencing events and people *before* there is a specific problem in the topic in question (thus saving the potential victims psychological if not physical pain, let alone the social and economic benefits that accrue). But we suspect that much heavy traffic on this bridge between child welfare and substance abuse will come from people in treatment, often involuntary clients who violated laws and are now forced to pay the penalty. This is rough traffic, and we have to deal with strong tools and structures to address it. Yet the concept of the whole problem is to recognize that a given aspect of it—say the child abuse or the substance abuse—rarely stops at this point. We have to explore other problems and other challenges.

It may be that by emphasizing the strengths of individuals, the natural supports of social groups, and the resources of the physical environment, we may be able to reduce individual limitations, social stresses, and physical environmental pressures. This too is a new orientation, away from the classic pathology orientation of traditional social work and related helping professions. It is like the strengths perspective (Saleebey, 1992) in giving equal weight—perhaps more than equal weight—to the strengths of persons, social groups, and physical environments as levers to use in resolving problems and achieving desired challenges. Indeed, instead of the pessimistic treatment of tough customers like drug abusers or child abusers, we may find we have optimistic preventive/promotive tools that emphasize strengths of clients and situations as ways of providing alternatives to antisocial actions as ways of meeting human needs.

This is not to go soft on rough customers; it is to make full use of these individuals and their social and physical contexts to induce them to do what we have had so much trouble trying to force them to do in the past. We do not give up on the use of strong laws; but we consider carefully how to include in these laws involving force the inducements involving persuasion and modeling. Clients have to agree that they have a problem, and then they have to learn how to deal with that problem. Force, even legal state force, may not convince people they have a problem—except that the state is breathing down their necks. We have to combine force and persuasion; awareness of the necessary protection of others with interest in self-development; and raise the level of moral awareness that the good of others is in one's own best interests. Arbuthnot's (1992) recent research with delinquents and moral behaviors is a delicious hint of what might be possible. His experimental/control group design moved the service group to higher levels of moral reasoning, but also to significantly more prosocial behaviors, such as better behavior in school, better grades, and fewer visits to the principal's office. Overall, this linkage building is not going to be an easy task because we have not ever built such a bridge before. We had better test the strength of the ideas and practices at each step of the way.

Is it possible to live together happily on such a house on the bridge? It will clearly take some getting used to, by proud but frustrated child welfare workers and accurately paranoid but beleaguered substance abuse workers. They share very similar problems at the basic structural levels, and the interventive efforts of the one may become solutions for the other. That is the nature of bridges, that they truly connect different territories, even if one has to make some shifts and transitions on the way.

To begin with, it might be worth an experiment to house such a group of workers from each territory in a bridging experiment in which they work together to see "all of the problem" when one problem comes along. Discussing, even brainstorming, problems and possibilities would be the first step. Let us offer an admittedly simplistic and rigid set of specifications for the house on the bridge and the rules by which a dual staff can live happily ever after—after a lot of rough times trying to understand where each is coming from and where each wants to go in its own terms.

Flow Diagram of Configural Problem Solving

We start, as with any professional problem-solving context, with the meeting of a stranger (client) in some context (office—including the office of a police station). The official context exudes the force of law and the power to control. The staff are recognized as belonging to that office and as having that power. However, the service worker—probably a team of workers at first, until each learns the other's perspectives and lines—speaks with courtesy and dignity to the client, informs the client of his or her legal rights and responsibilities, and makes the client as comfortable as possible in this context, such as offering food as appropriate.

When the client is comfortably situated, even in a room that exudes power and external control, the worker moves to an active listening mode, which involves the traditional triad: by being warm and respectful by verbal and nonverbal means; by showing empathic understanding by checking with the client on the worker's grasp of the messages and metacommunications from the client; and by facilitative genuineness, by allowing the client to reach closure on a topic and being as personable and sensitive to cultural differences as possible. When these core interview conditions are maximized, we can expect an initial working relationship between client and worker. The grounds are set for trust by means of honest and open communications. This is no easy task in areas, like child abuse and substance abuse, where the clients perceive enormous societal disapproval, possibly including that from society's "helping" professionals.

The next step is to assemble information on the whole configuration that reflects the client's life situation, recognizing the presenting problems—personal, social, and environmental—but also identifying the available strengths, supports, and resources of the person, the social contexts, and the physical environment, respectively. It is likely that a person's life contains strengths and limitations at all of the levels of a life situation, but that some are more important than others in a particular case situation. By literally listing the placement of these strengths and limitations at the personal, social, and environmental levels, the worker can begin to visualize a tentative causal framework that explains to some degree the client's behaviors and what courses of action are available to address them. The legal situation must be addressed as a priority, but simply hitting hard on the legal aspects may limit the personal or social strengths that are available in the situation. What conditions would be necessary not only to treat the existing problems, but also to prevent predictable ones, for the client as well as others in the extended context?

How does a proposed change in one area with one client affect events in other related areas with other clients or collateral such as family and friends, employers or teachers? This question leads to another structural feature of the house on the bridge: that there are various rooms at any one level. We can engage in primary prevention with a client, but also, down the hall, we can engage in primary prevention with friends and relatives of the client. To make this example as complex as life ordinarily is, it is also possible to be in several rooms at several levels, doing preventive and treatment work with a given client and with relatives and friends of that client. The architecture of this social service arrangement is going to be complex but very likely in the meeting place between child welfare and substance abuse.

Another point that needs to be made is that the size of the rooms in the house on the bridge can also vary in size. We may address programs to large numbers of parents in need of family life education services, as well as more focused programs for small groups of abusers, and individual clinical sessions with given individual victims. Thus, the rooms must be large (for institutional programs or meetings for neighborhoods), medium (for small groups), and small (for private sessions).

Clients may enter the house on the bridge to go to any of these rooms, and may then be referred to other rooms/services at this same level, or at other levels. We have to be flexible enough to have the conception of interrelated services "all under one roof" available as we analyze the presenting problems/challenges. Clearly this conception requires an extensive structure, this house on the bridge.

Thus, the bridging function is to make the connections among problems and potentials so as to use current strengths to address current difficulties as well as to create the context for future enhancements. Indeed, it may be that one deals with a current problem by using the power of a future enhancement, for example, surviving the detoxification regime in order to achieve a desired goal for one's self and one's children/family.

Bridging is difficult enough for the helping professional to grasp, but it may be even more difficult for clients. Yet, it is by understanding the whole of a life situation that the client can begin to readjust his or her priorities. Frank recognition of the frustrations of life and of the seductions of drugs is necessary by the worker, but so is an equally frank understanding of the limited benefits of drugs for self and family in comparison to the alternative goals and possible highs. The worker has to offer a kind of three-dimensional ticktacktoe in which one problem at one level may be counteracted by one strength at another level. It is the linkage between problems and goals that the bridging worker is responsible for conveying to the client.

The construction of such a multidimensional bridge connecting strengths and limitations of person and the social and physical contexts has to be done graphically, a kind of architectural specification that will then offer clear directions about who is to do what, when, and under what conditions. In short, the service contract is clearly specified because of the complexity of the issues. Actually, the action steps may be far simpler than the conceptual analysis, and the worker will have to decide how much of the latter to discuss in order to clarify the former. Certain client actions, such as learning social skills management, or anger control, or whatever, may serve both to address abusive problems and to enhance social opportunities that provide different positive rewards. A single action may resolve several problems and objectives.

Once the service contract is understood and implemented, the worker has to engage in ongoing evaluation, to monitor the progress of the case as well as to have objective evidence of its successful outcome. There may be differential demands from either side of the bridge: The judge may demand objective evidence of the resolution of the causes of the child abuse, while the substance abuse agency may accept reasonable evidence of progress toward keeping sober or clean of drugs. The worker has to be clear about the relative demands of each side of the bridge, and perhaps educate the less demanding side to the virtues of the evaluation from the more demanding side.

Then, as evidence begins to mount that the client is both resolving problems and making progress in achieving objectives—all considered as part of one human context—the worker has both to begin to help the client maintain these skills when the service relationship terminates, and to open up relapse prevention training (Marlatt & George, 1984). This will do as much as is currently possible to maintain both the treatment and the prevention services from decaying or collapsing (Bloom, 1996).

The evaluation process will likely show the changes in individual factors, as in single-system designs (Bloom, Fischer, & Orme, 1995). That is, we read data in a horizontal time series to compare changes from baseline, through intervention, and possibly to follow-up. What single-system designs contribute to the bridging approach is the opportunity to view these changing graphs simultaneously, but from a vertical perspective. That is, they show what changes occur in concomitant variation at about the same time—which leads one to hypothesize about interaction effects. This offers systematic hypotheses, how each part of the whole appears to be influencing each other part.

As the worker observes the changing events in the client's life, he or she must begin to reconceptualize what is occurring as the basis for building a repertoire of bridging tools and strategies. What went right in connecting child welfare issues (strengths and limitations) with substance abuse issues (strengths and limitations)? What kinds of transfers or shifts had to occur on the bridge in order to make the whole enterprise work out successfully? What can we do to incorporate the successes into a new case situation, and to learn from the failures or setbacks in individual cases? (It may be useful to have "postcase autopsies" to analyze the complex interactions of factors and services. More so than usual, these postcase analyses will likely be helpful in building a working repertoire of multidimensional skills and methods.)

Costs and Benefits of the Bridge Between Child Welfare and Substance Abuse

One of the costs or prices of this form of cooperation between two fields of practice is the sacrifice of field-specific sacred cows. Among this wild herd are forms of language for the cognoscenti, traditions of blessed but unread ancestors, and institutional rigidities in which professionals may have grown up, grown used to, and grown old—and that they may not want to change. It may be that a new cohort of workers has to be nurtured, fresh from schools that teach multidisciplinary thinking and cooperation. It may be that this new cohort has to have a belief in the strengths perspective and a systemic point of view. It may be that this new cohort of workers would need internships in both child welfare and substance abuse before getting their degrees so that they know something of the rules of the game before they start constructing a new house of preventive, protective, and promotive practice while involved in treatment and rehabilitation.

What will be the actual costs of training such workers and setting up such institutions as described above? It is difficult to say, except that nothing is cheap in constructing an innovative service, and everything is difficult in trying to measure it. Theoretically, combining child welfare and substance abuse within one organization may produce some savings in nonduplicated services, and other savings in the snowballing effect of synergistic services—although these are mere pipe dreams at this moment. It is equally possible to win architectural awards for this house on the bridge—as did the architects of the ill-fated Pruit-Igoe high-rise public housing project in St. Louis not so long ago. Nothing is certain in bridge building.

References

Arbuthnot, J. (1992). Sociomoral reasoning in behavior-disoriented adolescents: Cognitive and behavioral change. In J. McCord & R. E. Tremblay (Eds.), *Preventing antisocial behavior from birth through adolescence*. Newbury Park, CA: Sage.

Barnett, W. S. (1993). Benefit-cost analysis of preschool education: Findings from a 25-year follow-up. *American Journal of Orthopsychiatry, 63*, 500-508.

Bloom, M. (1996). *Primary prevention practices*. Thousand Oaks, CA: Sage.

Bloom, M., Fischer, J., & Orme, J. (1995). *Evaluating practice: Guidelines for the accountable professional*. Boston: Allyn & Bacon.

Cohen, A. Y. (1975). *Alternatives to drug abuse: Steps toward prevention* (DHEW Publication No. ADM 75-79). Washington, DC: Government Printing Office.

Cowen, E. L., Wyman, P. A., Work, W. C., & Iker, M. R. (1995). A preventive intervention for enhancing resilience among highly stressed urban children. *Journal of Primary Prevention, 15*(3), 247-260.

Dryfoos, J. (1994). *Full-service schools: A revolution in health and social services for children, youth, and families*. San Francisco: Jossey-Bass.

Hairston, C. F. (1995). Family views in correctional programs. In R. Edwards et al. (Eds.), *Encyclopedia of social work* (19th ed.). Silver Spring, MD: NASW.

Howell, J. C. (Ed.). (1995). *Guide for implementing the comprehensive strategy for serious, violent, and chronic juvenile offenders* (U.S. Department of Justice, Office of Juvenile Justice and Delinquency Prevention). Washington, DC: Government Printing Office.

Kadushin, A. (1980). *Child welfare services* (3rd ed.). New York: Macmillan.

Marlatt, G. A., & George, W. H. (1984). Relapse prevention: Introduction and overview of the model. *British Journal of Addiction, 79*, 261-273.

Queralt, M. (1996). *The social environment and human behavior: A diversity perspective*. Boston: Allyn & Bacon.

Renzulli, J. S. (1973). Talent potential in minority group students. *Exceptional Children, 39*, 437-444.

Saleebey, D. (1992). *The strength perspective in social work practice*. New York: Longman.

Schweinhart, L. J., & Weikart, D. B. (1988). The High/Scope Perry preschool program. In R. Price et al. (Eds.), *14 ounces of prevention*. Washington, DC: American Psychological Association.

Werner, E. E. (1989). High-risk children in young adulthood: A longitudinal study from birth to 32 years. *American Journal of Orthopsychiatry, 59*(1), 72-81.

• CHAPTER 6 •

Bridging the Gap for Children as Their Parents Enter Substance Abuse Treatment

THOMAS J. MCMAHON

SUNIYA S. LUTHAR

Through inextricable links with child abuse, parental neglect, and other threats to normative child development, parental substance abuse remains one of the more pressing public health issues involving the children of this nation. Although concern about the impact of parental substance abuse on child development can be traced back hundreds, if not thousands of years (Pagliaro & Pagliaro, 1996), drug use during pregnancy continues at an alarming rate, and the well-being of millions of children is being compromised every day as the adults in their lives struggle to balance their addiction against the demands of parenting (for reviews, see Feig, Chapter 3 in this volume; National Institute on Drug Abuse [NIDA], 1996; U.S. Department of Health and Human Services, 1994). Unfortunately, after years of political rhetoric, public outcry, and repeated warnings from professionals who work with children, significant gaps persist in our ability to intervene effectively on behalf of children affected by parental substance abuse. Despite substantial advances in the treatment of all forms of substance abuse, comprehensive family-oriented approaches to intervention remain something we read about in policy statements, government documents, and professional journals but rarely see in our hospitals, schools, and community agencies.

Even more striking, given our concern about the social costs of parental substance abuse, are the gaps in our service delivery systems that allow us arbitrarily to treat substance-abusing parents as individuals in one system while simultaneously providing services to their children in other systems without mechanisms to ensure communication, collaboration, and compliance across settings. Although not typically thought of as a place to assess quality of family environment and the course of child development, substance abuse treatment systems may in fact be the most appropriate system within which to deliver family-oriented services to drug-dependent parents and their children. Given that a substantial number of adults seeking treatment for substance abuse are parents (Gerstein, Johnson, Larison, Harwood, & Fountain, 1997), substance abuse treatment programs may be the best place to address the needs of children who both figuratively, and quite often literally, accompany their parents when they seek help. Working from this perspective, the fundamental question we will be exploring in this chapter is: What can be done within drug abuse treatment systems to develop services that directly affect quality of life for children living with a drug-dependent parent?[1,2,3]

As we begin, we would like to highlight two general principles that will guide this discussion. First, as we think about closing gaps in service delivery systems, we need to think in terms of both immediate action and long-term plans. That is, we must think about what each of us can do immediately to begin bridging gaps in existing service delivery systems while simultaneously thinking about the development of programs that will better meet the needs of families, rather than individuals, affected by substance abuse. Second, recognizing that it is often difficult to untangle the best interests of parents from those of their children, we must be clear that, even when considering the needs of adults, the focus here is ultimately on the well-being of children. As much as the discussion might focus on drug-dependent parents, the primary concern is the right children have to be raised in a safe, structured family environment with biological parents whose day-to-day functioning is not being compromised by substance abuse.

Defining *the Gap*

In addition to simply acknowledging that there are gaps in existing patterns of service delivery, it is important to define the nature of these gaps and identify factors that support their existence. For purposes of this discussion, there are four factors that deserve our attention: (a) the nature of traditional substance abuse treatment, (b) problems in client-system interaction, (c) problems in collaboration across systems, and (d) problems using scientific knowledge to inform public policy, service delivery, and professional training.

The Adult Is the Client and Substance Abuse Is the Problem

When parents enter substance abuse treatment systems, the initial focus is almost always on the nature of the substance abuse and initial work to establish abstinence. Given at least limited evidence (e.g., Moos & Billings, 1982) that establishing and maintaining abstinence may have an immediate impact on the entire family system, the initial focus needs to be on control of the substance use. However, as clients move toward abstinence, two critical questions emerge: How do we address family issues that may influence the maintenance of abstinence, and how do we intervene to have an even greater impact on the well-being of parents and their children?

At this point, even if inclined to do so, substance abuse treatment systems are generally not able to provide the array of services families need. Even if there is consideration of marital issues, parent-child relationships, and the developmental status of children, drug abuse treatment teams rarely include professionals with advanced training in child and family assessment. Typically, as parents establish an alliance within the substance abuse treatment system, questions emerge about the well-being of their children; and if multiple systems are not yet already involved, it is not unusual to discover quickly a need for collaboration with public welfare agencies, child welfare systems, school systems, child guidance clinics,[4] and other health-care providers where understanding of substance abuse is limited at best. As this process unfolds, we almost always end up with professionals who know substance abuse but not children attempting to collaborate across systems with professionals who know children but not substance abuse. Therein lies *the gap* in services for drug-dependent parents and their children.

Problems in Client-System Interaction

As substance-abusing parents find themselves needing assistance, a second dimension of this gap emerges. Services are often pursued in what seems to be an ambivalent, provocative, or irresponsible manner, if they are pursued at all. This happens for a number of reasons. First, even if clients get to the point where they feel supported within the drug abuse treatment system, substance-abusing parents usually feel inadequate, guilty, shameful, and defensive when they have to leave that system to seek assistance elsewhere (for discussion, see Beckman, 1994; Eliason & Skinstad, 1995; Finkelstein, 1993, 1994; Luthar & Walsh, 1995; Sandmaier, 1992), and they usually fear that, as more and more professionals become aware of their substance abuse, they are more likely to lose custody of their children (Allen, 1995; Beckman, 1994). Consequently, trust, or lack thereof, is almost always a defining characteristic of their interactions with all service delivery systems; and depression, anxiety, limited frustration tolerance, antisocial attitudes, and cognitive deficits may be aggravating an already tenuous situation (Eliason & Skinstad, 1995).

In addition, as they seek substance abuse treatment and whatever other services their family might need, substance-abusing parents often find that access is limited by economic considerations, their need for child care, lack of transportation, and any number of other institutional barriers (for discussion, see Allen, 1995; Colten, 1980, 1982; Finkelstein, 1993, 1994; Hanke & Faupel, 1993; National Center on Addiction and Substance Abuse, 1996). Also, clients often expect that negative stereotyping, anger with them because of what happened during previous contacts, and limited understanding of substance abuse will influence their interaction with professionals in all systems. Unfortunately, things often do not go well for these very reasons. Furthermore, if clients actually do become engaged with the appropriate service delivery systems, they typically find themselves juggling competing demands on their time as multiple systems insist on compliance with inflexible policies and procedures, including inflexible policies and procedures within drug treatment programs.

Problems in Interagency Collaboration

Even when clients connect with providers, intentions are good, and agencies agree to work collaboratively with a particular family, interagency collaboration often fails. As much as professionals might be interested in working together, collaboration is extremely time-consuming, there is usually no financial incentive to work collaboratively, and people are typically working from different perspectives with different goals. As mentioned previously, the professionals involved may also already have a history of problematic contact that influences their willingness to collaborate, and even professionals working inside substance abuse treatment programs may be influenced by values, stereotypes, prejudices, and misconceptions involving the nature of parental substance abuse (for discussion, see Colby & Murrell, Chapter 7 in this volume; Eliason & Skinstad, 1995; Erickson & Murray, 1989; Finkelstein, 1993; Goldberg, 1995; Imhof, 1991). Many of these issues become even more poignant when a substance abuse treatment program working with a parent as the client needs to collaborate with a child welfare or child guidance agency working with a child as the client. Although more effective models of intervention are now being developed, collaboration across systems has generally not been the norm. In short, regardless of how difficult the clients might be and how easy it may be to blame them when things do not go well, provider-provider interaction is often the critical, and rarely acknowledged, factor in many of our service delivery failures.

Problems With the Utilization of Scientific Knowledge

Finally, this gap in service delivery exists because, on a more global scale, public policy, patterns of funding, professional training, and the organization of service delivery systems are not always informed by our understanding of social problems. This problem is not a new one. For innumerable reasons, research designed to expand our understanding of social problems does not always inform the decisions we make about how best to respond (for discussion, see Lorion, Iscoe, DeLeon, & VanderBos, 1996; Mattaini & Thyer, 1996). Perhaps more so than with any other social problem, government often ignores or responds very slowly to scientific knowledge generated by substance abuse research (for discussion, see Bickel & DeGrandpre, 1996).

Examples of inconsistencies in our approach to parental substance abuse abound. At the federal level, we continue to allocate more money for interdiction and law enforcement than we do for treatment, despite evidence that every dollar spent on treatment probably produces greater long-term savings (Rydell, Caulkins, & Everingham, in press). Likewise, despite the prevalence of substance abuse in the general population, standards for the training of health, social service, and educational professionals generally do not require even basic exposure to the world of substance abuse (for discussion, see Galanter et al., 1989). Despite acclamations that *Treatment Works!*,[5] we remain focused on largely ineffective crime-and-punishment approaches to drug use (e.g., see O'Neil, Eskin, & Satter, 1996; for discussion, see Garrity-Rokous, 1994; MacCoun, 1993; Merrick, 1993; Reuter, 1992); and at all levels of government, categorical approaches to funding keep legislators and administrators fighting about how best to divide a single pot of money to serve the same families across multiple systems.

Similarly, in the context of concern about the cost of health care, clear understanding of the chronic nature of substance abuse, and greater awareness of its impact on utilization of other medical services, we are forced to focus on the development of short-term, externally managed, poorly reimbursed, often ineffective approaches to substance abuse treatment that may save money immediately but probably cost more in the long run. Women, children, and substance abuse have been provided priority status within the National Institute of Drug Abuse (Leshner, 1995), but priority status on the federal research agenda has not yet translated into large-scale expansion of clinical services for substance-abusing women (Hagan, Finnegan, & Nelson-Zlupko, 1994; Reed, 1987). Furthermore, despite acclamations that *Prevention Works!*, we tend to be more concerned with the treatment, rather than the prevention, of substance abuse even though every dollar spent on prevention may produce even greater savings than money spent on treatment (Haaga & Reuter, 1995). Finally, although we have ample documentation of a relationship between parental substance abuse, maltreatment of children, and the failures of our child welfare system (for discussion, see Besharov, 1994; Feig, Chapter 3 in this volume; North American Commission on Chemical Dependency and Child Welfare, 1992), we have really only begun to think about better ways to link child welfare and substance abuse treatment systems. As much as we might like to think otherwise, public policy, funding streams, professional training, and the organization of service delivery systems are generally not informed by our understanding of substance abuse.

Bridging the Gap: Building Upon What We Know

As we think about bridging this gap to better meet the needs of children as their parents enter substance abuse treatment, we must ground our interventions in current understanding of substance abuse, its impact on family life, and the development of children affected by parental substance abuse. Of primary importance are four points highlighted in the results of research done with drug-dependent parents and their children. First, substance-abusing adults often present with histories of serious difficulty in their early relationships with their parents. Second, parental substance abuse does not occur in a vacuum; it usually occurs in the context of other threats to normative child development. Third, although most drug-dependent parents care about the well-being of their children, their substance abuse and related problems compromise their ability to function effectively as parents. Fourth, parental substance abuse and the problems that usually come with it increase risk for poor developmental outcomes in children of all ages.

The Childhood Experiences of Substance-Abusing Adults

Research done from several different perspectives indicates that, when compared with adults who have no history of drug dependence, those with a history typically report greater exposure to childhood trauma and parenting practices known to heighten risk for poor developmental outcomes. In these studies (e.g., Bennett & Kemper, 1994; Bernardi, Jones, & Tennant, 1989; Duncan, Saunders, Kilpatrick, Hanson, & Resnik, 1996; Lisak & Luster,

1994; Windle, Windle, Scheidt, & Miller, 1995; Wright, Garrison, Wright, & Stimmel, 1991), men and women consistently confirm extremely high rates of psychological maltreatment, parental neglect, economic hardship, physical abuse, sexual abuse, and generally chaotic family life during their childhoods. Psychiatric disturbance and substance abuse among parents and siblings is common (for reviews, see Luthar, Cushing, & McMahon, 1997; Ripple & Luthar, 1996), and drug-dependent adults consistently report exposure to parenting styles linked with poorer outcomes for children (Anasagasti & Denia, 1988; Bauman & Levine, 1986; Bernardi et al., 1989; for review, see Mayes, 1995). From a developmental perspective, these findings mean that, as a group, substance abusers have moved through adolescence into adulthood without the developmental experiences that provide the foundation for effective parenting of the next generation. When considered from a family systems perspective, this literature also suggests that parental substance abuse represents not just risk for intergenerational transmission of drug abuse, but also substantial risk for repetition of problematic parent-child interaction.

Multiple Risks and Chronic Adversity

Parental substance abuse typically occurs in a broader context characterized by the presence of other problems also known to compromise normative child development (for discussion, see Jones Harden, Chapter 2 in this volume; Mayes, 1995; Myers, Olson, & Kaltenbach, 1992; Smith, 1992). Families affected by substance abuse tend to manifest multiple problems across generations, and the drug use is rarely the only threat to the well-being of a child living with a substance-abusing parent. Poverty, comorbid psychopathology, domestic violence, child abuse, parental neglect, and a multiplicity of other problems tend to occur concurrently within families affected by parental substance abuse, and research (Hawley, Halle, Drasin, & Thomas, 1995; Kolar, Brown, Haertzen, & Michaelson, 1994; McMahon, Luthar, & Schottenfeld, 1996) shows that children living with a drug-dependent parent tend to be exposed to multiple risk factors in varying combinations. The message here is consistent with that emerging from other work (e.g., Sameroff, Seifer, & Bartko, 1997) being done with children living in high-risk situations. Although we may assume that the substance abuse is the primary risk factor in the lives of these children, it is usually only one dimension of a constellation of threats, and there is at least initial evidence (Bernstein & Hans, 1994) that it may be the number and persistent nature of these threats that best predict developmental outcomes for children.

Parents, Substance Abuse, and Parenting

Over the course of the past 20 years, there has been a notable increase in the number of people over 35 years of age using illicit drugs (Substance Abuse and Mental Health Services Administration, 1996), and epidemiologic surveys (e.g., Anthony, Warner, & Kessler, 1994) indicate that actual drug dependence occurs most frequently during early to middle adulthood when a substantial proportion of the general population is parenting minor children. Along with data concerning the childhood experiences of substance-abusing adults, these data suggest that a sizable number of clients seeking treatment are likely to be parents presenting with some degree of impairment in their capacity to function in that role on a day-to-day basis. Consistent with this, research (e.g., Marcus & Tisne, 1987; Tarter, Blackson, Martin, Loeber, & Moss, 1993) indicates that, probably evolving from their experiences in their family of origin, the parenting styles of substance abusers differ significantly from those of parents with no history of drug dependence in ways that leave children at greater risk. Furthermore, even if the individual has the psychological resources to function effectively as a parent, chronic substance abuse almost always interferes with ability to do so, and several authors (e.g., Kearney, Murphy, & Rosenbaum, 1994; Rosenbaum, 1979) have described very nicely the process whereby drug-dependent parents seek, usually unsuccessfully, to balance their addiction against their responsibilities to care for their children.

However, just as it is important to acknowledge the deficits in parenting skills and the negative influence of addiction, it is equally important to note that substance abuse is not prima facie evidence of parental incompetence. Although we know virtually nothing about the interests of drug-dependent men, research (e.g., Colten, 1980; Hawley et al., 1995; Kearney et al., 1994; Rosenbaum, 1979; Tunving & Nilsson, 1985) indicates that most drug-dependent mothers demonstrate appropriate concern about the impact of their substance abuse on the well-being of their children. Contrary to popular belief, parenting is often the only legitimate social role they value, children are often viewed as the only stabilizing influence in their lives, and most women are guilt-ridden, ashamed, and rather defensive about ways they have neglected their children while pursuing their addiction (for discussion, see Colten, 1980, 1982; Kearney et al., 1994; Luthar & Walsh, 1995; Tunving & Nilsson, 1985). Consequently, although there may be limitations on their ability to translate values, beliefs, and desires into behavior that has a positive impact on child development, most drug-dependent women enter treatment with the necessary prerequisites to function effectively as a parent. That is, most come with some basic affective attachment to their children, a desire to foster positive growth over time, and awareness of their need for assistance (Luthar & Suchman, in press).

Child Development and
Parental Substance Abuse

When compared with peers, children of substance abusers almost always demonstrate poorer developmental outcomes. In general, there are two major findings emerging from a growing volume of studies. First, children living with a substance-abusing parent are themselves at greater risk for early and persistent use of drugs. Although researchers (e.g., Chassin, Pillow, Curran, Molina, & Barrera, 1993; Molina, Chassin, & Curran, 1994; Wills, Schreibman, Benson, & Vaccaro, 1994) are just beginning to explore how and why this occurs, there is consistent evidence (e.g., Chassin & Barrera, 1993; Chassin, Presson, Sherman, & Mulvenon, 1994; Chassin, Rogosch, & Barrera, 1991) that exposure to parental substance abuse represents substantial risk for use by the next generation. Second, there is evidence (e.g., Bauman & Levine, 1986; Bennett, Wolin, & Reiss, 1988; Davis & Templer, 1988; Lynskey, Fergusson, & Horwood, 1994; Metosky & Vondra, 1995; Ozkaragoz & Noble, 1995; van Baar & de Graaff, 1994; Wilens, Biederman, Kiely, Bredin, & Spencer, 1995) that children affected by parental drug abuse are also at risk for poorer physical, intellectual, emotional, and social development. Though often still within the normative range, the development of children living with a substance-abusing parent tends to be poorer when compared with that of other children, and they tend to have higher rates of clear developmental difficulty. As suggested previously, some of this disadvantage may be directly attributable to the effects of the substance abuse, but much of it is probably the nonspecific, multidetermined consequence of exposure to the broader context in which parental substance abuse occurs (Bernstein & Hans, 1994; Hans, 1996; Mayes, 1995; Myers et al., 1992; Smith, 1992).

Although several authors (e.g., Rivinus, 1991) have presented clinical formulations of psychosocial disturbance common in children of substance abusers, research (e.g., Bernstein & Hans, 1994; Johnson, Glassman, Fisks, & Rosen, 1990; Luthar, Cushing, Merikangas, & Rounsaville, in press; Werner & Smith, 1992) indicates that, even within relatively homogenous populations, outcomes for individual children vary considerably for reasons we do not understand very well. Therefore, while it is important to acknowledge the risks and higher rates of difficulty, it is as important to acknowledge that there is no predetermined outcome, even for children living in what appear to be similar circumstances. Mechanisms of influence appear to be very complex, they are poorly understood, and research designed to expand our understanding is just beginning. It is also important to note that, thus far, we have been preoccupied with documentation of risk for poor outcomes and we know virtually nothing about factors that promote positive development despite the presence of parental substance abuse (Johnson et al., 1990; Logue & Rivinus, 1991; Luthar et al., in press; Mayes, 1995). Although we know why some children seem to do relatively well in the face of other adversity (for reviews, see Luthar & Zigler, 1991; Masten & Coatsworth, 1995), as researchers (e.g., Johnson et al., 1990; Luthar et al., in press; Luthar, McMahon, & Rounsaville, 1996; Seracini, Siegel, Wills, Nunes, & Goldstein, 1995; Werner & Smith, 1992), we are just beginning to consider why some children affected by parental substance abuse seem to be doing better than others.

Bridging the Gap: Structural Components

As we think about using existing knowledge to develop interventions that better meet the needs of substance-abusing parents and their children, we should begin by acknowledging that the options are only limited by our interest in developing more responsive programs and our ability to think creatively about parents and children in systems of care. However, although the possibilities may be infinite, there are seven structural components that we need to begin developing within drug abuse treatment programs: (a) prenatal intervention, (b) child care services, (c) family therapy, (d) parent intervention, (e) consultation-liaison services for children, (f) special intervention for children, and (g) interagency collaboration.[6]

Prenatal Intervention

Intervention for pregnant substance-abusing women needs to be an integral component of any family-oriented approach to substance abuse treatment. Although there are many unanswered questions about the long-term consequences of prenatal exposure to some drugs of abuse (for reviews, see Carta et al., 1994; Peterson, Burns, & Widmayer, 1995), there is consensus that substance abuse during pregnancy represents an immediate threat to the well-being of newborn infants (for reviews, see Finnegan & Kandall, 1992; Jones Harden, Chapter 2 in this volume; Mayes, 1995; Zagon & Slotkin, 1992), and decreasing drug abuse during pregnancy remains a priority in our public health policy as we move into the next century (U.S. Department of Health and Human Services, 1991). Unfortunately, the National Pregnancy and Health Survey (NIDA, 1996) recently documented persistently high rates of alcohol, cigarette, and illicit drug use by pregnant women, and other surveys (e.g., Chavkin, 1990; Zellman, Jacobsen, DuPlessis, & DiMatteo, 1993) indicate that services needed to address the problem are not readily available. For a number of reasons, most women in need of intervention during pregnancy do not receive it.

Consequently, administrators, clinicians, and researchers working within substance abuse service delivery systems need to begin developing programs that will fill this void. Because substance-abusing women often use before they know they are pregnant, all women need to be educated about the impact drug use has on their reproductive systems and the risks associated with in utero exposure to drugs of abuse (National Center on Addiction and Substance Abuse, 1996). Health care professionals who work with women also need to have a better understanding of these issues, and we need to develop better systems of outreach, screening, and identification so that we can intervene with pregnant, substance-abusing women as early as possible (National Center on Addiction and Substance Abuse, 1996). Although funding for demonstration projects (for listing, see U.S. Department of Health and Human Services, 1992) has contributed to the design and testing of an array of interventions for pregnant substance-abusing women, short-term demonstration projects will never meet the need. At this juncture, the challenge is to take what we have learned from treatment-research projects and develop effective programs of prevention, screening, and intervention for women while thinking about ways to help men better understand how their drug use might also be affecting the health of their unborn children (National Center on Addiction and Substance Abuse, 1996).

Child Care Services

When considering ways to make drug abuse treatment more responsive to the needs of parents and children, we also need to find ways to make child care services more available to our clients. Wherever we might be seeing clients, we must know that children are being safely cared for while their parents are participating in treatment. This is neither a new nor a particularly novel idea. Consistently, lack of child care has been highlighted as one of the issues that needs to be addressed to make substance abuse treatment more accessible for women (for reviews, see Finkelstein, 1993, 1994), and more than 15 years ago, Blasinsky (1981) told us how to make it more available. Unfortunately, although some progress has been made, again largely within demonstration projects, child care services have generally not been integrated into treatment programs despite evidence that on-site child care promotes enrollment and compliance (Finkelstein, 1993, 1994).

Furthermore, although often viewed as an enhancement that makes treatment more accessible for women, child care centers can also serve a number of other purposes (Blasinsky, 1981). Among other things, they provide a setting within which to engage parents in informal discussion of child development issues, observe parent-child interaction, and evaluate the developmental status of children. Child care can also provide children with an important source of socialization and stimulation, and the presence of on-site child care services can facilitate the delivery of therapeutic services to preschool children. If parents do not have custody of their children, child care rooms can also be used for supported, supervised visitation.

Family Therapy

Family therapy, in some form, also needs to be an integral component of any family-oriented approach to substance abuse treatment. Substance abusers inevitably enter treatment with a history of difficulty within both their family of origin and their family of procreation. Clinical experience (e.g., Greif & Drechsler, 1993; Hardesty & Greif, 1994) and empirical investigations (e.g., Jacob, Krahn, & Leonard, 1991; Moos & Moos, 1984; Reich, Earls, & Powell, 1988; for review, see Ripple & Luthar, 1996) indicate that families affected by substance abuse are often characterized by a blurring of generational boundaries, maladaptive patterns of communication, interpersonal conflict, role reversal, and domestic violence. Substance-abusing parents are also often alienated from their extended family and other sources of social support (Greif & Drechsler, 1993; Luthar & Walsh, 1995; McMahon & Luthar, 1997). Significant others are often angry with them for neglecting their family responsibilities, friends and relatives are often caring for their children, and battles are often being waged over custody and parenting issues (Greif & Drechsler, 1993; Hardesty & Greif, 1994). Substance abusers also typically enter treatment with difficulty in their relationships with spouses, sexual partners, and the other parent of their children (Eliason & Skinstad, 1995); and the children involved almost always have unspoken thoughts and feelings about the substance abuse and its impact on their families. Consequently, as we conceptualize more family-oriented approaches to intervention, we should consider the work of those professionals (e.g., Stanton & Todd, 1982; Treadway, 1989) who have shown us how we might utilize family therapy so that, as the parent moves into recovery, the family system becomes a more stable, supportive environment for everyone involved.

Parent Intervention

Because most substance abusers come to treatment with deficits in their capacity to function effectively as parents, it is important that substance abuse treatment for clients with children include

some type of parent intervention (VanBremen & Chasnoff, 1994).
Even if we can demonstrate that traditional approaches to substance
abuse treatment have indirect effects on the family environment
and the psychological well-being of children, we need to continue
developing interventions designed specifically to promote more
effective parenting. However, it is important to recognize that,
although everyone is enthusiastic about this type of intervention,
the immediate and longer-term impact of most parent interventions
have not yet been documented. In addition, because the problems
of substance-abusing parents are extremely complex and extend
beyond simple lack of knowledge, it is important to acknowledge
that traditional approaches to parent education may not be sufficient to produce lasting change in actual behavior that affects the
psychosocial adjustment of children. Instead, there appears to be
need for more intense, clinically oriented interventions that will
adequately address the social isolation, childhood trauma, skill
deficits, and other problems common among substance-abusing
parents (for discussion, see Armistead & Forehand, 1995; Hardesty
& Greif, 1994; Luthar & Walsh, 1995).

Child Development Specialists in
Substance Abuse Treatment Systems

Administrators of substance abuse treatment programs that admit
parents must also consider their need for a child development
specialist who can serve as a resource for staff and parents, coordinate parent intervention, evaluate children on-site, and serve as a
liaison with child guidance, school, and child welfare systems.
Although not often thought of as an appropriate work site for a
child psychiatrist, child psychologist, pediatric nurse practitioner,
or pediatric social worker, there is clear need for a developmental
perspective in our understanding of substance abuse and our conceptualization of intervention (Luthar, Cushing, & McMahon,
1997). Regardless of professional discipline, the ideal person for
this role is a child development specialist who knows children,
family systems, and the world of substance abuse. Assuming professionals with these credentials are not readily available, those of us
administering substance abuse treatment programs need to consider
recruiting child and family-oriented clinicians willing to learn
about substance abuse while thinking creatively about how to

support the development of this unique and, from this perspective, necessary position on the drug abuse treatment team.

Special Intervention for Children

As more family-oriented approaches to substance abuse treatment evolve, we must also carefully consider questions about how best to intervene directly with children. Although it is relatively easy to conceptualize the consultative-liaison function of a child development specialist, it is more difficult to conceptualize models of psychotherapeutic intervention for children that move beyond therapeutic child care and family therapy. This is due, at least in part, to a general lack of knowledge about the needs of children whose parents are entering substance abuse treatment, particularly the needs of school-age children and adolescents. There are also philosophical, ethical, and practical questions about whether clinical services for children should be delivered within substance abuse treatment systems, as well as inevitable legal, administrative, and fiscal issues that may make it difficult to do so even if we were convinced we should and knew exactly what to do.

Clearly, this is the area where we must begin systematically developing interventions grounded in developmental theory and empirical knowledge. Although a number of authors (e.g., Frankel, 1992; Goldman & Rossland, 1992; Gross & McCaul, 1992; LePantois, 1986; Springer, Phillips, Phillips, Cannady, & Kerst-Harris, 1992) have described group interventions for children affected by substance abuse, the impact of most of these interventions has not been documented, and the results of the studies (e.g., Gross & McCaul, 1992) that have attempted to do so have not been encouraging. As with parent intervention, the problems of at least some children may be too serious to be addressed adequately in the brief psychoeducationally oriented groups that seem to account for much of the work that has been done in this area. As time goes on, complementary, more psychotherapeutically oriented group interventions for children whose parents are participating in parent interventions may prove beneficial (Springer et al., 1992), and interventions designed specifically to moderate risk for substance abuse as children grow older must be developed. Furthermore, although we may be enthusiastic about the advantages of group intervention, diversity in patterns of psychosocial difficulty evident in children living with a substance-abusing parent may reflect a need for an approach to individual psychotherapy that addresses both the unique needs of individual children and the concerns they share as a group. Given the gaps in our knowledge and the limited amount of work that has been done, this may be the area where we need to begin moving forward with some sense of urgency.

Collaboration, Networks, and Systems Inside Systems

As substance abuse treatment systems for parents and their children evolve, we should also be thinking about interagency networks, innovative approaches to interagency collaboration, and systems of care within systems of care. Clearly, given the fragmented nature of service delivery, we need to find ways to locate services for parents and children in the same building. Although often viewed as a negative influence by clinicians and administrators of treatment systems, the managed-care initiative under way in this country may actually help foster the development of interagency collaboratives and satellite clinics within clinics. In the not-too-distant past, few of us would have been enthusiastic about locating a substance abuse treatment program within a primary care clinic or a satellite child guidance clinic within a methadone maintenance treatment program. Today, although still novel ideas, these concepts are not as unthinkable.

However, although we might believe family-oriented services should all be available under one roof, the needs of families affected by substance abuse are probably too complex to be met exclusively within any one service delivery system. Even if we develop more family-oriented approaches to clinical intervention, there will always be need for collaboration with professionals working with children and families in other ways. In particular, given clear links between parental substance abuse, child abuse, and parental neglect (for review, see Feig, Chapter 3 in this volume), a number of authors (e.g., Azzi-Lessing & Olsen, 1996; National Center on Child Abuse and Neglect, 1995a, 1995b, 1995c; North American Commission on Chemical Dependency and Child Welfare, 1992) have high-lighted the need for communication and collaboration across child welfare and substance abuse treatment systems. Consequently, when thinking about closing this gap, we have to think about ways more effectively to coordinate services being provided by different organizations using special points of entry, interagency treatment teams, concrete statements of goals and guiding principles, and clearly defined service plans for individual families (for discussion, see Colby & Murrell, Chapter 7 in this volume). No matter how we end up rearranging service delivery systems, we must develop more effective ways of working together across agencies.

Bridging the Gap: Critical Considerations

In addition to the structural components described above, we need to consider a number of specific issues when developing more family-oriented approaches to intervention. Again, although the possibilities are limited only by our creativity, our final decisions about how to intervene must evolve from consideration of five critical factors: (a) the cultural context, (b) the treatment setting, (c) the age of the children, (d) gender, and (e) the primary drug of abuse. Once the intervention has been conceptualized, we will also need to think about (f) resolving questions of values, ethics, and law; (g) demonstrating efficacy; and (h) securing financial support.

The Cultural Context

As we begin developing interventions to better address the needs of substance-abusing parents and their children, we must acknowl-edge the importance of culture. Doing so means being aware that values, beliefs, parenting styles, family structures, and patterns of drug use vary with ethnicity and socioeconomic status (for reviews, see Garcia Coll, Meyer, & Brillon, 1995; Hoff-Ginsberg & Tardif, 1995; McGoldrick, Giordano, & Pearce, 1996; NIDA, 1995, 1996). Current understanding of these influences cannot be ig-nored. For example, the focus of intervention with poor families who may need help securing basic necessities like food, clothing, and shelter will differ from that pursued with middle-income families where these concerns will be less pressing. Likewise, when designing programs that will serve immigrant populations, issues of acculturation and intergenerational conflict will have to be considered. When developing programs that will serve urban neighborhoods, ambivalence about the role children play in the economics of drug trafficking and stress in the lives of grandparents caring for children largely abandoned by drug-dependent parents will need to be addressed. Similarly, intervention pursued in Native American communities will need to be different from that pursued in largely Hispanic or African American communities; and even if working primarily with families of European descent, we will need to be sensitive to ways, generations later, values, beliefs, and attitudes prevalent in European cultures may be affecting family life in this country (for review, see McGoldrick et al., 1996). To be effective, family-oriented intervention will need to be sensitive to differences both within and across demographic groups. As the examples suggest, sensitivity to the influence of socioeconomic status may prove to be as important as sensitivity to differences associated with ethnicity (for discussion, see Schnitzer, 1996).

The Treatment Setting

The integration of family-oriented intervention into traditional systems of substance abuse treatment will also be influenced to a large extent by the level of care and the philosophical orientation of the program. Family-oriented intervention in a residential therapeutic community will be different from that integrated into a day program. A smoking cessation program for pregnant, nicotine-dependent women delivered in a private medical practice will be different from one delivered in a methadone maintenance program. Intervention developed to complement traditional 12-step programming will be different from that developed to complement relapse-prevention therapy. Again, the message here should be obvious. Rather than simply thinking about family-oriented interventions as optional enhancements, we should be thinking about ways to integrate traditional conceptualizations of intervention and innovative family pieces into theoretically consistent packages that address the substance use, its antecedents, and its impact on the family system.

Infants and Toddlers Grow Up

As we consider the development of services designed to better accommodate the needs of children living with parents seeking substance abuse treatment, we must be aware that the needs of younger children will differ in important ways from those of older children. As we move forward, we may find, for example, that infants and preschool children need basic care, intervention to strengthen tenuous attachments to their parents, and opportunities for therapeutic play while finding that school-age children need intervention to promote positive adaptation in school, integration into peer groups, and involvement in social and recreational activities. Adolescents moving toward greater autonomy may need consistent, supportive contact with adults outside the household and direct intervention to address heightened risk for substance abuse. Rather than being prescriptive, the intent here is simply to highlight the idea that the nature of the intervention must be firmly grounded in an understanding of the developmental tasks children face as they move from infancy through childhood into adolescence. With children of all ages, the goal of the intervention must be to support, as much as possible, normative child development and positive adaptation.

As interventions evolve, we must acknowledge that most children living with a substance-abusing parent are not infants or toddlers and move beyond the historical focus on preschool children. Surveys (e.g., McMahon, Luthar, & Schottenfeld, 1996) indicate that substance-abusing parents are often living with school-age, adolescent, and even adult children when they enter treatment; and for a number of reasons, this is a less visible group of children affected by substance abuse. They are literally less visible because they tend to be in school, working, at home, or elsewhere when their parents come for treatment. They are also less visible in the literature on children affected by substance abuse because of a historical focus on prenatal exposure, infants, and toddlers (Hans, 1996). Therefore, as we think about the needs of children, it is important to remember that less visible does not mean less needy. In fact, there is evidence (for illustrative review, see Cummings & Davies, 1994) that psychosocial difficulty may actually increase as children living in high-risk situations grow older, and we are beginning to see evidence (e.g., Luthar et al., in press) that this trend is probably also true for children living with a drug-dependent parent. Less visibility may actually mean greater need.

Gender

When thinking about more family-oriented intervention, we also cannot ignore gender. Research (e.g., Anglin, Hser, & McGlothlin, 1987; Kosten, Rounsaville, & Kleber, 1985; Luthar, Cushing, & Rounsaville, 1997; Hser, Anglin, & Booth, 1987; Hser, Anglin, & McGlothin, 1987) consistently indicates that, within populations of substance-abusing adults, developmental precursors, patterns of use, drug-seeking behaviors, comorbid psychopathology, and concurrent problems common among men differ in important ways from those of women. Researchers (e.g., Gerstein et al., 1997; Kolar et al., 1994; Kosten et al., 1985) have also shown that, when compared with men, women are much more likely to be living with minor children when they enter treatment, and there is also at least limited evidence (e.g., Brook, Whiteman, Balka, & Cohen, 1995; Kandel, 1990; Luthar et al., in press) that outcomes for children differ depending on whether mother, father, or both parents are drug dependent. Consequently, as we think about how best to intervene and with whom, we need to know what the research says about gender differences in the nature of substance abuse and plan accordingly.

When thinking about the gender gap, we must also remember that, although women frequently enter treatment with minor children in their care, many substance-abusing men are also parents (Gerstein et al., 1997; U.S. Department of Health and Human Services, 1994). Because of traditional notions of gender, concern about the consequences of prenatal exposure to drugs of abuse, and funding of demonstration projects designed to better meet the needs of substance-abusing women, we have been conditioned to think about children as issues of concern to women. However, as Phares (1992) recently reminded us, we have largely ignored fathers when exploring risk for child psychopathology; and with some notable exceptions (for review, see Phares, 1996), the impact of paternal drug use on child development, the needs of substance-abusing fathers, and father-child interaction in the context of substance abuse have not been the focus of either empirical research or clinical intervention (Luthar, Cushing, & McMahon, 1997).

Consequently, to better inform the development of intervention that improves quality of life for children, we need to better understand parenting issues from the perspective of substance-abusing men and women. Given at least limited evidence (e.g., Gerstein et al., 1997) that there are men with parenting concerns seeking treatment, we need to think about ways to make room for fathers in the lives of children affected by parental substance abuse so that they benefit from whatever positive contribution both parents might be able to make to their psychosocial development.

Similarly, just as we cannot ignore gender when thinking about parents, gender of the children will undoubtedly prove to be an important consideration in the conceptualization of services. At this time, we know there are gender differences in risk for psychopathology and substance abuse throughout childhood and adolescence (American Psychiatric Association, 1994; Johnston, O'Malley, & Bachman, 1995). Given this, it is reasonable to expect that the developmental needs and presenting problems of boys living with a drug-dependent parent may not be the same as those of girls, particularly as children approach adolescence and developmental pathways to both positive and negative adjustment move more strikingly in different directions (for discussion, see Hans, 1994). As time goes on, we undoubtedly will see even clearer evidence of gender differences in genetic risk, risk for exposure to specific environmental influences, and patterns of outcome. Therefore, while thinking about ways the needs of boys and girls might be alike, we must also be looking to understand how they may be different so that our interventions are grounded as much as possible in an adequate understanding of gender differences within populations of children affected by parental substance abuse.

Primary Drug of Abuse

When thinking about alternative systems of care, we must also consider the primary drug of abuse. Although there are common dimensions across addictions, all substance abuse is not the same, and different drugs of abuse may represent differential risk for exposure to both biological and environmental threats to positive child development (Johnson, 1991; Mayes, 1995). Research indicates that prenatal exposure to different drugs of abuse represents differential exposure to an array of biological risks (for reviews, see

Finnegan & Kandall, 1992; Jones Harden, Chapter 2 in this volume; Mayes, 1995; Zagon & Slotkin, 1992), and there is also evidence that parental abuse of specific drugs may represent differential risk for exposure to any number of environmental threats (for discussion, see Johnson, 1991; Mayes, 1995). For example, when compared with children whose parents abuse licit drugs and even parents using other illegal drugs, children living with a parent dependent on cocaine may be at greater risk for exposure to, or actual involvement in, criminal activity (Johnson, 1991; Mayes, 1995). Similarly, through links with needle sharing and high-risk sexual activity, cocaine and heroin addiction imply greater risk for HIV infection at time of birth and early loss of a parent to AIDS (Johnson, 1991). Research (Famularo, Kinscherff, & Fenton, 1992) also suggests that parental abuse of alcohol may represent greater risk for physical abuse, whereas cocaine abuse may represent greater risk for sexual abuse. As we think about programming for children and families, we need to be sensitive to ways parental use of different drugs may represent differential risk for exposure to potential threats to the well-being of children.

Consideration of primary drug of abuse also means understanding how developmental outcomes vary for children living with parents abusing different drugs. Regardless of what form the intervention takes, there is need to understand as clearly as possible the consequences of prenatal exposure to the primary drug of parental abuse and patterns of psychosocial adjustment within populations of children affected by parental abuse of that drug. Although there are a number of unanswered questions about ways that abuse of different drugs affects the development of children from conception through adolescence, there is accumulating evidence that the consequences of in utero exposure to different drugs of abuse vary considerably (for reviews, see Finnegan & Kandall, 1992; Jones Harden, Chapter 2 in this volume; Mayes, 1995; Zagon & Slotkin, 1992). Research (e.g., Bernstein & Hans, 1994; Luthar et al., in press; Seracini et al., 1995) designed to increase understanding of the development of children living with parents addicted to specific drugs of abuse is also becoming more prevalent and more sophisticated. Recognizing that the existing knowledge base is limited, we must be sensitive to ways developmental outcomes for children vary both within and across populations, and we need to structure our interventions accordingly.

Values, Ethics, and Law

As we work to bridge this gap for families affected by substance abuse, we must be aware that innumerable ethical and legal issues will arise when intervening with children and adults in the same setting. What is substance abuse? Who is the client? What happens when the best interests of the child conflict with those of the parent? What exactly is in the best interests of the child? What constitutes parental neglect? What happens when a parent leaves treatment and a child needs additional intervention? Obviously, the list could go on and on (for discussion, see Feig, Chapter 3 in this volume; Colby & Murrell, Chapter 7 in this volume). The point is that there will be some difficult questions that must be resolved before we begin offering services. Through consultation with knowledgeable attorneys and administrators, we need to understand relevant statutes and administrative policies. We will also have to develop internal policies and procedures that address as many of these issues as possible so that we have some principles to guide our thinking as we get involved in difficult situations, and we must develop specific mechanisms to resolve questions of values, ethics, and law both in general and on a case-by-case basis.

Proving It Works

After conceptualizing what we intend to do, we also need to think about how to evaluate the impact of our intervention. To survive, family-oriented intervention that may initially be more costly than traditional services must be proven more effective (Luthar, Cushing, & McMahon, 1997). To do this, we will need to develop creative, comprehensive plans for the systematic evaluation of innovative programs, and the data generated by these evaluations should then inform the ongoing development of the intervention. In addition, while demonstrating that family-oriented programs are better for drug-abusing parents, we have to demonstrate that they also have an impact on the well-being of children, and we must generate data that prove they are cost-effective. In the current political climate, proving we can preserve families while also saving money will generate more interest than just proving we can preserve families.

Deciding Who Pays

As we plan to demonstrate that family-oriented intervention works and saves money, we also need to think about how we will market our program to funding authorities who usually think about financing services categorically. If we are going to make child care, family therapy, parent intervention, and intervention for children available within drug abuse treatment programs, we must begin thinking creatively about questions of financial support. Which state funding source assumes jurisdiction? How do we bill third-party payment systems? How do we convince managed-care networks that these services are necessary and more likely to produce real savings over time? Given the focus on cost containment and short-term treatment, how do we convince funding authorities to buy intermediate to longer-term intervention for high-risk families? In a political-economic environment preoccupied with immediate savings, who will invest in our long-term future and buy preventive services? Clearly, as we develop plans for programming, we also need to develop concrete plans to secure ongoing funding that take advantage of, rather than leave us victims of, some of the changes occurring in the financing of health-care services.

Bridging the Gap: Evolving Models of Family-Oriented Substance Abuse Treatment

Although we have just begun to close this gap in service delivery for substance-abusing parents and their children, there are a number of bridges that have already been built. These initiatives represent important efforts to develop innovative programs to better meet the needs of substance-abusing parents and their children, and the organization and evaluation of these evolving models of service delivery can provide valuable direction for those of us committed to closing the gap even farther. However, it is important to note that this listing is not meant to be exhaustive. Instead, the intent is simply to illustrate the diverse nature of the work some of us have already begun with hope that it will provoke others to think about what might be in their communities.

Prenatal Intervention

Although programs for pregnant drug-dependent women have been in existence for more than 20 years (e.g., see Suffet & Brotman, 1984), many of the projects described in the literature have been funded by the Perinatal-20 Treatment Research Demonstration Program (for brief description, see Rahdert, 1996), and data demonstrating the efficacy of different types of intervention during pregnancy are now becoming available. These programs usually serve only pregnant women. Some programs focus on the treatment of women abusing a specific drug, others target pregnant adolescents, while others admit pregnant women of all ages abusing any number of different drugs. Typically, there is some provision for outreach and recruitment as early in the pregnancy as possible, prenatal and perinatal care is provided on-site through links with existing clinics, and intensive outpatient or day treatment throughout the pregnancy and perinatal period is becoming increasingly popular. Almost all include a therapeutic nursery program, and most offer an array of support services ranging from clothing banks to transportation to case management and liaison with existing social service programs.

In terms of specific projects, Kaltenbach and Finnegan (1992) described the components of most prenatal addiction programs, using the Family Center in Philadelphia as an example of a prototypical program. Likewise, Carroll (Chang, Carroll, Behr, & Kosten, 1992; Carroll, Chang, Behr, Clinton, & Kosten, 1995) described the organization and efficacy of an enhanced methadone maintenance program for pregnant opioid-dependent women that includes daily medication, prenatal care, relapse-prevention therapy, and contingency reinforcement of negative urine screens. Palinkas and colleagues (Palinkas, Atkins, Noel, & Miller, 1996) described Positive Adolescent Life Skills (PALS), a program of intervention for adolescent girls at risk for substance use during pregnancy that focuses on the teaching of social skills, restructuring of social networks, and delivery of case management services; and Kaplan-Sanoff and Leib (1995) described the integration of a drug treatment program into an existing pediatric clinic at Boston City Hospital where mothers receive substance abuse treatment and parent intervention while their children receive primary pediatric care, developmental assessment, and play therapy. In the second phase of a Perinatal-20 program (Grossman & Schottenfeld, 1992), Schottenfeld and his colleagues (1995) recently began exploring the utility of some of the new behavioral treatments for cocaine dependence when used with pregnant and postpartum women. Although far from complete, this listing illustrates the diverse nature of programs being designed specifically to provide children of substance-abusing women with a better start in life.

Residential Treatment for Drug-Dependent Women With Children

Over the years, the therapeutic community has evolved into one of the better defined, better researched approaches to residential drug abuse treatment (for review, see Tims, DeLeon, & Jainchill, 1994). Consistently, researchers have shown that therapeutic community treatment produces positive outcomes over an extended period of time, and positive outcomes have repeatedly been linked directly to time spent in treatment. However, drug-dependent women have usually refused this type of intervention because of the need to be separated from their children for an extended period of time. To address this problem, selected programs began admitting women with their children more than 30 years ago, and soon after, the National Institute on Drug Abuse started funding evaluative studies (for review, see Glider et al., 1996).

More recently, the Perinatal-20 Treatment Research Demonstration Program (Rahdert, 1996) funded the continued development of two programs that allow women to enter therapeutic community treatment with their children. PAR Village in Largo, Florida, admits cocaine dependent women with children less than 10 years of age to a therapeutic community where up to 14 women live in separate residences with their children. Amity, a therapeutic community in Tucson, Arizona, admits substance-abusing women with children less than 8 years of age to live in a special residence where up to 40 women live with a maximum of 80 children. The structure of both programs and the results of studies comparing outcomes for women admitted with their children with those for women receiving other forms of treatment have been presented in a series of publications (Coletti et al., 1992; Coletti et al., 1995; Glider et al., 1996; Hughes et al., 1995; Stevens & Arbiter, 1995; Stevens, Arbiter, & Glider, 1989). In general, there is growing enthusiasm for this type of intervention, there are data suggesting that it may be both more efficacious and more cost-effective, and similar programs are now being developed throughout the country.

Intensive Outpatient and Day Treatment Programs

As enthusiasm grows for admitting mothers to residential treatment with their children, there is also recognition that doing so removes women and their children from the communities to which they typically return. Also, for older children, the move into a residential facility usually means a change in school placement, disruption of peer relationships, and less access to extended family who may be important sources of social support. While many families may need this level of intervention to remain together, intensive, family-oriented outpatient and day treatment programs are emerging as an alternative. For parents without vocational placements, intensive outpatient and day programming are becoming increasingly popular ways of providing a greater degree of structure and support.

Surprisingly, although known to be increasingly popular, there have been relatively few published descriptions of intensive outpatient and day treatment programs that include special services for parents and children, and most of the published reports (e.g., Grossman & Schottenfeld, 1992) describe programs for pregnant and postpartum women. With funding provided by the Center for Substance Abuse Treatment, The APT Foundation (Bryant, 1992) in New Haven, Connecticut, has been developing an enhanced methadone maintenance program for women that includes provisions for different levels of outpatient treatment. After several weeks of orientation and stabilization, clients in need of more intense treatment begin a regimen of individual and group counseling scheduled around a daily lunch. When stable, the clients move to a less intense phase of the program where contact for counseling services decreases from between two and four times weekly to once weekly. Women enrolled in all phases also have access to child care, parent intervention, a consulting child psychologist, case management services, health promotion workshops, and psychiatric consultation. As federal support for the project ends, the program is being expanded and integrated into a managed network of substance abuse treatment programs while several state agencies consider providing support for those aspects of the program not currently supported by third-party reimbursement.

Parent Intervention

Although a number of different authors (e.g., Greif & Drechsler, 1993; Lief, 1981; Plasse, 1995) have described interventions for substance-abusing parents, Luthar and her colleagues (Luthar & Suchman, in press; Luthar, Suchman, & Boltas, 1996; Luthar & Walsh, 1995) at the Yale School of Medicine are using an empirical approach to the conceptualization and testing of psychosocial treatments for substance abuse to develop a promising parent intervention for drug-dependent women. The Relational Psychotherapy Group for Mothers (RPMG) is a 24-week group therapy for substance-abusing mothers that is grounded in developmental theory and current understanding of gender differences in the nature of drug dependence (for discussion, see Luthar & Walsh, 1995). The intervention represents the integration of interpersonal, group, and skill-building approaches into a semi-structured group therapy designed to provide social support, increase self-esteem, and promote capacity for effective parenting. Ongoing evaluation of the intervention indicates that, when compared with women receiving traditional methadone maintenance, women who complete the treatment are reporting positive changes in their attitudes toward parenting, less emotional distress, and fewer signs of emotional-behavioral disturbance in their children while the children are reporting significant changes in the parenting behavior of their mothers.

Special Intervention for Children

At this time, a number of authors have also described an interesting array of interventions for children living with a substance-abusing parent. Most of the intervention pursued with children has been designed to complement intervention for parents, and it usually focuses on clinical themes, psychological symptoms, and coping styles thought to characterize children of substance abusers (for review, see Rivinus, 1991). Until recently, short-term, supportive, psychoeducationally oriented interventions seemed to be most prevalent (Deutsch, DiCicco, & Mills, 1982), and much of the work being done in this area seems to have originated in alcohol treatment systems (for brief review, see Goldman & Rossland, 1992). Of note is the relative absence of conceptual models of intervention for use with children on an individual basis, intervention designed specifically for adolescents, and intervention designed to decrease risk for early substance abuse.

In one of the more recent descriptions of a group therapy for children, Springer et al. (1992) outlined the development and initial evaluation of a semi-structured intervention for younger children that utilizes play and art therapy techniques to address psychotherapeutic issues common among children affected by substance abuse. Group sessions are conducted with parents and children and with children alone. Likewise, Frankel (1992) described an 8-week, structured intervention for parents that included concurrent groups for children. While parents with children of all ages are being seen together, two complementary groups designed to meet the needs of younger versus older children are conducted separately. Goldman and Rossland (1992) recently described a longer-term, semi-structured group therapy for younger children living with an alcoholic parent that included collateral contact with the parents, and Stratton and Penney (1993) illustrated how brief educational presentations done in high school and college classrooms might be used to identify children of alcoholics interested in psychotherapeutic intervention. In one of the few discussions of individual psychotherapy, Levy (1994) presented a con- ceptual model of intervention and illustrated the approach using the case of a 14-year-old boy affected by parental substance abuse.

Links With Child Welfare Systems

Given that parental substance abuse has repeatedly been linked with heightened risk for child abuse, parental neglect, and out-of-home placement (for review, see Feig, Chapter 3 in this volume), policymakers and administrators of child welfare systems have repeatedly emphasized the need for effective intervention for children affected by parental substance abuse (Besharov, 1994; North American Commission on Chemical Dependency and Child Welfare, 1992). In response to the dramatic increase in the number of children entering child welfare systems during the recent cocaine epidemic, a number of initiatives were developed to expand capacity and generate alternatives to traditional foster care (for reviews, see Resnik, Gardner, & Rogers, Chapter 4 in this volume; North American Commission on Chemical Dependency and Child Welfare, 1992), and the characteristics of some of the more effective programs have been described by the National Center on Child Abuse and Neglect (1995a, 1995b, 1995c). Given the theme of this chapter, however, it is important to note that, despite calls for better integration of the two systems, there have been relatively few descriptions of programs that have attempted to link substance abuse treatment directly with child welfare intervention. Much of what has been described focuses on intervention for children who have been removed from the custody of their drug-dependent parents despite data (for summaries, see Barth, 1994; Feig, Chapter 3 in this volume) indicating that the overwhelming majority of minor children affected by parental substance abuse remain in the custody of their parents.

Focusing on the need for community-based, in-home services for children living with a drug-dependent parent, Sabol (1994) recently described a number of programs in New York City that provide substance abuse treatment and family preservation services to drug-dependent parents in an integrated, coordinated manner. Barth (1994) also described a longer-term, community-based approach to intervention that utilizes extended case management, shared family care, therapeutic child care, developmental monitoring, and intensive family preservation services. In a unique program currently being developed, the Connecticut Department of Children and Families has attempted to establish direct links between the child welfare and the substance abuse treatment systems by making voluntary substance abuse assessment available to parents involved in protective services investigations. Through use of a telephone referral system maintained by a managed-care company with a network of 43 providers, child welfare workers with questions about the severity of parental substance abuse can secure appointments for evaluation on a priority basis with provisions for rapid reporting of results and priority access to treatment when it is indicated. By directly linking the two systems, the agency hopes to decrease risk for continued abuse or neglect, enhance decision making about service needs, facilitate admission to substance abuse treatment, and reduce need for out-of-home placement.

Moving Toward Prevention

While most of the family-oriented intervention presently being developed focuses on the treatment of substance-abusing parents, there has also been extensive discussion (e.g., Emshoff & Anyan, 1991) of our need for preventive intervention that targets children of substance abusers. At this time, several research groups have begun to develop specific approaches to prevention that target relatively asymptomatic children living in high-risk situations. Interestingly, Catalano and his colleagues (Catalano, Haggerty, & Gainey, 1993) have conceptualized their parent intervention for clients enrolled in methadone maintenance treatment as substance abuse prevention for children living with those parents. Using a skill-building approach that includes regular home visits to facilitate generalization of skills taught to groups of parents, Focus on Families was designed to reduce risk of relapse in parents while simultaneously reducing risk for drug use in their children by having the parents teach their children refusal skills. Similarly, Zucker and his associates (Maguin, Zucker, & Fitzgerald, 1994; Nye, Zucker, & Fitzgerald, 1995) recently described the conceptualization and initial evaluation of a prevention program for preschool boys living with an alcoholic father. Building upon research (for review, see Zucker, Fitzgerald, & Moses, 1995) that indicates boys living with alcoholic fathers are at risk to develop conduct problems that represent long-term risk for antisocial behavior and substance abuse, Zucker and his colleagues developed a 10-month, parent-oriented intervention that focuses on parental alcohol abuse, marital functioning, and parenting practices in an effort both to prevent the escalation of antisocial behavior and to promote the development of prosocial behavior in 3- to 6-year-old boys.

Conclusions: Building Bridges
Into the Next Century

Despite more than 20 years of concern about the impact of parental substance abuse on the well-being of children, significant gaps still exist in our understanding of ways parental drug use affects child development, and we have only begun to consider how best to meet the needs of this diverse group of parents and children.

As we move into the next century, it is time to heed the advice of the North American Commission on Chemical Dependency and Child Welfare (1992; also, see Heath, 1996) and take a different view of this war on drugs we have been waging for so long. Regardless of our vantage point, we need to recognize that the real casualties in this never-ending battle are the millions of children living with, or separated from, their drug-dependent parents. Like innocent civilians during other times of war, these children often find themselves involved in situations they would rather not have to confront as their parents struggle with their addiction. Regardless of how well they might be functioning on a day-to-day basis, these children cannot escape the experience of having been abused, neglected, or otherwise disappointed by an intoxicated parent; and even if we accept notions of resilience and invulnerability, we have to acknowledge that their wounds may just not show until we look from another perspective (Luthar, Doernberger, & Zigler, 1993).

Furthermore, as we think about gaps in our battle lines that must be closed as this war drags on, we need to think about service delivery systems that tend to divorce the needs of substance-abusing parents from those of their children. Spurred to action by calls for substance abuse treatments designed to better meet the needs of women, we have begun to develop more family-oriented approaches to intervention. We have, however, just begun; and although we should be encouraged by what we have done thus far, we must acknowledge that there is more to do. With some sense of urgency, those of us working with children need to begin building bridges to substance abuse treatment systems while those of us working with drug-dependent parents need to begin building in the same direction from the opposite shore so that children on the front lines today receive the assistance they need immediately. Those of us fortunate enough to be somewhere in between need to begin thinking about the design of new bridges so that the children of tomorrow receive the assistance they need as their parents enter substance abuse treatment.

Notes

1. Before we begin this discussion, we would like to acknowledge the extent to which our thoughts about many of the issues outlined in this chapter have been

influenced by our involvement in research and service delivery projects pursued by the Division of Substance Abuse at the Yale School of Medicine and The APT Foundation in New Haven, Connecticut. In addition to having a history within the substance abuse literature, many of the issues presented here have been the focus of ongoing discussion in our setting as we have worked with the leadership of The APT Foundation, the Division of Substance Abuse Services within the Connecticut Department of Children and Families, and others to expand our understanding of this topic and improve service delivery. In particular, we would like to thank Bruce Rounsaville, Rosalyn Liss, and Richard Schottenfeld for their ongoing support of our work, and we would like to thank our colleague, Nancy Suchman, for her thoughtful comments about the content of this chapter. Thomas McMahon would also like to thank Commissioner Linda D'Amario Rossi, Peter Panzarella, and Joseph Sheehan from the Connecticut Department of Children and Families for initiating the nomination that led to his selection as a Gimbel Child and Family Scholar. Support for the preparation of this chapter was provided by the National Institute on Drug Abuse (Grants P50 DA09241, K21 DA00202, and RO1 DA10726).

2. Throughout this chapter, the terms *substance abuse* and *drug dependence* are used generically and interchangeably to refer to the entire class of psychoactive substance use disorders described in the *Diagnostic and Statistical Manual of Mental Disorders* (American Psychiatric Association, 1994). *Substance abusing* and *drug dependent* are used generically and interchangeably to describe people with any one of these disorders, and *substance abuse treatment* and *drug abuse treatment* are used interchangeably to refer to the broad range of interventions used in the treatment of these conditions. Although these terms are used generically, most of the research and clinical intervention described throughout this chapter has been done with adults abusing alcohol, cocaine, or heroin and children affected by parental abuse of these three substances.

3. Our goal in this chapter is to highlight themes, summarize approaches to intervention, describe a few projects, and provide a listing of relevant references. However, the reader should be aware that the discussion, descriptions of programs, and reference list is not exhaustive. There are other issues, other innovative programs, and other references that we could not include in this overview.

4. Throughout this chapter, a distinction is made between child guidance services and child welfare services. The term *child guidance services* refers to clinical assessment and treatment rendered to children experiencing emotional-behavioral difficulty while the term *child welfare services* refers to protective intervention pursued with children living in abusive, neglectful family systems.

5. The slogans *Treatment Works!* and *Prevention Works!* have been used extensively the past few years in references and public relations material prepared by the Center for Substance Abuse Treatment (CSAT), the Center for Substance Abuse Prevention (CSAP), and the National Institute on Drug Abuse (NIDA). The origin of both phrases is not clear to us. A literature search suggests that *Treatment Works!* first appeared as the title of a report published by the National Association of State Alcohol and Drug Abuse Directors in 1990 while *Prevention Works!* seems to have first appeared in 1992 as the title of a news bulletin published by the Center for Substance Abuse Prevention.

6. Although highlighted here, it is important to note that more than 15 years ago all seven of these components were described in one of the early publications

(Beschner, Reed, & Mondanaro, 1981, 1982) calling for the development of services more responsive to the needs of drug-dependent women.

References

Allen, K. (1995). Barriers to treatment for addicted African-American women. *Journal of the National Medical Association, 87,* 751-756.

American Psychiatric Association. (1994). *Diagnostic and statistical manual of mental disorders* (4th ed.). Washington, DC: Author.

Anasagasti, J. I., & Denia, M. (1988). Opiate addicts and their perceived parental rearing. *Acta Psychiatrica Scandinavia, 78,* 344, 121-126.

Anglin, M. D., Hser, Y., & McGlothlin, W. H. (1987). Sex differences in addict careers: 2. Becoming addicted. *American Journal of Drug and Alcohol Abuse, 13,* 59-71.

Anthony, J. C., Warner, L. A., & Kessler, R. C. (1994). Comparative epidemiology of dependence on tobacco, alcohol, controlled substances, and inhalants: Basic findings from the National Comorbidity Survey. *Experimental and Clinical Psychopharmacology, 2,* 244-268.

Armistead, L., & Forehand, R. (1995). For whom the bell tolls: Parenting decisions and challenges faced by mothers who are HIV seropositive. *Clinical Psychology: Science and Practice, 2,* 239-250.

Azzi-Lessing, L., & Olsen, L. J. (1996). Substance abuse-affected families in the child welfare system: New challenges, new alliances. *Social Work, 41,* 15-23.

Barth, R. P. (1994). Long-term in-home care. In D. Besharov (Ed.), *When drug addicts have children* (pp. 175-194). Washington, DC: Child Welfare League of America.

Bauman, P. S., & Levine, S. A. (1986). The development of children of drug addicts. *International Journal of the Addictions, 21,* 849-863.

Beckman, L. J. (1994). Treatment needs of women with alcohol problems. *Alcohol Health and Research World, 18,* 206-211.

Bennett, E. M., & Kemper, K. J. (1994). Is abuse during childhood a risk factor for developing substance abuse problems as an adult? *Journal of Developmental and Behavioral Pediatrics, 15,* 426-429.

Bennett, L., Wolin, S., & Reiss, D. (1988). Cognitive, behavioral, and emotional problems among school-age children of alcoholic parents. *American Journal of Psychiatry, 145,* 185-190.

Bernardi, E., Jones, M., & Tennant, C. (1989). Quality of parenting in alcoholics and narcotic addicts. *British Journal of Psychiatry, 154,* 677-682.

Bernstein, V. J., & Hans, S. L. (1994). Predicting the developmental outcome of two-year-old children born exposed to methadone: Impact of social-environmental risk factors. *Journal of Clinical Child Psychology, 23,* 349-359.

Beschner, G. M., Reed, B. G., & Mondanaro, J. (Eds.). (1981). *Treatment services for drug dependent women: Vol. 1* (Treatment Research Monograph Series, DHHS Publication No. ADM 81-1177). Rockville, MD: National Institute on Drug Abuse.

Beschner, G. M., Reed, B. G., & Mondanaro, J. (Eds.). (1982). *Treatment services for drug dependent women: Vol. 2* (Treatment Research Monograph Series, DHHS Publication No. ADM 82-1219). Rockville, MD: National Institute on Drug Abuse.

Besharov, D. (Ed.). (1994). *When drug addicts have children.* Washington, DC: Child Welfare League of America.

Bickel, W. K., & DeGrandpre, R. J. (1996). *Drug policy and human nature: Psychological perspectives on the prevention, management, and treatment of illicit drug abuse.* New York: Plenum.

Blasinsky, M. (1981). Child care support services for female clients in treatment. In G. M. Beschner, B. G. Reed, & J. Mondanaro (Eds.), *Treatment services for drug dependent women: Vol. 1* (Treatment Research Monograph Series, DHHS Publication No. ADM 81-1177, pp. 408-454). Rockville, MD: National Institute on Drug Abuse.

Brook, J. S., Whiteman, M., Balka, E. B., & Cohen, P. (1995). Parent drug use, parent personality, and parenting. *Journal of Genetic Psychology, 156,* 137-151.

Bryant, J. (1992). *Women in treatment* (Center for Substance Abuse Treatment Grant No. 5H87 TI00313). Unpublished manuscript, The APT Foundation, New Haven, CT.

Carroll, K. M., Chang, G., Behr, H., Clinton, B., & Kosten, T. R. (1995). Improving treatment outcome in pregnant, methadone-maintained women. *American Journal on Addictions, 4,* 56-59.

Carta, J. J., Sideridis, G., Rinkel, P., Guimaraes, S., Greenwood, C., Baggett, K., Peterson, P., & Atwater, J. (1994). Behavioral outcomes of young children prenatally exposed to illicit drugs: Review and analysis of experimental literature. *Topics in Early Childhood Special Education, 14,* 184-216.

Catalano, R. F., Haggerty, K. P., & Gainey, R. R. (1993). *Prevention approaches in methadone treatment settings: Children of drug abuse treatment clients* (SDRG Publication No. 127). Seattle: University of Washington, Social Development Research Group.

Chang, G., Carroll, K. M., Behr, H. M., & Kosten, T. R. (1992). Improving treatment outcome in pregnant opiate-dependent women. *Journal of Substance Abuse Treatment, 9,* 327-330.

Chassin, L., & Barrera, M. (1993). Substance use escalation and substance use restraint among adolescent children of alcoholics. *Psychology of Addictive Behaviors, 7,* 3-20.

Chassin, L., Pillow, D. R., Curran, P. J., Molina, B. S., & Barrera, M. (1993). Relation of parental alcoholism to early substance use: A test of three mediating mechanisms. *Journal of Abnormal Psychology, 102,* 3-19.

Chassin, L., Presson, C. C., Sherman, S. J., & Mulvenon, S. (1994). Family history of smoking and young adult smoking behavior. *Psychology of Addictive Behaviors, 8,* 102-110.

Chassin, L., Rogosch, F., & Barrera, M. (1991). Substance use and symptomatology among adolescent children of alcoholics. *Journal of Abnormal Psychology, 100,* 449-463.

Chavkin, W. (1990). Drug addiction and pregnancy. Policy crossroads: Public health and the law. *American Journal of Public Health, 80,* 483-487.

Coletti, S. D., Hughes, P. H., Landress, H. J., Neri, R. L., Sicilian, D. M., Williams, K. M., Urman, C. F., & Anthony, J. C. (1992). PAR Village: Specialized intervention for cocaine abusing women. *Journal of the Florida Medical Association, 79,* 701-705.

Coletti, S. D., Schinka, J. A., Hughes, P. H., Hamilton, N. L., Renard, C. G., Sicilian, D. M., Urman, C. F., & Neri, R. L. (1995). PAR Village for chemically dependent women. *Journal of Substance Abuse Treatment, 12,* 289-296.

Colten, M. E. (1980). A comparison of heroin-addicted and non-addicted mothers: Their attitudes, beliefs and parenting experiences. In M. M. Basen (Ed.), *Heroinaddicted parents and their children: Two reports* (NIDA Services Research Report, DHHS Publication No. ADM 81-1028, pp. 1-18). Washington, DC: Government Printing Office.

Colten, M. E. (1982). Attitudes, experiences, and self-perceptions of heroin-addicted mothers. *Journal of Social Issues, 38,* 77-92.

Cummings, E. M., & Davies, P. T. (1994). Maternal depression and child development. *Journal of Child Psychology and Psychiatry, 35,* 73-112.

Davis, D. D., & Templer, D. I. (1988). Neurobehavioral functioning in children exposed to narcotics in utero. *Addictive Behaviors, 13,* 275-283.

Deutsch, C., DiCicco, L., & Mills, D. J. (1982). Services for children of alcoholic parents. In National Institute on Alcohol Abuse and Alcoholism (Ed.), *Prevention, intervention, and treatment: Concerns and models* (Alcohol and Health Monograph No. 3, pp. 147-174). Washington, DC: Government Printing Office.

Duncan, R. D., Saunders, B. E., Kilpatrick, D. G., Hanson, R. F., & Resnik, H. S. (1996). Childhood physical assault as a risk factor for PTSD, depression, and substance abuse. *American Journal of Orthopsychiatry, 66,* 437-448.

Eliason, M. J., & Skinstad, A. H. (1995). Drug/alcohol addictions and mothering. *Alcoholism Treatment Quarterly, 12,* 83-96.

Emshoff, J. G., & Anyan, L. L. (1991). From prevention to treatment: Issues for school aged children of alcoholics. In M. Galanter (Ed.), *Recent developments in alcoholism: Vol. 9. Children of alcoholics* (pp. 327-346). New York: Plenum.

Erickson, P. G., & Murray, G. F. (1989). Sex differences in cocaine use and experiences: A double standard revived. *American Journal of Drug and Alcohol Abuse, 15,* 135-152.

Famularo, R., Kinscherff, R., & Fenton, T. (1992). Parental substance abuse and the nature of child maltreatment. *Child Abuse & Neglect, 16,* 475-483.

Finkelstein, N. (1994). Treatment issues for alcohol and drug-dependent pregnant and parenting women. *Health and Social Work, 19,* 7-15.

Finkelstein, N. (1993). Treatment programming for alcohol and drug-dependent pregnant women. *International Journal of the Addictions, 28,* 1275-1310.

Finnegan, L. P., & Kandall, S. R. (1992). Maternal and neonatal effects of alcohol and drugs. In J. H. Lowinson, P. Ruiz, R. B. Millman, & J. G. Langrod (Eds.), *Substance abuse: A comprehensive textbook* (2nd ed.). Philadelphia: Williams & Wilkins.

Frankel, A. J. (1992). Groupwork with recovering families in concurrent parent and children's groups. *Alcoholism Treatment Quarterly, 9*(3/4), 23-37.

Galanter, M., Kaufman, E., Taintor, Z., Robinowitz, C. B., Meyer, R., & Halikas, J. (1989). The current status of psychiatric education in alcoholism and drug abuse. *American Journal of Psychiatry, 146,* 35-39.

Garcia Coll, C. T., Meyer, E. C., & Brillon, L. (1995). Ethnic and minority parenting. In M. H. Bornstein (Ed.), *Handbook of parenting: Vol. 2. Biology and ecology of parenting* (pp. 189-209). Mahwah, NJ: Lawrence Erlbaum.

Garrity-Rokous, F. E. (1994). Punitive legal approaches to the problem of prenatal drug exposure. *Infant Mental Health Journal, 15*, 218-237.

Gerstein, D. R., Johnson, R. A., Larison, C. L., Harwood, H. J., & Fountain, D. (1997). *Alcohol and other drug treatment for parents and welfare recipients: Outcomes, costs, and benefits.* (Available from the U.S. Department of Health and Human Services, Office of the Assistant Secretary for Planning and Evaluation, 200 Independence Avenue, SW, Washington, D.C. 20201)

Glider, P., Hughes, P., Mullen, R., Coletti, S., Sechrest, L., Neri, R., Renner, B., & Sicilian, D. (1996). Two therapeutic communities for substance abusing women. In E. Rahdert (Ed.), *Treatment for drug exposed women and their children: Advances in research methodology* (NIDA Research Monograph No. 166, NIH Publication No. 96-3632, pp. 32-49). Rockville, MD: National Institute on Drug Abuse.

Goldberg, M. E. (1995). Substance-abusing women: False stereotypes and real needs. *Social Work, 40*, 789-798.

Goldman, B. M., & Rossland, S. (1992). Young children of alcoholics: A group treatment model. *Social Work in Health Care, 16*, 53-65.

Greif, G. L., & Drechsler, M. (1993). Common issues for parents in a methadone maintenance group. *Journal of Substance Abuse Treatment, 10*, 339-343.

Gross, J., & McCaul, M. E. (1992). An evaluation of a psychoeducational and substance abuse risk reduction intervention for children of substance abusers. *Journal of Community Psychology*, 75-87.

Grossman, J., & Schottenfeld, R. (1992). Pregnancy and women's issues. In T. R. Kosten & H. D. Kleber (Eds.), *Clinician's guide to cocaine addiction: Theory, research, and treatment* (pp. 374-388). New York: Guilford.

Haaga, J., & Reuter, P. (1995). Prevention: The (lauded) orphan of drug policy. In R. Coombs & D. Ziedonis (Eds.), *Handbook on drug abuse prevention: A comprehensive strategy to prevent abuse of alcohol and other drugs* (pp. 3-17). Boston: Allyn & Bacon.

Hagan, T. A., Finnegan, L. P., & Nelson-Zlupko, L. (1994). Impediments to comprehensive treatment models for substance dependent women: Treatment and research questions. *Journal of Psychoactive Drugs, 26*, 163-171.

Hanke, P. J., & Faupel, C. E. (1993). Women opiate users' perceptions of treatment services in New York City. *Journal of Substance Abuse Treatment, 10*, 513-522.

Hans, S. L. (1994). Sex differences in children of substance abusing parents. In R. R. Watson (Ed.), *Addictive behaviors in women* (pp. 401-416). New York: Humana.

Hans, S. L. (1996). Prenatal drug exposure: Behavioral functioning in late childhood and adolescence. In C. L. Wetherington, V. L. Smeriglio, & L. P. Finnegan (Eds.), *Behavioral studies of drug-exposed offspring: Methodological issues in human and animal research* (NIDA Research Monograph No. 164, NIH Publication No. 96-4105, pp. 261-276). Rockville, MD: National Institute on Drug Abuse.

Hardesty, L., & Greif, G. L. (1994). Common themes in a group for female IV drug users who are HIV positive. *Journal of Psychoactive Drugs, 26*, 289-293.

Hawley, T. L., Halle, T. G., Drasin, R. E., & Thomas, N. G. (1995). Children of addicted mothers: Effects of the "crack epidemic" on the caregiving environment and the development of preschoolers. *American Journal of Orthopsychiatry, 65,* 364-379.

Heath, D. B. (1996). The war on drugs as a metaphor in American culture. In W. K. Bickel & R. J. DeGrandpre (Eds.), *Drug policy and human nature: Psychological perspectives on the prevention, management, and treatment of illicit drug abuse* (pp. 279-300). New York: Plenum.

Hoff-Ginsberg, E., & Tardif, T. (1995). Socioeconomic status and parenting. In M. H. Bornstein (Ed.), *Handbook of parenting: Vol. 2. Biology and ecology of parenting* (pp. 161-188). Mahwah, NJ: Lawrence Erlbaum.

Hser, Y., Anglin, M. D., & Booth, M. W. (1987). Sex differences in addict careers: 3. Addiction. *American Journal of Drug and Alcohol Abuse, 13,* 231-251.

Hser, Y., Anglin, M. D., & McGlothlin, W. H. (1987). Sex differences in addict careers: 1. Initiation of use. *American Journal of Drug and Alcohol Abuse, 13,* 33-57.

Hughes, P. H., Coletti, S. D., Neri, R. L., Urman, C. F., Stahl, S., Sicilian, D. M., & Anthony, J. C. (1995). Retaining cocaine-abusing women in a therapeutic community: The effect of a child live-in program. *American Journal of Public Health, 85,* 1149-1153.

Imhof, J. E. (1991). Countertransferential and attitudinal considerations in the treatment of drug abuse and addiction. *International Journal of the Addictions, 18,* 491-510.

Jacob, T., Krahn, G. L., & Leonard, K. (1991). Parent-child interactions in families with alcoholic fathers. *Journal of Consulting and Clinical Psychology, 59,* 176-181.

Johnson, H. L., Glassman, M. B., Fisks, K. B., & Rosen, T. S. (1990). Resilient children: Individual differences in developmental outcome of children born to drug abusers. *Journal of Genetic Psychology, 151,* 523-539.

Johnson, J. L. (1991). Forgotten no longer: An overview of research on children of chemically dependent parents. In T. M. Rivinus (Ed.), *Children of chemically dependent parents* (pp. 29-54). New York: Brunner/Mazel.

Johnston, L. D., O'Malley, P. M., & Bachman, J. G. (1995). *National survey results on drug use from the Monitoring the Future Study, 1975-1994: Vol. 1. Secondary school students.* Rockville, MD: National Institute on Drug Abuse.

Kaltenbach, K. A., & Finnegan, L. P. (1992). Studies of prenatal drug exposure and environmental research issues: The benefits of integrating research within a treatment program. In M. M. Kilbey & K. Asghar (Eds.), *Methodological issues in epidemiological, prevention, and treatment research on drug-exposed women and their children* (NIDA Research Monograph No. 117, DHHS Publication No. ADM 92-1881, pp. 259-269). Rockville, MD: National Institute on Drug Abuse.

Kandel, D. B. (1990). Parenting styles, drug use, and children's adjustment in families of young adults. *Journal of Marriage and the Family, 52,* 183-196.

Kaplan-Sanoff, M., & Leib, S. A. (1995). Model interventions programs for mothers and children impacted by substance abuse. *School Psychology Review, 24,* 186-199.

Kearney, M. H., Murphy, S., & Rosenbaum, M. (1994). Mothering on crack: A grounded theory analysis. *Social Science and Medicine, 38,* 351-361.

Kolar, A. F., Brown, B. S., Haertzen, C. A., & Michaelson, B. S. (1994). Children of substance abusers: The life experiences of children of opiate addicts in methadone maintenance. *American Journal of Drug and Alcohol Abuse, 20*, 159-171.

Kosten, T. R., Rounsaville, B. J., & Kleber, H. D. (1985). Ethnic and gender differences among opiate addicts. *International Journal of the Addictions, 20*, 1143-1162.

LePantois, J. (1986). Group therapy for children of substance abusers. *Social Work With Groups, 9*, 39-51.

Leshner, A. I. (1995, January/February). Filling the gender gap in drug abuse research. *NIDA Notes* [On-line]. (Available World Wide Web: http://www.health. org)

Levy, A. J. (1994). A community based approach to clinical services for children of substance abusers. *Child and Adolescent Social Work Journal, 11*, 221-233.

Lief, N. R. (1981). Parenting and child services for drug dependent women. In G. M. Beschner, B. G. Reed, & J. Mondanaro (Eds.), *Treatment services for drug dependent women: Vol. 1* (Treatment Research Monograph Series, DHHS Publication No. ADM 81-1177, pp. 455-498). Rockville, MD: National Institute on Drug Abuse.

Lisak, D., & Luster, L. (1994). Educational, occupational, and relationship histories of men who were sexually and/or physically abused as children. *Journal of Traumatic Stress, 7*, 507-523.

Logue, M. E., & Rivinus, T. M. (1991). Young children of substance-abusing parents: A developmental view of risk and resiliency. In T. M. Rivinus (Ed.), *Children of chemically dependent parents* (pp. 55-73). New York: Brunner/Mazel.

Lorion, R. P., Iscoe, I., DeLeon, P. H., & VanderBos, G. R. (1996). *Public policy and psychology: Balancing public service and professional need.* Hyattsville, MD: American Psychological Association.

Luthar, S. S., Cushing, G., & McMahon, T. J. (1997). Interdisciplinary interface: Developmental principles brought to substance abuse research. In S. S. Luthar, J. A. Burack, D. Cicchetti, & J. Weisz (Eds.), *Developmental psychopathology: Perspectives on adjustment, risk, and disorder* (pp. 437-456). New York: Cambridge University Press.

Luthar, S. S., Cushing, G., Merikangas, K. R., & Rounsaville, B. J. (in press). Multiple jeopardy: Risk and protective processes among addicted mothers' offspring. *Development and Psychopathology.*

Luthar, S. S., Cushing, G., & Rounsaville, B. J. (1997). Gender differences among opioid abusers: Pathways to disorder and profiles of psychopathology. *Drug and Alcohol Dependence, 43*, 179-189.

Luthar, S. S., Doernberger, C. H., & Zigler, E. (1993). Resilience is not a unidimensional construct: Insights from a prospective study of inner-city adolescents. *Development and Psychopathology, 5*, 703-717.

Luthar, S. S., McMahon, T. J., & Rounsaville, B. J. (1996). *Maternal drug use, psychopathology, and child adaptation* (National Institute on Drug Abuse Grant R01 DA10726). Unpublished manuscript, Yale University, New Haven, CT.

Luthar, S. S., Suchman, N. E., & Boltas, D. (1996). *Relational Parenting Mothers' Group: A therapist's manual.* Unpublished manuscript, Yale University, New Haven, CT.

Luthar, S. S., & Suchman, N. E. (in press). Developmentally informed parenting interventions: The Relational Psychotherapy Mothers' Group. In D. Cicchetti & S. L. Toth (Eds.), *Rochester Symposium on Developmental Psychopathology: Vol. 10. Developmental approaches to prevention and intervention.* Rochester, NY: University of Rochester Press.

Luthar, S. S., & Walsh, K. G. (1995). Treatment needs of drug addicted mothers: Integrated parenting psychotherapy interventions. *Journal of Substance Abuse Treatment, 12,* 341-348.

Luthar, S. S., & Zigler, E. (1991). Vulnerability and competence: A review of research on resilience in childhood. *American Journal of Orthopsychiatry, 61,* 6-22.

Lynskey, M. T., Fergusson, D. M., & Horwood, L. J. (1994). The effect of parental alcohol problems on rates of adolescent psychiatric disorders. *Addiction, 89,* 1277-1286.

MacCoun, R. J. (1993). Drugs and the law: A psychological analysis of drug prohibition. *Psychological Bulletin, 113,* 497-512.

Maguin, E. T., Zucker, R. A., & Fitzgerald, H. E. (1994). The path to alcohol problems through conduct problems: A family-based approach to very early intervention with risk. *Journal of Research on Adolescence, 4,* 249-269.

Marcus, A. M., & Tisne, S. (1987). Perception of maternal behavior by elementary school children of alcoholic mothers. *International Journal of the Addictions, 22,* 543-555.

Masten, A. S., & Coatsworth, J. D. (1995). Competence, resilience, and psychopathology. In D. Cicchetti & D. J. Cohen (Eds.), *Developmental psychopathology: Vol. 2. Risk, disorder, and adaptation* (pp. 32-71). New York: John Wiley.

Mattaini, M. A., & Thyer, B. A. (1996). *Finding solutions to social problems: Behavioral strategies for change.* Hyattsville, MD: American Psychological Association.

Mayes, L. C. (1995). Substance abuse and parenting. In M. H. Bornstein (Ed.), *Handbook of parenting: Vol. 4. Applied and practical parenting* (pp. 101-125). Mahwah, NJ: Lawrence Erlbaum.

McGoldrick, M., Giordano, J., & Pearce, J. K. (1996). *Ethnicity and family therapy* (2nd ed.). New York: Guilford.

McMahon, T. J., & Luthar, S. S. (1997). *Women in treatment: Different from men and different from one another.* Manuscript submitted for publication.

McMahon, T. J., Luthar, S. S., & Schottenfeld, R. S. (1996, June). *With their children at their side: A comprehensive description of inner-city women entering methadone maintenance treatment.* Poster session presented at the annual meeting of the College on the Problems of Drug Dependence, San Juan, Puerto Rico.

Merrick, J. C. (1993). Maternal substance abuse during pregnancy: Policy implications in the United States. *Journal of Legal Medicine, 14,* 57-71.

Metosky, P., & Vondra, J. (1995). Prenatal drug exposure and play and coping in toddlers: A comparison study. *Infant Behavior and Development, 18,* 15-25.

Molina, B. S., Chassin, L., & Curran, P. J. (1994). A comparison of mechanisms underlying substance use of early adolescent children of alcoholics and controls. *Journal of Studies on Alcohol, 55,* 269-275.

Moos, R. H., & Billings, A. G. (1982). Children of alcoholics during the recovery process: Alcoholic and matched control families. *Addictive Behaviors, 7,* 155-163.

Moos, R. H., & Moos, B. S. (1984). The process of recovery from alcoholism: III. Comparing functioning in families of alcoholics and matched control families. *Journal of Studies on Alcohol, 45,* 111-118.

Myers, B. J., Olson, H. C., & Kaltenbach, K. (1992). Cocaine-exposed infants: Myths and understandings. *Zero to Three, 13,* 1-5.

National Center on Addiction and Substance Abuse. (1996). *Substance abuse and the American woman.* New York: Author.

National Center on Child Abuse and Neglect. (1995a). *Descriptive analysis of comprehensive emergency services projects.* Washington, DC: Author.

National Center on Child Abuse and Neglect. (1995b). *Descriptive analysis of projects to improve services to substance abuse-affected families.* Washington, DC: Author.

National Center on Child Abuse and Neglect. (1995c). *Keys to success for the service delivery projects.* Washington, DC: Author.

National Institute on Drug Abuse. (1995). *Drug use among racial/ethnic minorities* (NIH Publication No. 95-3888). Rockville, MD: Author.

National Institute on Drug Abuse. (1996). *National Pregnancy and Health Survey. Drug use among women delivering live births: 1992* (NIH Publication No. 96-3819). Rockville, MD: Author.

North American Commission on Chemical Dependency and Child Welfare. (1992). *Children at the front: A different view of the war on alcohol and drugs.* Washington, DC: Child Welfare League of America.

Nye, C. L., Zucker, R. A., & Fitzgerald, H. E. (1995). Early intervention in the path to alcohol problems through conduct problems: Treatment involvement and child behavior change. *Journal of Consulting and Clinical Psychology, 63,* 831-840.

O'Neil, A. M., Eskin, L., & Satter, L. (1996, September 9). Under the influence: Drunk while pregnant, a woman is charged with trying to kill her baby. *People Magazine,* pp. 53-55.

Ozkaragoz, T. Z., & Noble, E. P. (1995). Neuropsychological differences between sons of active alcoholic and non-alcoholic fathers. *Alcohol and Alcoholism, 30,* 115-123.

Pagliaro, A. M., & Pagliaro, L. A. (1996). *Substance use among children and adolescents: Its nature, extent, and effects from conception to adulthood.* New York: John Wiley.

Palinkas, L. A., Atkins, C. J., Noel, P., & Miller, C. (1996). Recruitment and retention of adolescent women in drug treatment research. In E. Rahdert (Ed.), *Treatment for drug exposed women and their children: Advances in research methodology* (NIDA Research Monograph No. 166, NIH Publication No. 96-3632, pp. 87-109). Rockville, MD: National Institute on Drug Abuse.

Peterson, L. M., Burns, W. J., & Widmayer, S. M. (1995). Developmental risk for infants of maternal cocaine abusers: Evaluation and critique. *Clinical Psychology Review, 15,* 739-776.

Phares, V. (1992). Where's Poppa? The relative lack of attention to the role of fathers in child and adolescent psychopathology. *American Psychologist, 47,* 656-664.

Phares, V. (1996). *Fathers and developmental psychopathology.* New York: John Wiley.

Plasse, B. R. (1995). Parenting groups for recovering addicts in a day treatment center. *Social Work, 40,* 65-75.

Rahdert, E. (1996). Introduction to the Perinatal-20 Treatment Research Demonstration Program. In E. Rahdert (Ed.), *Treatment for drug exposed women and their children: Advances in research methodology* (NIDA Research Monograph No. 166, NIH Publication No. 96-3632, pp. 1-4). Rockville, MD: National Institute on Drug Abuse.

Reed, B. G. (1987). Developing women-sensitive drug dependence treatment services: Why so difficult? *Journal of Psychoactive Drugs, 19,* 151-164.

Reich, W., Earls, F., & Powell, J. (1988). A comparison of the home and social environments of children of alcoholic and non-alcoholic fathers. *British Journal of Addiction, 83,* 831-839.

Reuter, P. (1992). Hawks ascendant: The punitive trend of American drug policy. *Daedalus, 121,* 15-52.

Ripple, C. H., & Luthar, S. S. (1996). Familial factors in illicit drug abuse: An interdisciplinary perspective. *American Journal of Drug and Alcohol Abuse, 22,* 147-172.

Rivinus, T. M. (1991). Treatment of children of substance-abusing parents: Selected developmental, diagnostic, and treatment issues. In T. M. Rivinus (Ed.), *Children of chemically dependent parents* (pp. 263-287). New York: Brunner/Mazel.

Rosenbaum, M. (1979). Difficulties in taking care of business: Women addicts as mothers. *American Journal of Drug and Alcohol Abuse, 6,* 431-446.

Rydell, C. P., Caulkins, J. P., & Everingham, S. S. (in press). Enforcement or treatment: Modeling the relative efficacy of alternatives for controlling cocaine. *Operations Research.*

Sabol, B. J. (1994). The call on agency resources. In D. Besharov (Ed.), *When drug addicts have children* (pp. 125-143). Washington, DC: Child Welfare League of America.

Sameroff, A. J., Seifer, R., & Bartko, W. T. (1997). Environmental perspectives on adaptation during childhood and adolescence. In S. S. Luthar, J. A. Burack, D. Cicchetti, & J. Weisz (Eds.), *Developmental psychopathology: Perspectives on adjustment, risk, and disorder* (pp. 507-526). New York: Cambridge University Press.

Sandmaier, M. (1992). *The invisible alcoholics: Women and alcohol* (2nd ed). New York: McGraw-Hill.

Schnitzer, P. K. (1996). "They don't come in!" Stories told, lessons taught about poor families in therapy. *American Journal of Orthopsychiatry, 66,* 572-582.

Schottenfeld, R. S., Mayes, L., Forsyth, B. W., Ball, S., Carroll, K., & Mody, S. (1995). *Behavioral treatment for cocaine-dependent women* (National Institute on Drug Abuse Grant No. R01 DA06915). Unpublished manuscript, The APT Foundation, New Haven, CT.

Seracini, A. M., Siegel, L. J., Wills, T. A., Nunes, E. V., & Goldstein, R. B. (1995, August). *Coping, social support, and adjustment in children of heroin addicts.* Poster session presented at the annual convention of the American Psychological Association, New York City.

Smith, I. (1992). An ecological perspective: The impact of culture and social environment on drug-exposed children. In Office of Substance Abuse Prevention (Ed.), *Identifying the needs of drug-affected children: Public policy issues* (OSAP

Prevention Monograph No. 11, DHHS Publication No. ADM 92-1814, pp. 93-108). Rockville, MD: Office of Substance Abuse Prevention.

Springer, J. F., Phillips, J. L., Phillips, L., Cannady, L., & Kerst-Harris, E. (1992). CODA: A creative therapy program for children in families affected by abuse of alcohol or other drugs. *Journal of Community Psychology*, 55-74.

Stanton, M. D., & Todd, T. C. (Eds.). (1982). *The family therapy of drug abuse and addictions*. New York: Guilford.

Stratton, P. D., & Penney, A. (1993). High school and college student children of alcoholics: A pilot education program and assessment of readiness for assistance. *Journal of Alcohol and Drug Education, 38*, 100-112.

Stevens, S. J., & Arbiter, N. (1995). A therapeutic community for substance-abusing pregnant women and women with children: Process and outcome. *Journal of Psychoactive Drugs, 27*, 49-56.

Stevens, S. J., Arbiter, N., & Glider, P. (1989). Women residents: Expanding their role to increase effectiveness in substance abuse treatment. *International Journal of the Addictions, 24*, 425-434.

Substance Abuse and Mental Health Services Administration. (1996, August). *Preliminary estimates from the 1995 National Household Survey on Drug Abuse* (Advanced Report No. 18) [On-line]. (Available World Wide Web: http://www.health.org)

Suffet, F., & Brotman, R. (1984). A comprehensive care program for pregnant addicts: Obstetrical, neonatal, and child development outcomes. *International Journal of the Addictions, 19*, 199-219.

Tarter, R. E., Blackson, T. C., Martin, C. S., Loeber, R., & Moss, H. B. (1993). Characteristics and correlates of child discipline practices in substance abuse and normal families. *American Journal on Addictions, 2*, 18-25.

Tims, F. M., DeLeon, G., & Jainchill, N. (Eds.). (1994). *Therapeutic community: Advances in research and application* (NIDA Research Monograph No. 144, NIH Publication No. 94-3633). Rockville, MD: National Institute on Drug Abuse.

Treadway, D. C. (1989). *Before it's too late: Working with substance abuse in the family*. New York: Norton.

Tunving, K., & Nilsson, K. (1985). Young female drug addicts in treatment: A 12 year perspective. *Journal of Drug Issues, 15*, 367-382.

U.S. Department of Health and Human Services. (1991). *Healthy people 2000: National health promotion and disease prevention objectives* (DHHS Publication No. PHS 91-50212). Washington, DC: Government Printing Office.

U.S. Department of Health and Human Services. (1992). *Maternal drug abuse and drug exposed children: A compendium of HHS activities* (DHHS Publication No. ADM 92-1948). Washington, DC: Government Printing Office.

U.S. Department of Health and Human Services. (1994). *Substance abuse among women and parents*. Washington, DC: Author.

van Baar, A., & de Graaff, B. M. (1994). Cognitive development at pre-school-age of infants of drug-dependent mothers. *Developmental Medicine and Child Neurology, 36*, 1063-1075.

VanBremen, J. R., & Chasnoff, I. J. (1994). Policy issues for integrating parenting interventions and addiction treatment for women. *Topics in Early Childhood Special Education, 14*, 254-274.

Werner, E. E., & Smith, R. S. (1992). *Overcoming the odds: High risk children from birth to adulthood.* Ithaca, NY: Cornell University Press.

Wilens, T. E., Biederman, J., Kiely, K., Bredin, E., & Spencer, T. J. (1995). Pilot study of behavioral and emotional disturbance in the high-risk children of parents with opioid dependence. *Journal of the American Academy of Child and Adolescent Psychiatry, 34,* 779-785.

Wills, T. A., Schreibman, D., Benson, G., & Vaccaro, D. (1994). Impact of parental substance use on adolescents: A test of a mediational model. *Journal of Pediatric Psychology, 19,* 537-555.

Windle, M., Windle, R. C., Scheidt, D. M., & Miller, G. B. (1995). Physical and sexual abuse associated with mental disorders among alcoholic inpatients. *American Journal of Psychiatry, 152,* 1322-1328.

Wright, L. S., Garrison, J., Wright, N. B., & Stimmel, D. T. (1991). Childhood unhappiness and family stressors recalled by adult children of alcoholics. *Alcoholism Treatment Quarterly, 8(4),* 67-80.

Zagon, I. S., & Slotkin, T. A. (Eds.). (1992). *Maternal substance abuse and the developing nervous system.* New York: Academic Press.

Zellman, G. L., Jacobsen, P. D., DuPlessis, H., & DiMatteo, M. R. (1993). Detecting prenatal substance exposure: An exploratory analysis and policy discussion. *Journal of Drug Issues, 23,* 373-387.

Zucker, R. A., Fitzgerald, H. E., & Moses, H. D. (1995). Emergence of alcohol problems and the several alcoholisms: A developmental perspective on etiologic theory and life course trajectory. In D. Cicchetti & D. J. Cohen (Eds.), *Developmental psychopathology: Vol. 2. Risk, disorder, and adaptation* (pp. 677-711). New York: John Wiley.

• CHAPTER 7 •

Child Welfare and Substance Abuse Services: From Barriers to Collaboration

SUZANNE M. COLBY

WILBERT MURRELL

Maternal substance abuse has sparked an intense debate among policymakers in child welfare and substance abuse practices (Tracy, 1994). In studying the provision of child welfare and substance abuse services for parental substance abusers, practitioners and researchers have focused almost exclusively on what they know best and have ignored other family factors (Thompson, 1990). Substance abuse treatment evaluation studies typically fail even to measure outcomes related to child care and custody, parenting skills, or family stability. Conversely, child welfare studies have tended to focus on mandated services with little orientation to the nature of alcohol and other drug addiction (Child Welfare League of America, 1992).

Child Welfare Research and Policy. As early as 1917, Richmond's classic report recognized that child welfare workers needed to combat alcoholism within their targeted population. Eight decades later, the problem persists and remains largely unaddressed. Contemporary studies of the link between parental substance abuse and child maltreatment have found that substance abuse is present in at least 50% of the families known to the public child welfare system (Murphy et al., 1991), with most prevalence estimates ranging between 50% and 80% (Curtis & McCullough, 1993; Famularo, Kinscherff, & Fenton, 1992; Ways and Means Committee, 1990). In the case of child abusers and incest perpetrators, a large proportion have been found to be problem drinkers, with abusive acts frequently being preceded by drinking or other drug use (Famularo, Stone, Barnum, & Wharton, 1986; Leonard & Jacob, 1988; Widom, 1989).

Other evidence suggests that child welfare workers have limited training in alcohol and other drug (AOD) abuse treatment, resulting in an elevated risk for children of substance-abusing parents (Thompson, 1990). Traditional child welfare policies mandated termination of parental rights in the case of substance abuse, based on either parental incapacity or abandonment. In fact, the definition of *incapacity* specifically included excessive use of alcohol or a controlled substance (Horowitz, 1990). A related basis for termination occurs when a written case plan includes substance abuse treatment, but the parent fails to remedy his or her substance abuse with appropriate and comprehensive services (Horowitz, 1990). For almost two centuries, American family law has asserted that it places children and their welfare at the heart of custody and parentage determination. This principle is referred to as the "best-interest" standard. Recent child welfare policies have mandated child protection within the context of family preservation with greater emphasis on the goal of keeping parents and children together whenever possible (Adoption Assistance and Child Welfare Act of 1980). Still, placement of children in care outside the home has increased significantly since 1985. Children of parents addicted to crack cocaine are especially likely to be removed from the home (McCullough, 1991; Tatara, 1990). Several reports have documented that once children from substance-abusing families enter placement they tend to be in care longer and are less likely to be reunified with their biological parent compared to children from non substance-abusing parents (Besharov, 1990; Fanshel, 1975; Feig, 1990; Walker, Zangrillo, & Smith, 1991).

Substance Abuse Research and Policy. Research regarding the delivery of substance abuse treatment indicates that women are underrepresented in substance abuse treatment (Van Den Bergh, 1991). This may be attributed to the many gender-specific barriers to treatment that women face (Beckman, 1994). These include *internal barriers,* such as fear of stigmatization (Reed, 1987) and concern about leaving or losing their children (Wilsnack, in press), as well as *external barriers,* such as opposition by family and/or friends (Beckman & Amaro, 1986). Also, *institutional barriers* exist, illustrated by the fact that men are more likely to be referred to treatment than women (Duckert, 1987). There is considerable empirical evidence that men are more likely to be referred by physicians, employers, or the legal system than women (Beckman & Korel, 1982; Moore et al., 1989). Moreover, residential drug and alcohol treatment programs have traditionally been designed primarily for adult men (Harvey, Comfort, & Johns, 1993), and there is a shortage of appropriate treatment programs that are designed to address the specific needs of substance-abusing women and their children (Horowitz, 1990). Treatment must be tailored to address issues that are highly prevalent among female substance abusers, including sexual abuse and domestic violence (Beckman, 1994; Reed, 1987).

Until recently, research focusing on the prevalence of AOD problems among women and their impact on children was rare. Until the 1970s, alcohol research of all forms (e.g., epidemiological, clinical, and experimental) either excluded women entirely or focused disproportionately on men (Wilsnack, Wilsnack, & Sturmhofel, 1994). An extensive review of substance abuse research published from 1966 to 1975 (Davidson & Bemko, 1978) identified only 50 articles that specifically addressed the problem of substance-abusing women, and all of these ignored the issue of impact on children. In addiction treatment outcome studies that do include both women and men, the outcomes are typically less positive for women than for men (Beckman, 1994). Again, outcomes related to parenting are not reported even though approximately 80% of women entering substance abuse treatment are known to have children, and close to 50% have children living with them when they enter treatment (Stevens, Arbiter, & McGrath, 1994).

The Call for Collaboration. There is an obvious need for collaboration between child welfare and substance abuse treatment services to meet the dual goals of parental recovery from alcohol and other drug abuse and of protection of children from abuse and neglect. The dual problems of substance abuse and of child abuse and neglect are too complex, varied, and pervasive for a single discipline to have an adequate impact. Unfortunately, there are significant barriers to collaboration that must be recognized and removed (Mulwanda, Thornburg, Filbert, & Klein, 1995).

Collaboration is a word that sounds wonderful when two or more practices are trying to work together to achieve a common goal. However, two agencies deciding to work together does not constitute collaboration. There are differences between collaboration and cooperation. Cooperation may be achieved or defined simply as people just working together (Boyd et al., 1992; Hord, 1986; Lieberman, 1986a, 1986b). But collaboration goes beyond cooperation; it is defined as an organizational and interorganizational structure in which resources, power, and authority are shared, and people are brought together to achieve a common goal that could not be accomplished by a single entity, individual, or organization independently (Kagan, 1991). There are some key elements in collaboration. Collaborating agencies need to work through "turf" issues, and to develop clear roles and responsibilities. Grievance procedures should also be established before collaboration occurs. A set of common goals must be jointly constructed and agreed upon, responsibility must be shared for obtaining those goals, and finally, agency members must work together to achieve those goals using the combined expertise of the collaborators (Bruner, 1991).

Historically, child welfare and substance abuse treatment have operated as separate and independent entities. This separation has been reinforced and maintained by real differences in mission, philosophical perspectives, education and training, administrative structure, and institutional characteristics. However, it has become impossible to deny that these two service realms are largely treating an overlapping population of clients. An evaluation of whether to change the current structure of service delivery must begin with a consideration of the consequences of inaction. It is clear from the description presented here and in other chapters of this volume that the current system of fragmented care delivery and the lack of communication among these two fields is inefficient and ineffective. Professionals from both fields recognize that the problems of child abuse and neglect and substance abuse are complex problems. Where they co-exist within a family, they are inseparable from each other and inseparable from other aspects of family functioning. It follows that the resolution of these problems must be directed toward the family as a whole. If substance abuse treatment occurs without screening or intervention of associated child abuse or neglect, the interests of neither the parent nor the child are optimally served in the long run. First, the likelihood of the parent's relapse to substance use is probably high as the unresolved issues are likely to persist when he or she returns to the home environment. Second, children who are being abused or neglected remain undetected by the family's only contact with intervention professionals, as child welfare workers have no way to come in contact with the family. Similarly, interventions on the part of child welfare professionals are almost guaranteed to fail if parental substance abuse is not addressed. Although a *causal* relationship between substance abuse and child abuse and neglect has not been unequivocally proven, the evidence clearly indicates that a causal relationship is plausible. The current method of providing only a partial range of services to families is therefore inadequate for all parties involved. Even while professionals from the different fields insist that they are serving the interests of their own clients (i.e., parent vs. child) as a primary concern, the case can be convincingly made that no one in the family is receiving adequate services when the services are not coordinated.

The child welfare system has been principal in assessing, acknowledging, and trying to address this shortcoming in treatment delivery and coordination of services. However, in the absence of meaningful collaboration with the substance abuse field, the child welfare system has attempted to duplicate substance abuse treatment within the child welfare agencies. This solution is unsatisfactory for several reasons, including: (a) the fact that child welfare caseworkers are already overextended with large caseloads; (b) the lack of cost-effectiveness as preexisting services are being duplicated; and (c) substance abuse services are delivered by people who lack addiction training and expertise.

In summary, the consequences of not changing the current structure of service delivery are dire. Incomplete and inadequate services are delivered to troubled, multiproblem families. Outcome evaluations indicate poor prognosis in both fields. In substance abuse treatment, cases of child abuse and neglect go undetected, leaving children to be victimized. In the child welfare domain, substance abuse treatment may be mandated but not facilitated; most of those referred never attend treatment. Alternatively, inferior substance abuse services are delivered to child welfare clients, who in turn face serious consequences when their substance abuse does not abate. There is no uniform delivery of services; service delivery to families is an accident of the client's point of entry into the system. Both systems are ultimately inefficient and ineffective, thus eroding public support for maintaining these increasingly expensive structures.

Barriers to Collaboration

Different Professional Missions. There are a number of differences between substance abuse and child welfare professionals that impede meaningful collaboration between the two sets of services. Among the many differences described in an earlier chapter (Feig, Chapter 3 in this volume), perhaps the most fundamental difference is one of professional perspective of responsibility. That is, these professionals may be distinguished in terms of their determination of who their client is, and what the goals of intervention are.

From the child welfare perspective, the client is the child. The mission is clear and straightforward: Child welfare workers are children's advocates. Their conviction is that the child needs protection and takes priority over the parent, because the child cannot protect himself or herself. Thus, the primary responsibility of a child welfare professional is the well-being of the child. From this perspective, all suspected cases of child abuse and neglect must be investigated, because the risk of an undetected case resulting in the victimization of a child outweighs the risk of stigma and other negative consequences associated with being suspected of child abuse or neglect in unsubstantiated cases.

From the substance abuse treatment perspective, the substance abuser is the client, and his or her treatment and outcome are the primary targets of intervention. As primary advocates of the substance-abusing parent, treatment providers are primarily oriented toward adults. Treatment decisions are primarily made with respect to their impact on the substance-abusing client; considerations of how treatment decisions affect the client's children are not ignored, but they are secondary. This orientation has been reinforced by recent reductions in insurance coverage for substance abuse treatment. The resulting reductions in lengths of stay in treatment have led to even more intensive focus on the individual, because there is inadequate treatment time available to deal with the issues of the family—the individual's substance abuse treatment is the priority.

Resolution of Different Missions. On the face of it, this distinction in missions should be fairly easily resolved. As described above, the mission of child welfare workers as child advocates is straightforward, and this mission is sanctioned by federal and state laws. Mental health workers outside the child welfare field, including substance abuse professionals, are also required to comply with these laws. (Mandatory reporting laws do vary from state to state, however. For complete coverage of this issue as it applies to mental health workers outside the child welfare field, see Liss, 1994.) Convergent with relevant federal and state laws are professional codes of ethics for substance abuse treatment professionals that specify that although the rights of all parties involved must be recognized, when conflict arises regarding who is the client, one must decide in favor of the child (see McMahon, 1993).

While there is official agreement in laws and professional and ethical standards of conduct, there is not yet agreement in practice. Despite clearly articulated ethical guidelines, substance abuse treatment providers perceive themselves to be in an advocacy dilemma, whereby advancing the needs of the child sets aside the best interests of their client (McMahon, 1993). As agonizing as this dilemma is, there is no resolution without the acceptance of ethical requirements that mandate protection of the child. Furthermore, this acceptance cannot be purely academic; it must be a practical acceptance that is integral to the manner in which both child welfare and substance abuse professionals conduct their work. Meaningful collaboration between the child welfare and substance abuse treatment fields begins at this mutual agreement regarding intervention priorities.

Professional Distrust. A related barrier to collaboration is the tradition of clinical autonomy, a strong force in health professions. Many clinicians believe that their personal judgment should determine the course of all care and services received, based on their therapeutic relationship with, and knowledge of, the client. Clinicians will therefore tend to resist external pressures that mandate that they alter or standardize their own system of treatment delivery (Edmunds, 1996). Clinicians will also be resistant to policies that mandate that they betray the confidentiality upon which the successful therapeutic relationship is based. By placing a higher priority on provision of supportive treatment for the client, substance abuse professionals do not report the illicit activities of their clients, including the use of illicit drugs, prostitution, breaking and entering, and other crimes associated with illicit drug use. To do so would be to violate the confidentiality with the client, betray the client's trust, and consequently undermine the client's treatment. Likewise, many treatment providers are concerned that referring their clients to a child welfare agency changes the nature of the intervention from one of supportive treatment to punitive intervention. Although mandated to report suspected cases of child abuse and neglect, treatment providers may be motivated to avoid discussion of family issues that may uncover these concerns. Most are certainly reluctant to screen their clients proactively in an attempt to detect cases of child abuse or neglect.

Resolution of Professional Mistrust. The first step in resolving this issue is actively to involve both substance abuse professionals and child welfare professionals in the development and implementation of practice guidelines. The training and experience of professionals on both sides will provide unique contributions to policy formulation, and joint input will facilitate consensus building in favor of the policies. Policy formulation should be followed by dissemination of guidelines. Clinicians should become familiar not only with the guidelines, but also with the implementation recommendations of professional organizations in their field and with the implementation practices of similar institutions, and ensure that the guidelines are implemented.

It is critical that dissemination of policies and guidelines related to the collaboration of substance abuse treatment and child welfare professionals be two-sided. In other words, clinicians must know what their screening, documentation, notification, and follow-up responsibilities are, and at the same time, they must be able to anticipate what the action taken by the child welfare agency will be. Therefore, child welfare policies must also be documented and disseminated, *after* being informed by the substance abuse treatment field in issues related to treatment, relapse, recovery, and maintenance.

Lack of Expertise. Professionals in the substance abuse field may place more weight on the negative consequences of identifying cases of suspected child abuse or neglect that are later unsubstantiated. The consequences of incorrectly alleging child abuse or neglect include stress and stigmatization for the parent and family, as well as jeopardizing treatment with the parent. Since many professionals in the substance abuse field are not trained to screen or intervene professionally around child welfare issues, they are hesitant to refer a client incorrectly.

Resolution to Lack of Expertise. Cross-training is an essential element of the collaboration between substance abuse and child welfare services. Barriers to cross-training are real, and include: the need to develop a training curriculum; the need for consensus regarding competence criteria; and additional time and cost to students, professionals, and faculty. However, the benefits of better service to multiproblem families, more professional expertise on both sides, more empathy for each field's professional mission, and greater understanding of the relationship between substance abuse and child abuse and neglect outweigh the relatively modest pragmatic barriers.

Undergraduate and graduate training programs should add and require a cross-registration course for all students who are prospective professionals with the potential to be handling issues of substance abuse and child abuse/neglect in the future. At minimum, a cross-training curriculum should include coverage of cross-prevalence research from both fields; screening methods for substance abuse (as opposed to non-problem use of alcohol, for example) and screening methods for child abuse and neglect; legal responsibilities; confidentiality issues; institutional procedures; rights of adult and child clients; and potential for biased implementation of policy guidelines. In addition, clinical sites that are utilized for student internships (e.g., social work, clinical psychology, etc.) should also be required to establish their guidelines for compliance with policies related to child abuse/neglect and substance abuse. Competence in these areas should also be assessed and required for licensure or certification of clinical professionals.

Further Complications: Welfare Reform

More recently, child welfare has been confronted with a new politically conservative context for provision of services. Changes are being proposed from the top down that shift away from a public health approach of supportive interventions for substance-abusing parents. Instead, a judicial approach is being adopted, shifting toward punitive interventions with this population. Within the new zero-tolerance context, drug testing is being proposed for pregnant or parenting recipients of public financial assistance. Positive drug test results can result in dire consequences, including mandatory removal of children from the home and cessation of benefits from the government.

This policy initiative appears inconsistent with the framework of child protection laws from the same source as well as the ethical standards described above. The objectives of this policy initiative seem to prioritize punishing a drug-abusing parent above all other objectives; this will be explored below. Clearly, a relatively new conflict over the goals of child welfare and substance abuse treatment has emerged, and this too must be reconciled before collaboration between the fields occurs. Whereas the child welfare system was advocating on behalf of the child, and the substance abuse treatment provider was advocating on behalf of the substance-abusing client, governmental sources of public funding are now advocating on behalf of constituents. Constituents, by many accounts, are pushing for less waste in government programs and a greater emphasis on "family values." By this venue, public and social policy issues become service delivery issues.

Starting with the premise that it is ultimately protection of the child that must be the objective of child advocates, proposed consequences for positive drug testing must be considered.

The Child Welfare Perspective. In the field of child welfare, there has been a movement toward increased screening and referral for substance abuse problems. Child welfare caseworkers have complied with these relatively new areas of intervention, although they result in extra work for a workforce already stretched thin by limited resources and large caseloads. The compliance can be attributed to the fact that by addressing substance use issues, child welfare workers perceive themselves as providing better care for their client, the child, by providing better support and care for the family as a whole. They are securing more resources for the family and therefore indirectly for the child. Consider what will happen when policy mandates that identification of substance abuse results in a loss of resources to the parent and therefore to the child, removal of the child from the parent, or both. If these consequences are perceived to cause more harm to children and families than current policies, enforcement of the punitive policy will be resisted. It is plausible and even likely that child welfare workers will move away from proactively locating those in need of substance abuse treatment. Resistance to enforcing perceived harmful policies will probably take a form similar to the current ways that substance abuse treatment providers handle identification of child abuse and neglect cases. That is, they will identify those cases that they cannot avoid identifying, but they won't proactively attempt to identify problems, because once a problem is located, they must implement a policy that they believe is counterproductive.

The Substance Abuse Treatment Perspective. In the field of substance abuse, there has been a successful effort to remove barriers for pregnant and parenting women, in particular, to attend substance abuse treatment. Treatment for these women is supportive and confidential, and thereby attempts to avoid the stigma attached to receiving substance abuse treatment while pregnant or parenting. Progress in this area has been slow; it has been difficult in many treatment settings to assure women in this population that treatment was a safe place for them. As a result of these efforts, unprecedented numbers of women are receiving substance abuse treatment. This increase in the number of women should *not* be taken as evidence that the prevalence of substance-abusing mothers is up, only as evidence that women are receiving help for their substance abuse problems in greater numbers. Substance abuse treatment providers surely perceive this as contributing to the well-being of those women's families. If treatment for women receiving public assistance cannot be assured to be supportive and confidential, the numbers of women presenting for substance abuse treatment will rapidly decrease. This means that pregnant or parenting women will not get treatment for substance abuse out of fear of losing monetary support they depend on and/or out of fear of having their children removed from the home. Both of these dire consequences are salient enough to assure that these women will not present for treatment. Likewise, making drug screens mandatory during pregnancy will assure a decrease in the already inadequate rates at which substance-abusing women receive prenatal care. In summary, if treatment becomes a source of detection and punishment, women in need of treatment will go without. Approaches that drive substance-abusing families away from intervention rather than toward treatment and support will endanger children.

Implications for Children From Both Perspectives. Evaluated from either the child welfare or the substance abuse treatment perspective, a policy that is geared toward control rather than compassion will be seen as harmful to children and their families. Those people implementing policy decisions are the same people in the system now. They will likely make a personal, ethical decision about the client they are serving and what is best for the client, and that decision may not include implementation of a policy perceived to be punitive and destructive. The result will be decreased compliance with policy, which is tacitly accepted in the workplace as the lesser of two evils. It is widely known that professionals ranging from health care providers to educators to police officers will "look the other way" if information they receive will result in a mandated loss of resources that the implementers of policy deem too harsh.

Resolution to the Punitive Policy Dilemma. For resolution of these conflicting views to occur, it is important to acknowledge that each of the perspectives are legitimate and defensible. We do need to change the cultural norms; it is important to give a clear message that certain behaviors are not acceptable, and it is important not to reinforce mistakenly the wrong set of behaviors. While the objectives of the policy initiative are defensible, conflict derives from the fact that recent governmental policy is more oriented toward class advocacy for children than case advocacy, while implementers of policy will be more oriented toward case advocacy. In other words, control-related governmental policy is geared toward improving the well-being of children "in the long run" by breaking the cycle of dependency on public assistance, for example. This rationale is defensible from a class advocacy perspective; however it illustrates well the danger of getting away from focusing on the individual child: Action becomes more political as the issue becomes more abstract and more important than the actual children involved (Blatt, 1979; McMahon, 1993; Melton, 1987; Trachtman, 1981). At the case level, new policy mandates appear to jeopardize children by: removing resources from the family; keeping their parents out of substance abuse treatment; keeping mothers from receiving prenatal care; and in some cases unnecessarily removing children from their home, often to place them in an even worse situation. In short, better "in the long run" is not good enough for all the children affected in the meantime.

In order to make effective policy improvements, federal and state governments should consider the principles of changing policy from the top down, since unilateral coercive action will not typically secure meaningful change. It is important that frontline implementers of policy are consulted if they are to comply with new policies. Any resolution will also have to acknowledge the rights and responsibilities of all parties involved, including the children, the parents, the child welfare and substance abuse treatment professionals, the legislators of policy, and the constituents of those legislators. Most objectives of these parties are the same, but creative solutions may be required to make the means to attaining those solutions acceptable to all. However, our first premise must be to protect children. If we do not agree to this as a premise, there is no collaboration, no resolution to the dilemma.

Beyond Collaboration: Other Influences on the Implementation of Policy

It is well established that the implementation of policy is not unaffected by the personal characteristics of those implementing the policy. Institutional perspectives and individual characteristics such as moral judgment, values, stereotypes, and biases influence the way policies are executed. These influences must be anticipated by those creating policy as well as those overseeing its administration. For example, stereotypes and personal and institutional biases represent liabilities related to enforcing punitive interventions: They prevent the uniform and equitable delivery of these interventions.

The "Bad Families" Label. Unfortunately, policy in practice often isolates the most troubled families for punitive intervention, although other less troubled families engage in the same behaviors without detection or consequence. Empirical studies demonstrate, for example, that child abuse and substance abuse problems cut across all ethnic groups and levels of socioeconomic status; however, the system doesn't react that way. In practice, assumptions regarding suspected abuse of either type may be inappropriately made on the basis of race, ethnicity, economic status, or age of parents. The result is that we are primed to see abuse too readily in groups considered to be of low status and to ignore abuse in high-status groups (Scott-Jones, 1994). Minority, poor, and single-parent families are subjected to greater scrutiny and surveillance by professionals, who are less inclined to report abuse in middle-income white families (Baumrind, 1993; Daro, 1988; Scott-Jones, 1994). Reliance on government assistance for health care provides an opportunity for low-status groups to be singled out for more intense screening. For example, prenatal drug screening is common (and may become mandatory) in public clinics, while women treated in private clinics are often not even asked about possible alcohol, tobacco, or other drug use (Colby, Gulliver, O'Brien, & Kambin, 1996). In addition, adolescent parents are often targeted as likely child abusers, although there is not sufficient empirical evidence for doing so (Scott-Jones, 1994; see also Daro, 1988, and Jason, Andereck, Marks, & Tyler, 1982). Not surprisingly, differential surveillance results in greater detection in these low-status groups, thus serving to reinforce the preexisting stereotypes. Finally, with adolescents, minorities, and single-parent and poor families identified as high risk for child abuse and substance abuse, they become the target of research related to abuse, while studies of nonabusive parenting are conducted on predominantly white, affluent samples (Baumrind, 1993; Scott-Jones, 1994). The cycle is complete, with biases influencing surveillance, surveillance influencing detection, detection influencing research, and finally research influencing policy. The "scientific" label on research adds to the perceived legitimacy of the ultimately biased process of creation and implementation of policy.

The "Bad Mother" Label. Our societal values related to gender roles also influence the creation of policy. For example, the punitive aspects of welfare reform are essentially targeted at women, who face the loss of their children and all of their resources as the result of a positive drug test. As stated earlier in this chapter, drug use during pregnancy and while parenting is clearly a public health problem. However, the vitriolic nature of our policy response to this problem appears to be based on moral judgment and retribution, rather than oriented toward a public health solution. Having moved in the direction of improving the health of mothers and their children by increasing screening for abuse, and increasing the numbers of women who receive drug abuse treatment, we are now tempted to back away from that progress, seemingly out of a desire to punish these women with consequences unprecedented in public welfare policy.

It is plausible that the notion of a substance-abusing mother so violates our societal value on motherhood and our stereotype of the woman serving as the nurturing caregiver, that parenting women who abuse substances are singled out by a policy oriented toward punishment and control rather than compassion. Of course, it is the most troubled, least empowered women who are affected by this policy because they are dependent on governmental assistance.

Of note also is the absence of discussion of the "bad father." The lack of attention to the effects of alcohol and other drugs on male parenting may be attributable to several factors. First, the focus on drug-abusing mothers begins during pregnancy, when only the mother's alcohol and other drug abuse affects the developing fetus. Next, because single parenthood is largely, though not exclusively, a female phenomenon, the focus tends to remain on maternal drug abusers. Fathers tend to be perceived as outside the home; when they do receive attention, it tends to be as "deadbeat dads," and the focus of intervention is on receipt of financial resources rather than caregiving. Third, receipt of some types of government assistance require single parenthood, and it is widely believed that males who do live with families on assistance are kept hidden from the system so as not to jeopardize these government benefits. Thus, obtaining accurate statistics on male parenting among economically disadvantaged families is difficult. The situation precludes the identification of a potentially important population for intervention: the male child care provider.

In the field of substance abuse treatment, the parenting role of males is typically overlooked as well. Indeed, programs that provide child care, teach parenting skills, and collaborate with child welfare agencies are considered to be specifically tailored for women. Overlooking the male drug abuser as a parent or as an at least occasional member of a household with young children is a missed opportunity, and is potentially dangerous to children. Given that the positive relationship between substance abuse and child neglect and abuse is not limited to women, efforts to address this problem must be targeted at fathers as well as mothers. Perhaps this aspect of substance abuse treatment should be conceptualized as tailored to parents rather than tailored to women. Substance abuse clinicians should assess males as well as females for parenting problems related to their substance abuse, and parent training should be provided for males as well as females. Subsequent parenting outcomes should be measured for males as well as females when assessing the full impact of substance abuse treatment. Finally, the effects of alcohol and other drug abuse on male parenting should be studied to elucidate the nature of the problem and inform treatment policy.

The "Bad Drug" Label. Stereotypes and biases surrounding the evaluation of various drugs of abuse are often tied to information about the specific populations who use the drugs. In the law enforcement realm, this issue has been the source of controversy as users of crack cocaine, disproportionately minorities, were more often sentenced and received more severe sentences than users of other forms of cocaine (this distinction has recently been legally precluded from playing a role in sentencing). Similarly, the use of crack cocaine by pregnant or parenting women receives much more attention by child welfare workers and policy reformers than the use of amphetamines, marijuana, alcohol, or tobacco (disproportionately used by nonminorities).

It is a value judgment that crack cocaine is worse than alcohol, which is worse than amphetamines, which are worse than cigarettes. Unfortunately, the legality of a substance does not ameliorate the effects of prenatal exposure to that substance on a developing fetus (Bell & Lau, 1995). In fact, the prenatal effects of exposure to amphetamines, cocaine, and nicotine are not easily distinguished as they are actually quite similar, including: low birth weight; increased incidence of sudden infant death syndrome; delayed development; and increased perinatal morbidity and mortality.

The individual effects of these drugs is difficult to discern for several reasons. First, the use of one drug is highly associated with polydrug use, and so it is difficult to isolate the unique effects of an individual drug, separate from the combined effects. Second, it is also difficult to separate the effects of a drug on fetal, infant, and child development from other associated factors such as poor nutrition and poor parenting skills. Third, experimenter biases regarding drugs of abuse can affect how carefully they statistically control for these other associated factors when evaluating the effects of certain drugs. While research findings related to drug effects are inconsistent due to these methodological problems, many researchers agree that if families are provided with enough support (e.g., proper nutrition, parenting training, addiction treatment, and a safe environment), the majority of children will overcome the effects of prenatal drug exposure (Bell & Lau, 1995; Napiorkowski et al., 1996).

Provider Characteristics and Personal History. Knowing how personal biases affect the conduct of surveillance, treatment, and research related to abuse issues, it is clear that provider values, histories, and biases will impact on how policy is implemented and services are delivered. Influences on service delivery include, but are not limited to, personal or family history of substance abuse or physical abuse or neglect, religious background, and minority versus majority status. For this reason, a team approach to case management that provides checks and balances is critical, as is the establishment of procedures that are as objective as possible while maintaining enough flexibility to consider the unique aspects of each case. There is a rich theoretical and empirical literature developing in the psychotherapy field that is designed to inform the counselor about how best to intervene with culturally diverse populations. The interested reader is directed to Baker-Sinclair, Weist, and Petroff (1996), Leong (1996), and Rigazio-Digilio, Goncalves, and Ivey (1996).

Collaboration in Action

The balance of this chapter will be devoted to the description of three innovative programs that demonstrate the feasibility of attaining true collaboration between substance abuse and child welfare services, to the benefit of the populations they serve. These programs are: (a) the ADAPT (Alcohol and Drug Abuse Project Team) Program in Ohio; (b) the MAP (Maternal Addiction Program) in Miami, Florida; and (c) Project Discovery and other programs at the Women's Correctional Facility in Rhode Island.

The ADAPT Program

The ADAPT Program was initiated in part as a response to a 1986 lawsuit in which Cincinnati Legal Aid sued the Hamilton County Department of Human Services (DHS) for failure to implement fully the provisions of Public Law 96-272, the Child Welfare and Adoption Assistance Act of 1980. In this suit (*Roe v. Staples*), Hamilton County DHS was charged with failing to provide preplacement supportive services to prevent unnecessary placement of children into foster care as required by federal law. After negotiation between the parties, a consent decree was entered that now applies to all 88 counties in Ohio. There were three significant mandates incorporated into the *Roe v. Staples* consent decree: (a) A *child welfare tracking system* had to be developed in order to provide information regarding all children categorized as potentially entering the foster care system; (b) a *system to monitor case records* had to be developed to provide documentation by which accountability of the local agency in meeting and measuring family needs could be established; and (c) a *needs assessment* had to be conducted on a triennial basis to identify the met and unmet needs of the children and families served from the public child protection system (The Ohio Department of Human Services Office of Child Care and Family Services, 1996).

Three needs assessments have been completed for the state of Ohio under the consent decree. The first was conducted by the University of Southern Maine in 1988, the second was conducted by Case Western Reserve University Mondel School of Applied Social Sciences in 1990. The third was conducted in 1992 by the Ohio Department of Human Services. The federal court rejected each of these studies as inadequate for meeting the terms of the decree.

The ADAPT (Alcohol and Drug Abuse Project Team) model is one of the responses that the Ohio Department of Human Services funded to be in compliance with the federal mandate of Public Law 96-272. The program was designed to prevent the removal of children from their homes and to reunify children who had been removed from their families. ADAPT also addressed maternal and/or other familial adult substance abuse. The need for intervention was defined as when the "regular use of drugs affects the caretakers' ability to care for the child." The goal for ADAPT was to identify the met and unmet maternal needs for child welfare and substance abuse services in order to keep families together or to reunify families. In 1991, the Lucas County Children Services (LCCS) of Ohio conducted a survey that ascertained the prevalence of child welfare cases associated with substance abuse and the extent to which referrals were available. Consistent with national statistics, the survey indicated that a substantial proportion of cases had substance abuse as a factor, particularly the custody cases (75%), as compared with the 422 noncustody cases (40%) (personal communication, Laurie Swyers, LCCS, 1996).

Project ADAPT Client Characteristics. Clients in the ADAPT program present a somewhat greater challenge to service providers than their non-ADAPT counterparts. For example, ADAPT cases involve slightly more children on average (2.36 per case), which is 6.3% more than the non-ADAPT clients (2.22 children per case). Polysubstance abuse is much more prevalent among ADAPT cases, with 43% of the cases abusing more than one substance, compared with 18% of the non-ADAPT cases. Network providers are used more frequently in the ADAPT cases versus the non-ADAPT cases, requiring a higher level of alcohol/drug expertise for case manage-

Table 7.1 Tenets of the ADAPT Network

1. We acknowledge that recovery from addiction requires total abstinence. We support the recovery philosophy.
2. We believe that the neglect and abuse of children is often associated with maternal addiction. The potential for losing custody of her child is often the key to bringing the maternal addict to treatment.
3. We understand that since the other problems of the maternal addict are often rooted in the addiction, the initial focus of services should be directed toward assessment and treatment of the addiction.
4. We believe that a sober, supportive living environment is critical to the recovery process.
5. We are aware that no one agency contains the resources and expertise to respond adequately to the needs of the maternal addict.
6. We are committed to modifying agency policies or procedures which may impede the addict's cooperation with all service providers.
7. We commit ourselves to working cooperatively together with the addict to develop and implement plans.
8. We believe that keeping the mother and child closely connected is an essential factor to enhance or preserve their relationship.
9. We believe that when a child must be removed from his mother for protection, the child has the right to frequent visits with the mother during the mother's treatment.
10. We agree to work cooperatively toward a goal of reunification of mother and child as quickly as the child's protection can be assured.
11. We believe that both mother and child have the right to continuity of health care services.

ment. The ADAPT parent clientele also includes more minorities, in particular African Americans (68.3%), compared with the non-ADAPT child welfare population (46.7%).

Components of the ADAPT Program

Commitment to a Common Mission. The ADAPT model sought to establish common ground between substance abuse and child welfare professionals. The first goal was to join the two services together under a common mission of service to their clients. The tenets of that mission were negotiated and agreed upon by all ADAPT participants (see Table 7.1). These tenets became guiding principles for the ADAPT professionals in bridging the gap between their respective practices.

Specialized Service Delivery. To facilitate achieving the goals of the agencies' common mission, ADAPT changed the conditions under which services were delivered. For example, ADAPT caseworkers had a lower caseload, two caseworkers teamed up to manage each case, and all workers completed specialized addiction training. In addition, due to the high minority representation among the population of clients, staff development and training activities ensued related to cultural and ethnic sensitivity and to racial issues. With these changes, and stronger relationships among network providers in place, the ADAPT caseworker is better able to case manage the addicted client through the recovery process.

Avoiding Duplication of Effort. According to the developers of the ADAPT model, there were instances in which agencies were trying to be all things to all clients, in some cases providing services that were clearly outside the scope of their practices. In order to prevent duplication of service, the ADAPT participants worked together to revise each agency's case plan; plans were revised to spell out precisely what each agency would do and to specify what was expected of each client (Seybold, Wiford, Nussbaum, Rideout, & Swyers, 1990). With jointly developed and clearly documented division of responsibilities, delivery of services became more efficient, with each agency achieving better focus on its own area of expertise.

Cross-Training. Trusting the expertise of other professionals is essential to bridging the fields of child welfare and substance abuse, yet accepting the position of another professional in regard to the treatment plan for one's own client proves difficult. Anticipating this barrier to collaboration, ADAPT embarked on a cross-training venture in which people who worked in each part of the network (e.g., substance abuse services, child protection services) received training in the other parts of the network. Having workers trained in the other network areas successfully increased trust and respect among the professionals (Seybold et al., 1990). Feedback from the network was enthusiastic and positive. Substance abuse staff found that the legal training they received and the information regarding the time frames that needed to be followed helped them to understand and therefore implement the procedures better. Staff from other parts of the network reported having a better understanding of substance abuse treatment and the process of recovery. Child welfare staff at Lucas County Children Services (LCCS) described the addiction training as "invaluable" to them. Moreover, they perceived improved collaboration with substance abuse professionals as a result of the training that the latter received from LCCS (Seybold et al., 1990).

Outcome. To date, results from the ADAPT approach have been impressive; according to Comprehensive Addiction Services System and Lucas County Children Services, only 3% to 5% of women have relapsed after 4 years. In addition, only 5.8% of the ADAPT cases resulted in permanent custody outside the home versus 6.7% of the non-ADAPT cases. Although this difference does not appear significant, it must be evaluated in the context of the fact that the average ADAPT case involves significantly more substance abuse, which systematically increases the likelihood of permanent loss of custody by the parent.

Conclusions. The ADAPT model provides a good example of collaboration across provider agencies, particularly in terms of anticipating barriers to collaboration and implementing procedures to address these barriers and facilitate true collaboration. ADAPT's establishment of a common mission across agencies, cross-training, avoidance of duplicated effort, and teamed case management were essential to its success. A replication of this model approach is currently being undertaken in a large city in northwestern Ohio.

The Maternal Addiction Program

The Maternal Addiction Program (MAP) of the University of Miami/Jackson Memorial Medical Center/Highland Park Pavilion was developed to meet the special needs of a largely African American, indigent, inner-city female population (see Malow et al., 1994, for original article upon which this program description is based). It is a model inpatient and day treatment rehabilitation program specifically designed to treat substance-abusing women during and after pregnancy. The philosophy of this program is to target substance abuse for intervention first, and secure benefits for the women and their children through the attainment and maintenance of abstinence. The program was a response to the multiple needs that were apparent in this population. It was developed as part of the Addiction Research and Treatment Program in the Department of Psychiatry at the University of Miami. Unlike most substance abuse treatment programs, MAP uses a comprehensive, multilevel approach to intervene at both the individual level and at a systems level (e.g., including family interventions, coordination with child welfare, social service, legal, and other community resources).

MAP Client Characteristics. The clients at MAP are similar to those at ADAPT. The majority of women are ethnic minorities, including 77% African American, 14% Hispanic, and 9% non-Hispanic white. Most are unmarried with an average of 3 children; 41% have concerns regarding the custody of one or more of their children. About 25% are in treatment under court order, and over half report a past legal charge or conviction. Approximately two thirds of the women report being past or present victims of physical, emotional, or sexual abuse. Most of the women are severely socioeconomically disadvantaged and are dependent on family or public assistance for financial and housing support. Crack cocaine is the most common primary drug of abuse (75%); other substances typically used include alcohol, marijuana, and nicotine.

Components of MAP. A multidisciplinary team works together to address the myriad complex problems the clients present with in treatment. The team includes a psychiatrist and psychologist, a nurse practitioner, drug counselors, therapists, and other health care professionals. The treatment team is able to bridge substance abuse and child welfare services because it has specialized training in assessing and handling the psychosocial, legal, and financial problems that typically accompany maternal addiction. These include issues related to parenting, abuse, and neglect. MAP also tailors its program to address the special needs of substance-abusing women who are the sole caretakers of their children, as many of these clients are. The treatment team works to minimize the disruption of treatment on family life and to address the guilt that women may experience by not being available to their children during treatment. In order to facilitate treatment participation and retention, the team helps to coordinate appropriate arrangements for child care and transportation.

Program participation begins with 28 days of intensive inpatient treatment in a highly structured hospital environment. The women receive a comprehensive evaluation upon admission that includes assessments of psychosocial functioning and medical status, as well as substance abuse. The extent to which the client is a danger to herself or to others (e.g., her children) is assessed along with the quality of interpersonal and family relationships more broadly. Whenever possible, partners or other family members ("significant others") are involved in the assessment process to enhance the accuracy of the information provided. Information gathered during the evaluation is then used to develop the multilevel treatment plan. The plan is developed in collaboration with the client and her family members as appropriate. Progress toward specific treatment goals is documented weekly in the Patient Care Plan. The majority of the treatment is delivered in a group format, and includes couple and family therapy; HIV education and prevention; relapse prevention; social skills training; coping with and recovery from abuse; and 12-step program involvement, among other content areas. Some individual counseling is also delivered that focuses on addressing individual problems and dealing with interpersonal issues. Training is provided that emphasizes anger reduction, impulsivity control, and stress management. When parenting competence is in question, the treatment team is trained to identify and access community resources to help the client develop parenting skills.

To provide for a smooth transition back into the community, the treatment team, client, and family members develop a discharge plan within 48 hours of the client's leaving inpatient treatment. Like the inpatient treatment, the discharge plan is multilevel; it is designed to address child custody and care issues as well as substance abuse aftercare planning, housing, and organizing the return to home and family. Following inpatient treatment, an 8- to 12-month outpatient treatment phase ensues that is designed to facilitate reentry into society while preventing relapse to drugs. During this phase, the women attend treatment 5 hours per day, Monday through Friday, for individual, couple, and family counseling. This

phase of the treatment emphasizes resolution of psychosocial problems, construction of supportive networks, and development of
vocational skills.

Evaluation of Outcome. Women are contacted at 1, 3, 6, and 12
months for follow-up to evaluate their treatment success. Unlike
many substance abuse treatment evaluations, the MAP assessment
focuses on the client's functioning across many psychosocial domains, including substance use and family functioning; parenting
and other interpersonal relationships; legal status; and financial,
educational, vocational, and medical status. Outcome data are not
yet available for this program.

Conclusions. The MAP program provides a good illustration of
how multicomponent interventions can be done with pregnant and
parenting substance-abusing women. The promise of this program
lies in its identification of the complex set of problems and needs
this population has, and the recognition that *all* of these dimensions
need to be treated if successful outcomes are to be achieved in any
domain. A long-term intensive residential treatment program provides an excellent opportunity to handle the diversity of these
issues. MAP utilizes a multidisciplinary treatment team with specialized training outside the realm of substance abuse treatment,
and with contacts with relevant community and state agencies, to
achieve the goals documented in each client's treatment plan.
Elements of MAP that should be standard for all substance abuse
treatment programs include: assessment of parenting competence
at intake; referral to parenting training as appropriate; assistance
coordinating child care during maternal treatment attendance;
involvement of family members in treatment and planning; and
assessment of parenting functioning as an evaluation of treatment
efficacy.

Rhode Island Department of Corrections, Women's Facility

Another opportune setting for dealing with the dual problems of
child abuse and neglect and substance abuse is in correctional
facilities. In Rhode Island, women who are incarcerated in the
correctional facility (there is only one in the state) are able to

participate in five major interrelated treatment and counseling programs that operate full-time.

Characteristics of Incarcerated Women. In the past 10 years, the population of incarcerated women in Rhode Island has tripled. Approximately 75% of the incarcerated women are mothers of dependent children, and the majority of the women are single. Their median age is 31 years old. About 40% of the women are sentenced to 6 months or less; 37% are sentenced to more than 6 months to 3 years; and the remaining are sentenced to over 3 years to life. Based on a recent (September-December, 1995) quarterly report from the Department of Corrections, 42% of the women were sentenced for nonviolent crimes; 31% for drug-related crimes; 23% for violent crimes; and the rest (about 4%) for burglary or theft. Minority representation is higher than for the state as a whole; still, the majority (67%) of female inmates are non-Hispanic white; 20% are African American; and 12% are Hispanic. Compared to their male counterparts, incarcerated women are less likely to attempt escape from prison. They also tend to be less violent, thereby presenting reduced risk of physical harm to staff.

This is clearly a multiproblem population. The large majority are substance abusers, victims of sexual violence and childhood sexual abuse, victims of domestic violence, homeless, and unemployed upon release. They are poorly educated and have limited work experience. They are in poor physical condition and most have not received adequate medical or dental care prior to incarceration. They suffer from mental health problems ranging from depression to schizophrenia, which often require medication and therapeutic attention. They are generally unequipped to deal with the routine stress of daily life in the community and require strong support during transition and postrelease periods.

Description of Programs. The administration and staff at the Women's Facility recognize the opportunity that incarceration presents to intervene on the multiple problems that the women inmates have. While clinical lore would lead to skepticism about the motivation level for behavior change in an incarcerated population, there is empirical evidence that people who are coerced into substance abuse treatment (e.g., by court order or similar means) do not have poorer treatment retention or motivation than noncoerced treatment participants (Tsoh, 1993). The key is the participant's *perception* of coercion; in other words, if the participant feels that she is taking part in an intervention because it will be beneficial to her (regardless of how she arrived in treatment), motivation and retention in treatment are improved. To this end, practitioners who work with similar populations may benefit from learning Motivational Interviewing (Miller & Rollnick, 1991). Motivational Interviewing (MI) is a therapeutic technique designed to enhance motivation for behavior change. Using a nonconfrontational interaction style, a counselor using MI would highlight discrepancies between clients' behavior and their life goals and how they would like to view themselves as a person. Responsibility for behavior change rests with the client; the counselor facilitates change by helping the client to set goals for change, secure needed resources, and evaluate progress over time, from the client's perspective.

The five major programs operating in the correctional facility include: substance abuse treatment (Project Discovery); parenting education and supervised mother/child visits; a job training/mentoring program; education/GED and college classes; and discharge planning. In addition to security personnel, the Women's Facility is staffed with physicians and nurses, teachers, counselors, and program staff. Funding for the programs is derived from various sources including the Department of Corrections, state grants, and the United Way. The majority of programming also emphasizes and spans the transition from incarceration to reentry into the community.

Like Project ADAPT (described above), the Correctional Facility's staff are unified in their mission by a set of documented core values, thus bringing together the correctional/control staff with the rehabilitative staff under a common set of principles. The Mission Statement of the Women's Facility lists these core values as follows:

1. The community is entitled to protection from offenders.

2. The potential for offenders to become law-abiding citizens is enhanced through intervention.

3. The entire Department must operate with openness, integrity, and accountability, and on unwavering commitment to ethical conduct.

4. A sufficient array of treatment and control models must be available in order to achieve the mission.

5. The Department's strength and major resource in achieving the mission is its staff.

This mission statement again illustrates the feasibility of integrating the dual missions of control and treatment, which is directly analogous to the bridging of child welfare policy and substance abuse treatment policy. While there are no comprehensive evaluative data yet available on the success of the Women's Facility programs, preliminary evidence from various program components indicate reduced recidivism as a function of these program initiatives. A more comprehensive evaluation that assesses subsequent substance use and parenting outcomes would be advantageous. Regardless, the Rhode Island Women's Facility provides an excellent example of taking advantage of unique opportunities to intervene on this population, unifying diverse staffs with very different missions under one core set of common values, and intervening at multiple levels with this multiproblem population.

Conclusions

This chapter provides an overview of the institutional, professional, and interpersonal barriers to collaboration between the fields of child welfare and substance abuse. Principles for overcoming these barriers are also highlighted, with concrete examples of successful collaborative efforts presented at the end of the chapter. There are several underlying themes that repetitively surface throughout the chapter that will be delineated briefly.

Perhaps the most striking recurrent theme is the intertwining of two constructs: perpetrator and victim. The women who have contact with the child welfare and substance abuse services are replete with problems at multiple levels, including financial, legal, social, vocational, and psychological. Most are single mothers, many are indigent and have difficulty securing basic food and shelter for their families. The majority have experienced or currently experience sexual, physical, or emotional abuse, or a combination of these, and many have significant mental health problems. Although these women are in many senses victims, their own victimization or neglect of children cannot be disregarded. The most successful programs recognize the need to intervene on many different levels in order to achieve success. Missions to intervene with these women must also meet the dual objectives of compassion and control. A second theme that emerges is the need to *facilitate* treatment in this population. Successful programs remove barriers to attending treatment, for example, by coordinating for child care during treatment, by arranging for transportation, by creating interdisciplinary teams with diverse expertise that are able to coordinate and provide all aspects of treatment in one facility, and by intervening in opportune settings such as prisons. Child welfare services and courts must appreciate the difficulty this population has in complying with mandated treatment, and should follow these examples and work with other services and professionals to facilitate treatment. The final theme that we hope emerged is one of *optimism*. Barriers to collaboration can be overcome; there are several examples of meaningful collaboration in various settings.

References

Baker-Sinclair, M. E., Weist, M. D., & Petroff, H. J. (1996, September). Language and rapport in cognitive behavioral therapy with African American teenagers. *The Behavior Therapist,* pp. 118-119.

Baumrind, D. (1993). *Optimal caregiving and child abuse: Continuities and discontinuities.*

Beckman, L., & Amaro, H. (1986). Personal and social differences faced by females and males entering alcohol treatment. *Journal of Studies on Alcohol, 47,* 135-145.

Beckman, L. J. (1994). Treatment needs of women with alcohol problems. *Alcohol Health and Research World, 18*(3), 206-211.

Beckman, L. J., & Korel, K. M. (1982). The treatment-delivery system of alcohol abuse in women: Social policy implications. *Journal of Sociological Issues, 38*(2), 139-151.

Bell, G. L., & Lau, K. (1995). Perinatal and neonatal issues of substance abuse. *Substance Abuse, 42*(2), 261-280.

Besharov, D. J. (1990). Crack children in foster care. *Children Today, 19*(4), 21-35.

Blatt, B. (1979). Bandwagons also go to funerals: Unmailed letter 3. *Journal of Learning Disabilities, 12,* 288-291.

Boyd, B., Duning, B., Gomez, R., Hertzel, R., King, R., Patrick, S., & Whitaker, K. (1992, April). *Impacts of interagency collaboration on participating organizations.* Paper presented at the meeting of the American Educational Research Association, San Francisco. (ERIC Document Reproduction Service No. ED 346 566)

Bruner, C. (1991). *Thinking collaboratively: Ten questions and answers to help policy makers improve children's services.* Washington, DC: Education and Human Services Consortium.

The Child Welfare and Adoption Assistance Act of 1980: Roe v. Staples, OH. Pub. L. No. 96-272 (1986).

Child Welfare League of America, North America Commission on Chemical Dependency. (1992). *Children of the front: A different view of the war on alcohol and drugs.* Washington, DC: Author.

Colby, S. M., Gulliver, S. B., O'Brien, K., & Kambin, S. (1996, November). *A community reinforcement approach for smoking cessation in pregnant women and their partners.* Poster session presented at the annual meeting of the Association for Advancement of Behavior Therapy, New York City.

Curtis, P. A., & McCullough, C. (1993). The impact of alcohol and other drugs on the child welfare system. *Child Welfare, 72*(6), 533-542.

Davidson, V., & Bemko, J. (1978). International review of women and drug abuse (1966-1975). *Journal of the American Medical Women's Association, 33*(12), 507-518.

Daro, D. (1988). *Confronting child abuse research for effective program design.* New York: Free Press.

Duckert, F. (1987). Recruitment into treatment and effects of treatment for female problem drinkers. *Addictive Behavior, 12,* 137-150.

Edmunds, M. (1996). Clinical practice guidelines: Opportunities and implications. *Annals of Behavioral Medicine, 18*(2), 126-132.

Famularo, R., Kinscherff, R., & Fenton, T. (1992). Parental substance abuse and the nature of child maltreatment. *Child Abuse & Neglect, 16*(4), 475-483.

Famularo, R., Stone, K., Barnum, R., & Wharton, R. (1986). Alcoholism and severe child maltreatment. *American Journal of Orthopsychiatry, 56,* 481-485.

Fanshel, D. (1975). Parental failure and consequences for children: The drug abusing mother whose children are in foster care. *American Journal of Public Health, 65*(6), 604-612.

Feig, L. (1990). *Drug-exposed infants and children: Service needs and policy questions.* Washington, DC: Department of Health and Human Services.

Harvey, C., Comfort, M., & Johns, N. (1993, August/September). Integrating parent support into residential drug and alcohol treatment programs. *Zero to Three,* pp. 11-13.

Hord, S. M. (1986). A synthesis of research on organizational collaboration. *Educational Leadership, 43*(5), 22-27.

Horowitz, R. (1990). Prenatal substance abuse: A coordinated public health and child welfare response. *Children Today,* pp. 8-12.

Jason, J., Andereck, N. D., Marks, J., & Tyler, C. W., Jr. (1982). Child abuse in Georgia: A method to evaluate risk factors and reporting bias. *American Journal of Public Health, 72*(12), 1353-1358.

Kagan, S. L. (1991). *United we stand: Collaboration for child care and early education services.* New York: Teachers College Press.

Leonard, K. E., & Jacob, T. (1988). Alcohol, alcoholism, and family violence. In V. B. Hasselt, R. L. Morrison, A. S. Bellack, & M. Hersen (Ed.), *Handbook of family violence* (pp. 383-406). New York: Plenum.

Leong, F. T. L. (1996). Toward an integrative model for cross-cultural counseling and psychotherapy. *Applied & Preventive Psychology, 5,* 189-209.

Lieberman, A. (1986a). Collaborative research: Working with not working on. *Educational Leadership, 43*(5), 28-32.

Lieberman, A. (1986b). Collaborative work. *Educational Leadership, 43*(5), 4-8.

Liss, M. B. (1994). Child abuse: Is there a mandate for researchers to report? *Ethics and Behavior, 4*(2), 133-146.

Malow, R. M., Ireland, S. J., Halpert, E. S., Szapocznik, J., McMahon, R. C., & Haber L. (1994). A description of the maternal addiction program of the University of Miami/Jackson Memorial Medical Center. *Journal of Substance Abuse Treatment, 11*(1), 55-60.

McCullough, C. (1991). The child welfare response. *The Future of Children: Drug Exposed Infants,* (1), 61-71.

McMahon, T. J. (1993). On the concept of child advocacy: A review of theory and methodology. *School Psychology Review, 22*(4), 744-755.

Melton, G. B. (1987). Children, politics, and morality: The ethics of child advocacy. *Journal of Clinical Child Psychology, 16,* 357-367.

Miller, W. R., & Rollnick, S. (1991). *Motivational interviewing: Preparing people to change addictive behavior.* New York: Guilford.

Moore, R. D., Bone, L. R., Geller, G., Mamon, J. A., Stokes, E. J., & Levine, D. M. (1989). Prevalence detection and treatment of alcoholism in hospitalized patients. *Journal of the American Medical Association, 261*(3), 403-407.

Mulwanda, V., Thornburg, K. R., Filbert, K., & Klein, T. (1995). Collaboration of services for children and families: A synthesis of recent research and recommendations. *Family Relations, 44,* 219-225.

Murphy, J. M., Jellinek, M., Quinn, D., Smith, G., Poitrast, F. G., & Goshko, M. (1991). Substance abuse and serious child mistreatment: Prevalence, risk, and outcome in a court sample. *Child Abuse & Neglect, 15,* 197-211.

Napiorkowski, B., Lester, B. M., Freier, M. C., Brunner, S., Dietz, L., & Nadra, A. (1996). Effects of in utero substance exposure on infant neurobehavior. *Pediatrics, 98*(1), 71-75.

The Ohio Department of Human Services Office of Child Care and Family Services and The Public Children Services Association of Ohio. (1996). *An assessment of the service needs of families and children served by Ohio Public Children Services Agencies.* Columbus, OH: Author.

Reed, B. G. (1987). Developing women-sensitive drug dependence treatment services: Why so difficult? *Journal of Psychoactive Drugs, 19,* 151-164.

Rigazio-Digilio, S. A., Goncalves, O. F., & Ivey, A. E. (1996). From cultural to existential diversity: The impossibility of psychotherapy integration within a traditional framework. *Applied & Preventive Psychology, 5,* 235-247.

Scott-Jones, D. (1994). Ethical issues in reporting and referring in research with low-income minority children. *Ethics & Behavior, 4*(2), 97-108.

Seybold, E., Wiford, C., Nussbaum, D., Rideout, P., & Swyers, L. (1990). The ADAPT Network alcohol & drug abuse team, *Aurora project & comprehensive addiction service system.* Toledo, OH: Lucas County Children Services.

Stevens, S. J., Arbiter, N., & McGrath, R. (1994). Women and children: Therapeutic community substance abuse treatment and outcome findings. In G. DeLeon (Ed.), *Therapeutic communities for special populations in special settings.* New York: Greenwood.

Tatara, T. (1990). *Children of substance abusing-alcoholic parents referred to the public child welfare system: Summaries of key statistical data obtained from states. Final report.* Washington, DC: American Public Welfare Association.

Thompson, L. (1990). Working with alcoholics' families in a child welfare agency: The problem of underdiagnosis. *Child Welfare, 69*(5), 464-470.

Trachtman, G. M. (1981). On such a full sea. *School Psychology Review, 10,* 138-181.

Tracy, E. M. (1994). Maternal substance abuse: Protecting the child, preserving the family. *Social Work, 39*(5), 534-540.

Tsoh, J. Y. (1993). *Motivation and stages of change among drug addicts in drug abuse treatment programs.* Unpublished master's thesis, University of Rhode Island.

Van Den Bergh, N. (1991). *Feminist perspectives on addiction.* New York: Springer.

Walker, C. D., Zangrillo, P., & Smith, J. M. (1991). *Parental drug abuse and African American children in foster care: Issues and study findings.* Washington, DC: U.S. Department of Health and Human Services, Office of the Assistant Secretary for Planning and Evaluation.

Ways and Means Committee, U.S. House of Representatives. (1990). *The enemy within: Crack cocaine and American families.* Washington, DC: Government Printing Office.

Widom, C. S. (1989). *The intergenerational transmission of violence.* New York: Harry Frank Guggenheim Foundation.

Wilsnack, S. C. (in press). Alcohol use and problems in women. In A. L. Stanton & S. J. Gillonet (Eds.), *Psychology of women's health. Progress and challenges in research and application.* Washington, DC: American Psychological Association.

Wilsnack, S. C., Wilsnack, R. W., & Sturmhofel, S. H. (1994). How women drink: Epidemiology of women's drinking and problem drinking. *Alcohol Health and Research World, 18*(3), 173-181.

CHAPTER 8

Bridges to Effective Treatment: Family Therapy and Family Psychoeducational Interventions With Maltreating and Substance-Abusing Families

MICAH L. MCCREARY

JAMES MAFFUID

TONI A. STEPTER

The issues of child maltreatment, family violence, and substance abuse on the mental health of children and their families are some of the most pressing problems of modern society. Families afflicted by these problems are often overwhelmed and consumed by the multiplicity of difficulties these problems create. Consequently, many families become trapped in a cycle of abuse and despair. Some families are able to exit the cycle on their own, while others become liberated from the cycle through the support and intervention of extended family members or community organizations. There are still other families, however, who linger in the cycle for years struggling and looking for solutions to their challenges. The process of finding and achieving healthy solutions often occurs in treatment or on what we are calling the "bridge."

We define the "bridge" as effective treatment for maltreating and substance-abusing families, on which hurting and injured families move from the shores of injury and constraints to the shores of health and wholeness. In other words, the bridge is empowerment, and this bridge of treatment involves clinical observation, description, evaluation, and interpretation of family interactions and individual functioning. On this bridge, counselors motivate families to change their behavior, prevent the development of problems, and eliminate maladaptive behavior. As guides and bridge builders, counselors must help the abusing family to enhance interpersonal relationships, make work adjustments, increase personal effectiveness, enhance behavioral health, and promote mental health.

This chapter will focus on the clinician as a guide or contractor of the treatment bridge. Specifically, family therapy will be presented as an effective treatment strategy for maltreating and substance-abusing families. First, we will suggest that counselors are more effective guides and contractors for maltreating and substance-abusing families when counselors are able to master their own presuppositions and clinical biases. Second, we suggest that family therapy and family-based psychoeducational programs are effective treatment strategies with maltreating and substance-abusing families. Finally, we will discuss our own family-based psychoeducational program designed to reduce child maltreatment and positively impact and enhance family functioning.

The Clinician as a Guide and Contractor

The role of the clinician is critical to the healing process of maltreating and substance-abusing families. The clinical mental health professional plays an important role in helping families first to build the bridge and then to travel over it, thereby escaping the cycles of child maltreatment and substance abuse. Yet professional clinicians and mental health workers often unconsciously and unintentionally obstruct family relief and symptom remediation. As discussed elsewhere in this volume (see Feig, Chapter 3 in this volume), the variety and seemingly competing philosophical approaches of various mental health agencies may hinder the counselor's ability to construct the treatment bridge. When this occurs, the service rendered to children and families may be compromised (see Colby & Murrell, Chapter 7 in this volume). Thus, something must be done to prevent these type of barriers from interfering with the treatment of substance-abusing and maltreating families.

When barriers of philosophy and personal preferences hinder the clinician's ability to provide quality interventions, clinicians must examine and enhance their understanding of client dynamics with regard to their own experiences. We suggest that clinicians will become better guides and contractors by applying three strategies. First, they must guard against and overcome issues of countertransference (Friedlander, Siegel, & Brenock, 1989; Getz & Protinsky, 1994). Second, they must avoid the tendency to blame the victim or the system (Ryan, 1971; West, 1993), and third, they must develop sound theoretical conceptualizations to guide their practice (Ivey, 1980).

For therapists, the first aspect of constructing a quality treatment bridge is to address their countertransference issues through clinical supervision or peer consultation. Quality supervision or peer consultation helps clinicians to refine their abilities to observe precisely and to describe accurately both the client's behavior and their own behavior with regard to the therapeutic process (Friedlander et al., 1989: Stolenberg & Delworth, 1987). Quality supervision or consultation also helps counselors to integrate empathic awareness of the client's dynamics and environmental concerns with their conceptual framework, while exploring ways in which their own behavior influences clinical practice (Friedlander et al., 1989; Stolenberg & Delworth, 1987). A good clinical supervisor must not serve as a counselor to the counselor; rather, supervisors must operate in the role of an advisor or coach to help the counselor maintain emotional autonomy from the counselor's clients (Getz & Protinsky, 1994). Furthermore, good supervisors help counselors to realize when they are overfunctioning or underfunctioning with their clients based on the counselors' personal family-of-origin experiences.

Counselors show that they are being influenced by negative countertransference when they overfunction or underfunction in their clinical practice. Counselors are overfunctioning when they become excessively sensitive to the client's issues and find themselves desperately trying to "fix" the client, rather than allowing the client to solve his or her own problems using the expertise of the counselor. Counselors are underfunctioning when they are motivated by their own needs for clients to like them. When counselors are motivated by the need to be liked, they frequently fail to confront and evaluate the clients' difficulties. Interestingly, the problems of overfunctioning and underfunctioning are not idiosyncratic to new clinicians, rather they are hazards of the profession, particularly with counselors who work with substance-abusing and maltreating families. Thus, all counselors, regardless of years in the field, must continually guard against overfunctioning and underfunctioning. Quality supervision or consultation is one of the most effective ways to challenge the tendency to overfunction or underfunction and thereby avoid the problems associated with countertransference that would inevitably follow. In other words, clinicians become better guides and bridge contractors when they integrate their personal experiences with their attitudes and values, while not allowing these personal experiences to influence their counseling practices negatively.

Therapists' struggle against countertransference is ongoing, and as they strive to guard against countertransference, they must also strive to avoid the tendency to blame the victim or the system. Herein lies the second strategy counselors must apply in order to become better guides and contractors for their clients.

Professional training programs, according to Ivey (1980), frequently train mental health workers in the medical or disease model of treatment. The disease model views the problem as an abnormality or an illness, thus, the treatment goal of the medical professional is to search for a cure. Clinical practitioners, therefore, who embrace the disease model of treatment tend to diagnose the maltreating or substance-abusing family as sick and the practitioners attempt to "cure" the family. If the family does not respond affirmatively, or, in other words, does not "get well" as a result of the treatment the practitioners provide, the family may be labeled as treatment disordered or dysfunctional. Ryan (1971) called this "blaming the victim," and he suggested that this type of approach to treating clinical disorders lends itself to blaming the victim, which inhibits the healing process or the process of helping the clients build effective bridges toward their own healing. Healing should be understood as more of an ongoing process that continues over time as opposed to a cure, which is more of a once-and-for-all manifestation.

In addition to avoiding the tendency to blame the victim, counselors must also avoid the tendency to place unfair blame on the system (Danish, in press; West, 1993). According to Danish and to West, blaming looks backward at the unchangeable past rather than forward to an alterable future. It also infers that one is judging, but, perhaps most tragically, blaming can also misguide the counselors' efforts to provide the most effective intervention for the families with whom they work. For example, consider the question, "Is it better to protect the child or to reunite the family?" If clinicians operate from a blaming perspective, they must judge someone or something as "bad." If this issue is pressed to the extreme, the ultimate conclusion will be that someone in the family or something in the system failed, and therefore the culprit must be punished, not healed. Thus, rephrasing the question to, "How can the child be protected?" or "How can the family be reunited?" can help to avoid the tendency to blame the victim or the system and can cause the counselor to look for a means to help rather than punish. When counselors ask questions without blaming, they build bridges of cooperation rather than competition, and maltreating and sub-stance-abusing families tend to be more willing to travel on these types of bridges. One special note about the counselors' efforts to build bridges of cooperation: This does not absolve family members of their responsibility to protect and provide a healthy environ-ment. Quite frankly, bridges of cooperation will allow families to confront their own challenges and constraints in order to help themselves move toward healing and health.

A third suggestion to help clinicians who wish to help families build bridges of effective treatment is for clinicians to consider the theoretical conceptualizations that guide their practice. This means that clinicians must clarify their theoretical orientations, because the way they think about problems determines to a large degree how they will attempt to solve them (Krumboltz, 1966). Clinicians who have a clear theoretical orientation possess clear guiding principles about treatment and the therapy process (Parrott, 1997). This type of clear theoretical orientation helps clinicians determine (a) how their decision-making process functions as they analyze human behavior, (b) whether or not their assumptions about human behavior are accurate, and (c) which features of well-validated theories they accept or reject.

Bloom (Chapter 5 in this volume) has presented the three theo-retical dimensions of primary prevention, treatment, and rehabili-tation as foundational strategies for building a bridge between the fields of child welfare and substance abuse. As discussed by Bloom, clinicians will enhance their therapeutic efforts if they proceed from a well-defined and integrated theoretical orientation. A clear theoretical conceptualization is more than just an asset to the clinician. It is a necessity for building effective bridges. Placing a value or a hierarchy on the choice of theoretical perspectives is not necessary, but there is evidence to support the effectiveness of therapies that remediate psychological disorder, prevent the development of disorders, and educate the public about mental health issues (for further discussion see Garfield & Bergin, 1994; Lipsey & Wilson, 1993; Smith & Glass, 1977; Smith, Glass, & Miller, 1980). Research indicates that a counselor, more often than not, must possess the ability to conduct a multiplicity of psychological and social services. Furthermore, due to the complexity of family problems that tend to develop within substance-abusing and maltreating homes, the most effective intervention programs are usually multimodal and multisystemic (see McMahon & Luthar, Chapter 6 in this volume). Nevertheless, many clinicians tend to favor one theoretical perspective over another. Some traditional clinicians conduct therapy from a remediation and rehabilitation perspective. Others, like the authors, operate from a family systems theoretical approach and thereby have the goal of education, prevention, and remediation of interpersonal constraints (Ivey, 1980). No matter which therapeutic approach the clinician applies, it is critical for the clinician to have a clear theoretical conceptualization to guide his or her clinical efforts. We do, however, want to examine further the effectiveness of family therapy and psychoeducational intervention models as mechanisms for building bridges with maltreating and substance-abusing families.

Family Therapy and the Bridge

In general, family therapy has been proven to be an effective treatment for a variety of family difficulties (Gurman, Kniskern, & Pinsof, 1986). Under certain conditions, family therapy has been proven to be effective with substance-abusing and maltreating families (see Geffner, 1989; Geffner & Pagelow, 1990; Heath & Atkinson, 1988; Wolfe, Wolfe, & Best, 1988). Family therapy's effectiveness is largely attributed to its techniques and to its systemic and psychodynamic theoretical foundation (for review and discussion, see Andolfi, 1980; Breunlin, Rampage, & Eovaldi, 1995; Guttman, 1991; Minuchin, 1974).

Family therapy is grounded in systems theory, which sees the family as a system or unified whole that consists of interrelated parts, such that the whole can be identified as being different from the sum of its parts (Guttman, 1991). The systems perspective focuses on relationships and is concerned about the impact of one person's behavior on another's. From a systems perspective, family problems are viewed as circular, thus, the systems family therapist will focus on process, interactions, and patterns in the family, rather than on the content of who abused whom. The systems family therapist also looks for repetitive patterns of interactions and devises strategies to alter them. Furthermore, the systems family therapist understands the family system as the unit of treatment, and therefore treats the individual and the family simultaneously (Andolfi, 1980; Breunlin et al., 1995).

Family therapy is based on the systems theory concepts of homeostasis and negative and positive feedback loops. Systems theory purports that the family is a system that adapts to the changing demands of its environment and its members (Andolfi, 1980). It is this process of adapting that either stagnates or moves the family forward. Families who change use the positive feedback mechanism, whereas families who are constrained by rigid rules that serve to maintain homeostasis often develop dysfunctional ways of interacting (Minuchin, 1974). The family systems therapist observes, assesses, and then changes the patterns of interactions in constrained families.

Family systems therapists are also concerned with the external systems that affect the family. The multisystems family therapy model is an outgrowth of extended systems thinking. It integrates the ecological work of Bronfenbrenner (1977) as well as the social systems work of Aponte (1976, 1978, 1986). Boyd-Franklin (1989, 1995) developed a multisystems model that allows clinicians to conceptualize the various systems or levels that interact around the family and the constraints. Boyd-Franklin identified six levels:

- The Individual
- Nuclear Family

- Marital Dyad
- Extended Family
- External Systems (including child welfare and substance abuse services)
- Political and Governmental

Family therapy, like most psychotherapies, is grounded in psychodynamic theory, yet, according to Breunlin and colleagues (1995), many family therapists do not acknowledge or accept the psychodynamic aspect of family therapy even though they practice psychodynamic techniques. For example, when a family therapist focuses on how psychosocial development involves interpersonal processes, he or she is working from a psychodynamic perspective. As the family therapist emphasizes individual dynamics within the interpersonal context, or touches on issues such as splitting, projection identification to manage intolerable internal affective states, the therapist is being psychodynamic.

Why is it that family therapists seem to resist the integration of psychodynamic theory, even though they practice psychodynamic techniques? According to some theorists (see Garfield & Bergin, 1994) the answer is that psychodynamic theory seems to focus primarily on the individual, the individual's personality structure, and the influences of the individual's relationships with primary caregivers during early childhood. Family therapists may also reject pure psychodynamic theory because it is based on a disease or medical model of illness. As discussed earlier, the medical model generally seeks to cure the illnesses of the individual. Pure systems theory, however, focuses on the system's contributions to the problem and seeks to prevent problems rather than to alleviate them. Therefore, in light of the complexities involved in treating substance-abusing and maltreating families, clinicians will be more effective if they attend to the dynamics of the family system, as well as to the problems of individuals (Andolfi, 1980; Breunlin et al., 1995).

Breunlin and colleagues (1995) suggest that as family therapists integrate their systems orientation with their psychodynamic orientation, they should begin by working with the whole family. In the initial session, the family therapist should investigate the family system by exploring the various perspectives that tend to constrain the family from functioning to its fullest. Once the therapist forms

an alliance with each family member, the therapist may then move
to the individual level. On the individual level, the therapist then
uses a more psychodynamic approach to investigate the internal
constraints on individual functioning. The therapist must be careful
to maintain a health and wholeness perspective and only focus on
the internal processes as they are necessary to solve the family's
problem.

Another approach to integrating psychodynamic and systems
theories was offered by Bentovim and Kinston (1991). They presented a seven-level approach to describing family functioning as a
model. Briefly, the model is as follows:

Step 1: Develop your concepts and ideas about family interactions and
family life.

Step 2: Interrupt constraining interactions and interpersonal patterns.

Step 3: Organize the concepts and items into episodes (interactional cycle) that involve the whole family.

Step 4: Produce patterns of meaning by placing family episodes in
context.

Step 5: Develop a holistic formulation that provides a single complete
account of the family as it is now. In this step it is particularly
important for the therapist to answer the following four questions:
(a) How is the symptom a part of the interaction? (b) What is the
function of the current interaction? (c) What is the disaster feared
by the family? and (d) How is the current situation linked to past
trauma?

Step 6: Classify or categorize the family based on one or more of its
distinguishing characteristics (disengaged, enmeshed, *DSM-IV,* etc.).

Step 7: Develop an idealistic formulation or conceptualization of the
family as it might be after successful therapy.

Clinicians who utilize the multisystems family therapy model are
advised that they can conceptualize problems at any or all system
levels. Interventions, however, must be directed toward only the
level that will lead to change. Clinically, the goal is to coordinate
and interact with individuals, family members, community personnel, and professionals outside of the family in ways that lead to
removing the family's constraints.

Some systems-oriented family therapists may not feel fully comfortable with this discussion linking the theoretical orientations of

systems and psychodynamic theory. However, maltreating and substance-abusing families often present in therapy with intense opposition to change, deterioration in functioning, and resistance to verbalization and intellectual insight, and require a focus on altering the patterns of action in the system. The integration of systems theory and psychodynamic theory are important to the treatment of maltreating and substance-abusing families because of the additional and complicating family dynamics and problems these challenges create.

Regarding family therapy with maltreating families, three family dynamics of power, revictimization, and safety deserve mention because of their strong influence on family functioning. For example, treatment is more effective when clinicians understand how the power of coercion often overrides other system variables such as boundaries, roles, and values (Mikesell, Lusterman, & McDaniel, 1995). Likewise, understanding how resolving the issues of revictimization and safety help to create a therapeutic environment for family therapy is also critical to therapeutic success. Actually, in order to understand how these issues affect families in treatment, Geffner and Pagelow (1990) recommended that family therapists obtain additional training in domestic violence before they conduct family therapy with maltreating families.

Others (Geffner, 1989; Geffner & Pagelow, 1990; Wolfe et al., 1988) have recommended that maltreating families meet several conditions before beginning family therapy. First, they suggest that both the victim and the perpetrator consent to family treatment. Second, in cases of child abuse, clinicians must help the perpetrator and other adults in the system assume responsibility for the child abuse. Third, family therapy is not recommended when the perpetrator continues to harbor obsessive ideas toward the victim.

When substance abuse is the presenting family problem, it also strongly affects family dynamics and family functioning (Heath & Atkinson, 1988). Research has shown that substance-abusing families also present with a number of additional family characteristics, such as the following ones presented by Stanton, Todd, & Associates (1982):

- Higher frequency of multigenerational chemical dependency
- Higher observance and existence of symbiotic relationships, where the boundaries between two or more family members are blurred or fused

- More overt coalitions and alliances within the family system
- Overinvolvement, overfunctioning, and/or underinvolvement by family members
- More primitive and direct expression of conflict
- Focus more on themes related to death and more occurrences of untimely deaths
- More involvement by adolescents in drug-oriented peer groups

Taking these family characteristics into account, several additional treatment strategies are warranted. Initially, it is important for clinicians to label the substance abuse problem as a family problem and to convince substance-abusing families that the substance abuse problem is the most important problem to address (Heath & Atkinson, 1988; Stanton & Heath, 1995; Stanton, Todd, & Associates, 1982). Successful clinicians also help these families focus on working together to eliminate the "illness," rather than label the family as "dysfunctional." Moreover, successful clinicians must help these families to mobilize and use all of their resources in their efforts to illuminate the substance abuse problem and motivate the abuser to live a responsible substance-free life.

Family Psychoeducational Interventions and the Bridge

Family psychoeducational interventions can be understood as an attempt to deal with two realities simultaneously (McFarland, 1991). The first reality is that clinicians must offer a treatment that addresses a particular constraint or disorder, and second, clinicians must consider the needs of the family around the constraint or disorder. As a result of the integration of these two treatment realities, psychoeducational interventions frequently entail goal setting and teach specific skills (Ivey, 1980).

Years ago, when psychoeducational interventions were applied to families with schizophrenic members, clinicians who treated these families believed that the dysfunction in these families actually served to maintain the family members' schizophrenia. Thus, as a treatment application, clinicians believed that if they [therapists] could change the dysfunctional parent-child interactions the disorder would dissipate (Fromm-Reichmann, 1950; Lang & Esterson, 1970). McFarland (1991), however, pointed out that these early clinicians did not allow for the possibility of neurological causes for schizophrenic symptoms. He also found that later research on treatment of schizophrenia failed to offer empirical validation or to demonstrate that the interactions believed to cause schizophrenia were present and unique to families with schizophrenic patients. Still, according to McFarland, this early psychoeducational work revealed the effectiveness of family therapy techniques such as boundaries, knowledge and skills training, and structural and communication interventions. This work revealed that the interventions were most effective when clinicians and families were active throughout the intervention. McFarland also suggested that therapists need to recognize that while they may have more general knowledge of treatment issues, families in treatment know more about what they have experienced, tried, and endured. Thus, the critical component of the therapeutic bridge to recovery is an active ongoing collaboration among the patient, the family, and the clinician. This active collaboration must entail the patient's and the family's expectations about their experience and must utilize these experiences in collaboration with the clinician's expertise.

Parenting Psychoeducational Interventions and the Bridge

Researchers have conducted numerous studies investigating the general effectiveness of psychoeducational interventions with family difficulties and constraints (Ainsworth, 1996; Carlo, 1993; Cox & Ray, 1994; Eyberg, 1992; Schmidt, Liddle, & Dakof, 1996). Broadly defined, parent education interventions have a common educational component directed at parenting behavior, attitudes, styles, and practices (Eyberg, 1992). In these programs, clinicians teach parents to use behavioral procedures such as positive reinforcement and mild punishment to change their child's behavior. Parents also learn to give the child praise and tokens to reinforce positive behavior and to provide time-outs or to take away privileges to punish problem behaviors.

Investigators have shown that parent education programs are effective interventions for dealing with a wide range of child and adolescent related problems that occur as a result of maltreating and substance-abusing families (Cox & Ray, 1994; Maccoby & Martin, 1983; Schmidt et al., 1996). Cox and Ray (1994) suggested that clinicians who provide interventions with parents of substance-abusing adolescents should reject the tendency to blame and attribute the illness to the adolescent substance abuser. Rather, clinicians should realize that the adolescent's substance abuse is simply a dynamic aspect of the family's interactions. Maccoby and Martin (1983) suggested that parenting is a fundamental aspect of the family system and is critically related to adolescent and child functioning. Furthermore, researchers (Cox & Ray, 1994; Maccoby & Martin, 1983; Schmidt et al., 1996) interested in parenting suggested that the parent-child relationship, and the parents' attitudes about substance use and religion, are more related to adolescent problem behavior, including substance use, than individual child or individual parent behavior. Other factors that have been found to relate to child and adolescent problem behavior include poor family management, disrupted parenting, inappropriate discipline, inadequate parental monitoring, excessive parent irritability, and coercive family processes (Patterson, 1982). Almost all of these family constraints are often present in maltreating and substance-abusing homes.

Significant research has been done to examine the effectiveness of parent education programs and family therapy singly and in comparison to one another. Researchers have compared parent education programs with family therapy (Ainsworth, 1996; Carlo, 1993), evaluated the effectiveness of parent education programs and family therapy in research involving preschool children (Eyberg, 1992), and examined the effectiveness of family-based parent training provided to parents of adolescents with problem behavior, including substance abuse (Schmidt et al., 1996). While they found that both types of programs were effective, the parent and child/adolescent psychosocial interventions were found to be more effective and able to address a wider array of difficulties.

DeVoss and Newlon (1986) found that parents who were themselves survivors of nonviolent, nonincestuous child sexual abuse were usually less effective in protecting their children from sexual abuse. Thus, DeVoss and Newlon (1986) developed a program for parent survivors that was designed to help them talk about their childhood experience with grown siblings, extended family members, and their children. In addition, they recommended that clinicians give parents specific information about the effects of sexual abuse on their children, and DeVoss and Newlon (1986) found these two interventions to be very effective in helping parents to deal with their pain and thereby develop the ability to better help and protect their children.

Carlo (1993) investigated the effectiveness of parenting training on the reunification of families with children exhibiting problem behavior. The study examined the effectiveness of didactic learning interventions and experiential learning interventions. They applied the workshops separately to two groups and jointly to another. The investigator found that when parents received the joint intervention (didactic and experiential), their families moved toward reunification at a significantly higher rate than did families in which the parents received either the experiential or the didactic treatment alone. The researcher concluded that the joint intervention was more effective because adults learn better when they understand the connection between organized knowledge and general experience (Carlo, 1993).

Regarding the comparison of the effectiveness of parent education with family therapy, researchers have found that the specific conditions and contexts of the treatment are critical to this evaluation (Ainsworth, 1996; Carlo, 1993). In a study conducted with families whose children were in a residential treatment facility, Ainsworth (1996) found that poverty appeared to inhibit the capacity of the families to achieve control of their social condition. This lack of contextual control, in turn, increased the likelihood of adolescent delinquency. Thus, the investigator concluded that family therapists must guard against attributing adolescent problem behavior solely to parenting deficiencies. Ainsworth further concluded that interventions with parents whose children were in residential care might effectively address the contextual issues of the family by providing effective parent education that focuses on parental limit setting, child development, behavioral management skills, and should help these families develop support from extended family members, friends, and other people in their communities.

Frequently, members of society have the impression that parents of children with behavior problems are incompetent and incapable (Eyberg, 1992). However, researchers (Campbell, Szumowski, Ewing, Gluck, & Breaux, 1982; Weisz, Weiss, Alicke, & Klotz, 1987) have shown that the reports of parents of children with behavioral problems are consistent with the observations of professionals and with psychological testing. According to Schmidt and colleagues (1996), professionals who work with troubled adolescents should select and target their interventions to specific dysfunctions and problem behaviors. Based on their research with black and white middle-class mothers, Rowland and Wampler (1983) suggested that psychoeducational programs target the specific interests and preferences of parents, particularly regarding matters of race and socioeconomic status. They found that the African American mothers and less educated mothers were more willing than others to attend parenting workshops; however, the programs needed to cater to specific needs. For instance, these mothers preferred that the training be provided in churches, on weekends, and occasionally include children, because these factors were important to them.

Webster-Stratton (1985) developed and evaluated a parenting intervention targeted at parents with children having early-onset conduct disorder. Her research showed that the treatment program was successful over the short and long term at improving behavior and adjustment in two thirds of the children whose parents participated. Webster-Stratton and Hammond (1997) compared four conditions of treatment to evaluate the generalizability and clinical effectiveness of their parenting training programs over a wide range of risk factors. In this recent study, they examined the successful parenting treatment program, a children's treatment program, and a joint parent-child treatment program. When Webster-Stratton and Hammond (1997) combined the child training and parent training and compared it with the other two conditions, the combined program was far superior in improving parenting skills and child behavior problems. The combination of child training and parent training significantly improved the parent reports of problem behavior, parent-child interactions at home, child problem-solving skills, child conflict management, and consumer satisfaction.

We suggest that their interventions would also be effective with substance-abusing and maltreating families. That is, families in which the children have conduct disorders, like maltreating and substance-abusing families, often struggle with issues of family violence, family instability, family conflict, and stress. Thus, their study supports the need for a comprehensive approach in interventions with maltreating and substance-abusing families. This comprehensive program is another way in which clinicians can build a bridge that serves maltreating and substance-abusing homes.

Using the Extended Family as a Bridge to Effective Treatment

By definition, an extended family is a group of individuals consisting of the nuclear family—normatively consisting of a husband, wife, and children—and individuals related by ties of consanguinity (Sauber, L'Abate, Weeks, & Buchanan, 1993). The extended family can be a powerful support for all types of families. A core benefit of the extended family is the existence of mutual help (Hannah, 1991; Hill, 1977; Zollar, 1983). Healthy extended families offer rewarding and beneficial relationships, living arrangements, positive interactions, and mutual support (Zollar, 1983).

Family Network Systems Therapy (FNST). Counseling with the extended family or family network systems therapy is therapy that brings important people and resources together to address the family problem (Cole, 1995; Woolf, 1983). The therapist generally focuses FNST on sharing information among the family, extended family members, and other supportive social systems. Professionals can also use FNST to gather information and make sure that procedures and forms regarding a family are consistent across agencies and organizations. The aim of FNST is to uncover and prevent family and agency communication problems. FNST also provides an opportunity to model, role play, and show to the various systems healthy ways to function and support the family in treatment.

Frequently, family network systems therapy seeks to find and connect the child in a substance-abusing or maltreating home with a resourceful extended family member (Attneave, 1990). Network therapists use surrogate families to help children in substance-abusing and maltreating homes. Family network therapists focus on the needs of the entire family, and they are willing to conduct treatment in the home, school, and community. Network therapists use extrafamilial support to address resistance, build rapport, and empower specific family members.

One important aspect of FNST is family assessment. Many family therapists using FNST use the genogram to outline a family tree network. Problems that families experience tend to have their roots in patterns of dysfunction and difficulty. That is, they are handed down from generation to generation (Bowen, 1976). The FNST considers this multigenerational transmission and may use a genogram to help families better understand how their constraints have a multigenerational origin.

The genogram charts the relational and emotional aspects of a family across several generations. It includes the typical information found in a family tree, such as names, birth dates, marriages, divorces, deaths, and even illnesses. It also includes a brief description of family members, their particular strengths and weaknesses, and aspects of their lives that can have a continuing effect throughout the years.

There are three primary gains from using genograms. The first is to gain an understanding of the family as more than just a collection of individuals. Genograms enable the therapist to see the family as a whole system. They help the therapist to identify patterns that may have been pervasive in the family for years, and perhaps identify the impact of these patterns as they exist today. This enhanced understanding of the family system will apply not only to the family as a whole, but also to specific generations of the family and even to particular individuals.

The second gain from using genograms is that they help the families to identify and draw boundaries. Boundaries are the psychological and social parameters that exist within families. Family boundaries are the same as physical boundaries around property, city, state, or country. When helping a family to construct a genogram, the therapist is primarily concerned with three boundaries: (a) Personal boundaries that define who they are in relationship to others, (b) Intergenerational boundaries that define who are the parents and children, and (c) Family boundaries that define the family and make it distinct from other families.

Finally, the genogram helps the therapist identify roles of family members. A role is simply any fixed habitual pattern of relating that forces family members into set actions, behaviors, and responses. Roles can help or dehumanize family members. Roles allow family members to be responsible or scapegoated and cast by type. Thus, knowing the roles family members play inside and outside the family is important. FNST also uses another assessment tool called the ecomap (Hartman & Laird, 1983). The ecomap is a tool that depicts the family at the center of a complex system. In the ecomap, agencies and support systems outside of the family are diagramed through a series of circles. An ecomap identifies extended family, friends, associates, and professionals who either are currently involved with the problem or have experience with the problem. Like the genogram, the ecomap can be used to build bridges among the various organizations with which the family and extended family interact.

The family therapy interventions that network therapists use include here-and-now, transgenerational, and ecosystemic interventions. Here-and-now interventions are goal oriented and problem or solution focused. Therapists who use here-and-now interventions are active and directive, and their emphasis is on behavioral change rather than insight. Frequently, therapists use (a) reenactment and enactment family demonstrations; (b) reframing and a positive connotation of problems; (c) restructuring and physical positioning of the family in session; (d) defining the problem and establishing goals and action plans; (e) family psychoeducation training; (f) between-session homework tasks; and (g) the self with the family.

Transgenerational interventions include use of genograms, trips home, inviting extended family into therapy, and symbolic inclusion of the family of origin. The premise of transgenerational interventions is that the transgenerational process, which occurs across time, influences the development of current problems. These problems often arise during transitional periods such as family life changes, and solving current problems often involves resolving relationship issues from the past with family members.

Ecosystemic interventions are biopsychosocial and collaborative. They address power issues and use the family's network and larger support systems. Ecosystemic interventions are based on the premise that discussing multisystems issues with a family allows family members to communicate around the issues that brought them into treatment. It allows the therapist to join with the family while exploring the family's structure, resiliency, boundaries, and power structure (Boyd-Franklin, 1989, 1990, 1995).

Bridges to Effective Treatment

This chapter has focused on the ideological and philosophical bridges that a clinician must build in order to counsel substance-abusing and maltreating families effectively. This section of the chapter focuses on several practice issues that must be addressed during treatment.

Generally, clinicians who work with substance-abusing and maltreating families must overcome the obstacle of open conflict, defensiveness, low levels of warmth, and children and adolescents with severe behavioral problems (Robbins, Alexander, Newell, & Turner, 1996). Behavioral problems occur in clusters (Jessor & Jessor, 1977), so once the family develops one major problem, it is typical that other problems will follow.

Families with serious challenges like abuse frequently exist in environments that are inconsistent, nonresponsive, and emotionally distant. Family members whose family-of-origin or family-of-procreation is characterized by such conditions develop a fundamental insecurity that results in broader interpersonal difficulties (Scales, 1990). Members of families characterized by these environmental challenges will often misread and misrepresent messages they receive from others, often to the point of attributing blame and harm when there is none.

Herrenkohl, Herrenkohl, and Egolf (1994) examined the interaction of the individual and the environmental characteristics over time for a group of children (ages 18 months to 6 years) from maltreating families. In 1976, they identified a group of resilient children from maltreating homes and compared them to a group of less resourceful children from maltreating homes and a non-maltreated comparison group. They interviewed the children in late adolescence and found that the resilient group, in comparison to the others, had moderate but not stellar outcomes. Of the 23 resilient children, 14 had graduated from high school or were still in school. Of this 14, 6 had "B" averages, 2 had "C" averages, and 6 had "D" averages. Of the 9 who dropped out of high school, 6 continued to live in abusive homes and 3 had very unstable caregivers. The 3 resilient children who dropped out and lived with unstable caregivers were responsible and reliable. The other 6 adolescents were all exhibiting significant problems.

This study indicated that maltreating homes can have a devastating affect on the lives of children, and that even resilient children can be greatly affected by environmental influences. Herrenkohl and colleagues (1994) also presented a case in which they demonstrated the integration among environmental, maturational, and individual factors. They showed how the developmental trajectory of three siblings was a result of their gender, environment, and personalities. The study also demonstrated the importance of helping maltreating and substance-abusing families develop positive self-images and an internal sense of control in their members. It was not surprising that the results suggested that the ability to set goals and show planning behavior was predictive of future success. Thus, we maintain that family therapy and family psychoeducational interventions can and do help maltreating and substance-abusing families address challenging issues and help them create positive self-images, internal motivation, and positive goal-setting behavior.

The IMPACT Program: Constructing a Bridge

The "I Must Parent According to Christian or Cultural Teachings" (IMPACT) program is an example of a family therapy based intervention program designed to help maltreating and substance-abusing families create positive self-images and develop goal-setting behaviors. We specifically developed the intervention to be used with African American families. The intervention (see Table 8.1) helps parents and adolescents enhance their relationships and consider the effects of maltreatment and abuse through discussions about parenting, parent-child relationships, values and attitudes, cultural influences, and disciplinary skills. Realizing the difficulty of obtaining motivated participation from parents and adolescents in family training and education, our program has sought to engage family members in training through discussions of their religious values, cultural principles, or both. Thus, the IMPACT program provides either a Christian or a cultural focus. The program is taught in churches on Sunday mornings during the church school hour. We have found that using the church school hour provides accessibility and credibility to our program. We work within churches because the church is a healing community intensely

Table 8.1 The IMPACT Program

Principles	Workshops	Techniques & Concepts
Expressing High Value	1. Impact and winning 2. Impacting sons, impacting daughters	• The family blessing • Male empowerment • Female empowerment • Role modeling • Parent-child relationship
Spoken Messages (with substance-using and maltreating families)	3. Impact with a blessing 4. Impact with style	• Renewing and building new relationships • Addictive behaviors and their effects on the family • When parents are not available
Meaningful Touch	5. Impact through discipline	• Verbal and physical communication: Positive and negative touching • Appropriate disciplinary practices • Managing anger • Appropriate and inappropriate usages of power • Violence in intimate relationships
Picturing a Special Future	6. Impact and responsibilities 7. Impact and adult relationships	• Kinship networks • Stress management • Self-respect issues • Child and adolescent development • Single parenting • Poem: We Shall Rise
Having an Active Commitment	8. Impact and Culture 9. Impact, Racism, and Discrimination	• Building appropriate coping skills • Setting appropriate boundaries and rules for the home • Strengthening communication • Poem: Don't Quit

committed to the common interest of healing its members on the psychological, behavioral, and spiritual levels (Almond, 1974).

Conceptually, the IMPACT program has three components that address the issue of parental motivation. First, the Christian and the cultural IMPACT programs are rooted in the concept of "Blessing Your Family." The lessons on blessing your family are the foundational premise for our parent training. These lessons seek to engage family members in the training process and stress that they must further develop and maintain their relationships in order to promote spiritual growth and healing. The blessing lessons adopted from Smalley and Trent (1983) were designed to *motivate* family members to work cooperatively to develop a sense of wholeness. Smalley and Trent (1983, see pp. 23-29) identified the following five components of the special Blessing:

- *Expressing High Value* is attaching high value, valuing, or respecting your children in thought and deed.

- *Spoken Messages* consist of verbalized words of love, acceptance, and encouragement. It is not only the absence of yelling or hurtful criticism, but the presence of positive words.

- *Meaningful Touch* is providing your children with physical touch such as hugs, kisses, handshakes, and pats on the back. This touch communicates warmth, personal acceptance, affirmation, and as research shows, even promotes physical health.

- *Picturing a Special Future* is providing your children with a description of a special future. This means encouraging your children to set meaningful goals and having high but not unattainable or perfectionist expectations.

- *An Active Commitment* means that your words must be backed up by responsible action.

This "blessing" concept is used to teach family members that positive family relationships are more powerful and more important than coercive and substance-abusing behaviors. We have found that parents, from the Christian or community samples, are more likely to accept our disciplinary recommendations, and alter their disciplinary practices, if we begin the training with a focus on the blessing (McCreary, Nicholson, Stepter, Walker, & Berry, 1997).

A second component of the IMPACT program is on parenting style. We seek to make parents and adolescents aware of the influence and effect of parenting on family functioning. We teach that parents will have the greatest impact and give the greatest blessing to their children if they parent with maximum love and appropriate limits. Likewise, we teach children through play, discussion, and structured exercises the reciprocal effects of their behaviors on their family.

The third component of our program is discipline. We approach the topic of discipline from a cultural competency perspective, and we use the notion of family socialization to motivate and engage parents (Tharp, 1989; Winegar & Valsiner, 1992). Here socialization refers to the process through which ideas about what one should do (prescriptions) and the ideas about what one should not do (prohibitions) are transmitted to family members (Stech, McClintock, Fitzpatrick, & Babin, 1976).

Moreover, our program focuses on religious and racial socialization. Religious socialization involves helping parents discipline their children based on their religious life and religious values (Abbott, Berry, & Meredith, 1990; Brook, Lukoff, & Whiteman, 1977; Jessor & Jessor, 1977; Oetting & Beauvais, 1987). Our current research has found adolescents' self-reports that the higher their credal assent and the more their parents attend religious services, the lower their problem behavior (Berry, McCreary, & Kliewer, 1997). Racial socialization is an additional challenge that African American parents face in parenting their children within a prejudiced and racist society (Comer & Poussaint, 1992; Hopson & Hopson, 1990; Peters, 1985). This includes teaching their children about the majority culture, values, and behavior, while counteracting the negative stereotypes society attributes to African Americans. It further entails helping children learn to respect their own cultural heritage and to solve problems utilizing this knowledge. We also teach that both religious and racial socialization practices prohibit coercive, addictive, and abusive behaviors toward children, adolescents, and adults (see Table 8.1). That is, our intervention attempts to create a critical pedagogy based on religious and cultural values that promotes an empowerment, liberation, and problem-solving approach to family difficulties, which we suggest will help combat family maltreatment and substance abuse.

Historically, African Americans have used a "no nonsense" parenting style with a strong social norm that favors spanking (Genovese, 1972; McLeod, Kruttschnitt, & Dornfeld, 1994). Our applied research with African American parents suggests that they benefit from a comprehensive understanding of the issues surrounding physical punishment. We have motivated African American parents to participate in training that includes discussions about the quality of the parent-child relationship, skillful reasoning, nonpunitive discipline, and skillful periodic punishment. So far, we have received positive results, but our research continues with a longitudinal design so that we will be able to examine the effects of our program over time. In the meantime, there is evidence to indicate that this program is helping to build bridges that help families reconcile and resolve differences and that help restore them to healthy living.

Summary and Conclusions: Lesson and Reflections

Building a bridge to effective treatment for and with substance-abusing and maltreating families is not a simple matter. To construct a quality bridge, construction must begin with the therapist. The clinician is a guide and a contractor who helps families as they travel onto and across the bridge. This chapter purported that clinicians are more capable and helpful to families as they master issues of countertransference, move beyond seeking and assigning blame, and develop a sound therapeutic theory and orientation.

This chapter also suggested that family therapy, which integrates systems theory and psychodynamic theory, is an effective treatment strategy to address the systemic issues of substance-abusing and maltreating families. Several methods were discussed as ways to build the treatment bridges: (a) family and parent psychoeducational programs that enhance the knowledge and skills of struggling and hurting families, (b) applying multimodal and multisystems interventions, and (c) mobilizing extended family networks to help abusive families.

Finally, a family-based psychoeducational program that we are currently conducting in churches, communities, and group homes was described. The program has an adolescent and child component, and seeks to empower families to build and travel on bridges of healthy family functioning. As family issues continue to be an important concern, clinicians who are able to help families build effective bridges for healing will continue to provide a much needed and greatly appreciated service.

References

Abbott, D. A., Berry, M., & Meredith, W. H. (1990). Religious belief and practice: A potential asset in helping families. *Family Relations, 39,* 443-448.

Ainsworth, F. (1996). Parent education and training or family therapy: Does it matter which comes first? *Child and Youth Care Forum, 25,* 101-110.

Almond, R. (1974). *The healing community.* New York: Jason Aronson.

Andolfi, M. (1980). *Family therapy: An interactional approach.* New York: Plenum.

Aponte, H. (1976). The family-school interview: An ecostructural approach. *Family Process, 15,* 303-311.

Aponte, H. (1978). Diagnosis in family therapy. In C. B. Germain (Ed.), *Social work practice: People and environments.* New York: Columbia University Press.

Aponte, H. (1986). If I don't get simple, I cry. *Family Process, 25,* 531-548.

Attneave, C. L. (1990). Core network intervention: An emerging paradigm. *Journal of Strategic & Systemic Therapies, 9,* 3-10.

Bentovim, A., & Kinston, W. (1991). Focal family therapy: Joining systems theory with psychodynamic understanding. In H. S. Gurman & D. P. Kniskern (Eds.), *Handbook of family therapy* (Vol. 2, pp. 284-324). New York: Brunner/Mazel.

Berry, E. J., McCreary, M. L., & Kliewer, W. L. (1997). *The influence of religion, parenting styles and racial socialization on African American families.* Manuscript under review for publication.

Bowen, M. (1976). Theory in the practice of psychotherapy. In P. J. Guerin (Ed.), *Family therapy: Theory and practice* (pp. 42-90). New York: Gardner.

Boyd-Franklin, N. (1989). *Black families in therapy: A multisystems approach.* New York: Guilford.

Boyd-Franklin, N. (1990). Five key factors in treatment of black families. In G. W. Saba, B. M. Karrer, & K. V. Hardy (Eds.), *Minorities and family therapy* (pp. 53-69). New York: Haworth.

Boyd-Franklin, N. (1995). Therapy with African American inner-city families. In R. H. Mikesell, D. Lusterman, & S. H. McDaniel (Eds.), *Integrating family therapy: Handbook of family psychology and family theory* (pp. 357-371). Washington, DC: American Psychological Association.

Breunlin, D. C., Rampage, C., & Eovaldi, M. L. (1995). Family therapy supervision: Toward an integrative perspective. In R. H. Mikesell, D. Lusterman, & S. H. McDaniel (Eds.), *Integrating family therapy: Handbook of family psychology and systems theory* (pp. 547-560). Washington, DC: American Psychological Association.

Bronfenbrenner, U. (1977). Toward an experimental ecology of human development. *American Psychologist, 45,* 513-530.

Brook, J. S., Lukoff, I. F., & Whiteman, M. (1977). Correlates of marijuana use as related to age, sex, and ethnicity. *Yale Journal of Biology and Medicine, 50,* 383-390.

Campbell, S. B., Szumowski, E. K., Ewing, L. J., Gluck, D. S., & Breaux, A. M. (1982). A multidimensional assessment of parent-identified behavior problem toddlers. *Journal of Abnormal Child Psychology, 10,* 569-592.

Carlo, P. (1993). Parent education vs. parent involvement: Which type of effects work best to reunify families? *Journal of Social Service Research, 17,* 135-150.

Cole, E. S. (1995). Becoming family centered: Child welfare's challenge. 75th anniversary special issue: Social work: Challenges and directions. *Family in Society, 76,* 163-172.

Comer, J. P., & Poussaint, A. F. (1992). *Raising black children.* New York: Plume.

Cox, R. B., Jr., & Ray, W. A. (1994). The role of theory in treating adolescent substance abuse. *Contemporary Family Therapy, 16,* 131-144.

Danish, S. J. (in press). Interventions for enhancing adolescents' life skills. *The Humanistic Psychologist.*

DeVoss, J. A., & Newlon, B. J. (1986). Support groups for parents of sexually victimized children. *School Counselor, 34,* 51-56.

Eyberg, S. M. (1992). Assessing therapy outcome with preschool children: Progress and problems. American Psychological Association Convention Section on Clinical Child Psychology Presidential Address. *Journal of Clinical Child Psychology, 21,* 306-311.

Friedlander, M. L., Siegel, S., & Brenock, K. (1989). Parallel processes in counseling and supervision: A case study. *Journal of Counseling Psychology, 36,* 149-157.

Fromm-Reichmann, F. (1950). *Principles of intensive psychotherapy.* Chicago: University of Chicago Press.

Garfield, S. L., & Bergin, A. E. (Eds.). (1994). *Handbook of psychotherapy and behavior change* (4th ed.). New York: John Wiley.

Geffner, R. (1989). Treating spouse abuse with conjoint marital therapy. *Family Therapy Today, 4,* 1-5.

Geffner, R., & Pagelow, M. D. (1990). Victims of spouse abuse. In R. T. Ammerman & M. Hersen (Eds.), *Treatment of family violence: A sourcebook* (pp. 113-135). New York: John Wiley.

Genovese, E. D. (1972). *Roll, Jordan, roll: The world the slaves made.* New York: Vintage.

Getz, H. G., & Protinsky, H. O. (1994). Training marriage and family counselors: A family-of-origin approach. *Counselor Education and Supervision, 23,* 42-46.

Gurman, A. S., Kniskern, D. P., & Pinsof, W. M. (1986). Research on the process and outcome of marital and family therapy. In S. L. Garfield & A. E. Bergin (Eds.), *Handbook of psychotherapy and behavior change* (pp. 565-626). New York: John Wiley.

Guttman, H. A. (1991). Systems theory, cybernetics, and epistemology. In H. S. Gurman & D. P. Kniskern (Eds.), *Handbook of family therapy* (Vol. 2, pp. 41-62). New York: Brunner/Mazel.

Hannah, D. B. (1991). The black extended family: An appraisal of its past, present, and future statuses. In L. C. June (Ed.), *The black family: Past, present, and future* (pp. 33-56). Grand Rapids, MI: Zondervan.

Hartman, A., & Laird, J. (1983). *Family centered social work practice.* New York: Free Press.

Heath, A., & Atkinson, B. (1988). Systemic treatment of substance abuse: A graduate course. *Journal of Marital and Family Therapy, 14,* 411-418.

Herrenkohl, E. C., Herrenkohl, R. C., & Egolf, B. (1994). Resilient early school-age children from maltreating homes: Outcomes in late adolescence. *American Journal of Orthopsychiatry, 64,* 301-309.

Hill, R. (1977). *Informal adoptions among black families.* Washington, DC: National Urban League.

Hopson, D. P., & Hopson, D. S. (1990). *Different and wonderful: Raising black children in a race-conscious society.* New York: Fireside.

Ivey, A. E. (1980). Counseling 2000: Time to take charge! *The Counseling Psychologist, 8,* 12-16.

Jessor, R., & Jessor, S. L. (1977). *Problem behavior and psychosocial development: A longitudinal study of youth.* New York: Academic Press.

Krumboltz, J. D. (1966). Promoting adaptive behavior: Behavioral approach. In J. D. Krumboltz (Ed.), *Revolution in counseling.* Boston: Houghton Mifflin.

Lang, R. D., & Esterson, A. (1970). *Sanity, madness and the family.* Middlesex, UK: Penguin.

Lipsey, M. W., & Wilson, D. B. (1993). The efficacy of psychological, educational, and behavioral treatment: Confirmation from meta-analyses. *American Psychologist, 48,* 1181-1209.

Maccoby, E. E., & Martin, J. A. (1983). Socialization in the context of the family: Parent-child interaction. In E. M. Hetherington (Ed.), *Handbook of child psychology: Vol. 4. Socialization, personality, and social development* (pp. 1-101). New York: John Wiley.

McCreary, M. L., Nicholson, S. C., Stepter, T. A., Walker, T. D., & Berry, E. J. (1997). Making an IMPACT on our youth. In R. G. Murray, D. Riddick, & S. B. McDowney (Eds.), *Take me back: Empowering the family for kingdom readiness* (pp. 39-46). Richmond, VA: Baptist General Convention of Virginia.

McFarland, W. R. (1991). Family psychoeducational treatment. In H. S. Gurman & D. P. Kniskern (Eds.), *Handbook of family therapy* (Vol. 2, pp. 363-395). New York: Brunner/Mazel.

McLeod, J. D., Kruttschnitt, C., & Dornfeld, M. (1994). Does parenting explain the effects of structural conditions on children's antisocial behavior? A comparison of blacks and whites. *Social Forces, 73*(2), 575-604.

Mikesell, R. H., Lusterman, D., & McDaniel, S. H. (Eds.). (1995). *Integrating family therapy: Handbook of family psychology and systems theory.* Washington, DC: American Psychological Association.

Minuchin, S. (1974). *Families and family therapy.* Cambridge, MA: Harvard University Press.

Oetting, E. R., & Beauvais, F. (1987). Peer cluster theory, socialization characteristics, and adolescent drug use: A path analysis. *Journal of Counseling Psychology, 34*(2), 205-213.

Parrott, L., III. (1997). *Counseling and psychotherapy.* New York: McGraw-Hill.

Patterson, G. R. (1982). *Coercive family process: A social learning approach* (3rd ed.). Eugene, OR: Casilia.

Peters, M. F. (1985). Racial socialization of young black children. In H. P. McAdoo & J. L. McAdoo (Eds.), *Black children* (pp. 159-173). Beverly Hills, CA: Sage.

Robbins, M. S., Alexander, J. F., Newell, R. M., & Turner, C. W. (1996). The immediate effects of reframing on client attitude in family therapy. *Journal of Family Psychology, 10,* 28-34.

Rowland, S. B., & Wampler, K. S. (1983). Black and white mothers' preferences for parenting programs. *Family Relations, 32,* 323-330.

Ryan, W. (1971). *Blaming the victim.* New York: Random House.

Sauber, S. R., L'Abate, L., Weeks, G. R., & Buchanan, W. L. (Eds.). (1993). *The dictionary of family psychology and family therapy* (2nd ed.). Newbury Park, CA: Sage.

Scales, P. (1990). Developing capable young people: An alternative strategy for prevention. *Journal of Early Adolescence, 10,* 420-438.

Schmidt, S. E., Liddle, H. A., & Dakof, G. A. (1996). Changes in parenting practices and adolescent drug abuse during multidimensional family therapy. *Journal of Family Psychology, 10,* 12-27.

Smalley, G., & Trent, J. (1983). *The blessing.* Nashville, TN: Thomas Nelson.

Smith, M. L., & Glass, G. V. (1977). Meta-analysis of psychotherapy outcome studies. *American Psychologist, 32,* 752-760.

Smith, M. L., Glass, G. V., & Miller, R. L. (1980). *The benefits of psychotherapy.* Baltimore, MD: Johns Hopkins University Press.

Stanton, M. D., & Heath, A. W. (1995). Family treatment of alcohol and drug abuse. In R. H. Mikesell, D. Lusterman, & S. H. McDaniel (Eds.), *Integrating family therapy: Handbook of family psychology and systems theory* (pp. 529-541). Washington, DC: American Psychological Association.

Stanton, M. D., Todd, T. C., & Associates. (1982). *The family therapy of drug abuse and addiction.* New York: Guilford.

Stech, F. J., McClintock, C. G., Fitzpatrick, N. J., & Babin, C. A. (1976). When a cultural prohibition is effective: A field investigation. *Journal of Applied Social Psychology, 6,* 211-227.

Stolenberg, C. D., & Delworth, U. (1987). *Supervising counselors and therapists: A developmental approach.* San Francisco: Jossey-Bass.

Tharp, R. G. (1989). Psychocultural variables and constants: Effects on teaching and learning in schools. In Children and their development: Knowledge base, research agenda, and social policy application [Special issue]. *American Psychologist, 44,* 349-359.

Webster-Stratton, C. (1985). Comparisons of behavior transactions between conduct-disordered children and their mothers in the clinic and at home. *Journal of Abnormal Child Psychology, 13,* 169-183.

Webster-Stratton, C., & Hammond, M. (1997). Treating children with early-onset conduct problems: A comparison of child and parent training interventions. *Journal of Consulting and Clinical Psychology, 65,* 93-109.

West, C. (1993). *Race matters.* Boston: Beacon.

Weisz, J. R., Weiss, B., Alicke, M. D., & Klotz, M. L. (1987). Effectiveness of psychotherapy with children and adolescents: A meta-analysis for clinicians. *Journal of Consulting and Clinical Psychology, 9,* 217-219.

Winegar, L. T., & Valsiner, J. (Eds.). (1992). *Children's development within social context.* Hillsdale, NJ: Lawrence Erlbaum.

Wolfe, D. A., Wolfe, V. V., & Best, C. L. (1988). Child victims of sexual abuse. In V. B. Van Hasselt, R. L. Morrison, A. S. Bellack, & M. Hersen (Eds.), *Handbook of family violence.* New York: Plenum.

Woolf, V. V. (1983). Family network systems in transgenerational psychotherapy: The theory, advantages and expanded applications of the genogram. *Family Therapy, 10,* 219-237.

Zollar, A. C. (1983). *A member of the family: Strategies for black family continuity.* Chicago: Nelson-Hall.

Prevention Issues:
Some Cautionary Notes

DAVID F. DUNCAN

The preceding chapters in this volume have made it clear that parental abuse of alcohol and other drugs (AOD) is a very serious risk factor for the well-being of children. While I would urge the cautionary note that these children are neither so numerous nor so severely damaged as the recent media hysteria over "crack babies" would have led us to believe (Beckett, 1995; Duncan, 1997; Norton-Hawk, in press; Reinarman & Levine, 1994; Susman, 1996), their actual numbers and their very real problems do constitute a serious challenge to our educational, welfare, and health care institutions. As with other problems that reach the proportions of a public health issue, the promotion of health and the reduction of risk factors (primary prevention) should be the organizing principle behind our activities regarding children of drug-abusing parents.

In the field of public health, prevention has traditionally been conceptualized as occurring at three levels: primary, secondary, and tertiary (Duncan, 1988). By primary prevention we mean the prevention of new instances of the problem—lessening the frequency with which it happens in the first place. By secondary prevention we mean early intervention in the course of a problem, aimed at shortening the duration of cases of the problem and thus reducing the burden of those cases on the community at any given time. The term tertiary prevention is used to describe efforts aimed at mitigating the long-term consequences of the problem.

In the case of an infectious disease, this might mean primary prevention by means of vaccination to prevent people from catching the disease. Secondary prevention might consist of active screening aimed at channeling infected persons into treatment and returning them as quickly as possible to good health, with a primary prevention benefit of reducing spread of the infection from them to others. Medical measures aimed at preventing death and disability in those afflicted with the disease would constitute tertiary prevention.

These concepts have also been applied to the prevention of drug abuse. Primary prevention measures such as drug education, strengthening families, and teaching coping skills can serve to protect individuals against the onset of drug abuse. Teaching parents, physicians, and others to recognize the signs and symptoms of drug abuse, and providing accessible and acceptable treatment services can achieve secondary prevention by bringing abusers into treatment at as early a stage as possible in their disorder. Harm reduction measures such as needle exchanges, methadone maintenance, and street outreach medical workers can reduce the incidence of such dire consequences of drug abuse as HIV and other infections, overdoses, and involvement in acquisitive crime to pay for drugs.

Prevention of the harm to children that may result from parental abuse of alcohol or other drugs is conceptually more complex. It can be difficult to identify what is primary prevention and what is secondary or tertiary in this problem. For example, is getting a parent into an Alcoholics Anonymous (AA) program or a treatment facility an instance of secondary prevention or is it primary prevention? Or is intervention to prevent abuse of the child merely tertiary prevention of one of the long-term consequences of alcohol or other drug abuse? While at first glance these may seem to be mere semantic quibbles, on closer inspection they reflect fundamental assumptions about the problem of abuse and neglect of children by their substance-abusing parents. The soundness of those assumptions may make the difference between an effective prevention program or a waste of scarce resources.

If we view the problem solely from a drug-centered perspective, then the only interventions that make sense are those targeted at the parent's abuse of alcohol or other drugs. If such interventions are successful, then nothing more should be needed to protect the child's well-being. At the very least, such a perspective holds that nothing worthwhile can be done about an AOD-abusing parent's neglect or abuse of a child until that parent's drug problem has been resolved. The opposite view might hold that the parent's AOD abuse was a result of abuse by his or her parents early in life and can be resolved only in the context of a full confrontation with the intergenerational pattern of child maltreatment that exists in the family. While each perspective has its merits, neither alone is adequate to the task of guiding our prevention efforts in this area.

I would propose that in developing preventive interventions for this problem we should be explicit in accepting that both primary and secondary prevention of parental AOD abuse often will also be primary prevention of child abuse and neglect. At the same time we should accept that prevention of parental AOD abuse is neither necessary nor sufficient to prevent child abuse and neglect at primary, secondary, or tertiary levels. AOD-abusing parents do not necessarily abuse their children; nor is the absence of AOD abuse any guarantee of proper parenting behavior.

Within such a schema, I would suggest that strategies for primary prevention might be organized around three different objectives: (a) preventing the onset of AOD abuse among parenting-age women; (b) early intervention for drug abuse in pregnant or parenting women; (c) preventing the onset of child abuse by women or their spouses who continue to abuse alcohol or other drugs.

These primary prevention efforts, of course, should be supplemented by secondary and tertiary prevention. Secondary prevention would provide early intervention in child abuse by drug-abusing women and their spouses. Tertiary prevention would target the long-term sequelae of the child's exposure to child abuse and parental drug abuse. In this chapter, I will be concerned with primary preventive interventions.

Primary Prevention of Drug Abuse in Parenting-Age Women

The most obvious strategy is intended to achieve primary prevention of the entire complex problem of parental AOD abuse and child abuse or neglect by preventing the drug abuse from ever occurring in the first place. The great problem with this elegantly simple approach is that we have had very little success in preventing drug abuse, as was documented by the National Research Council's Committee on Drug Abuse Prevention Research (Gerstein & Green, 1993). It seems to me that there are three major reasons for our general failure to achieve noteworthy success in preventing drug abuse. First, most efforts have been mistargeted on preventing use rather than on preventing abuse. Second, techniques that we know don't work continue, nevertheless, to be the main techniques used in drug abuse prevention. Third, most prevention programs lie to their target audience.

Effective prevention of drug abuse by parenting-age women should be targeted precisely on abusive patterns of drug use, involving large doses, large weekly intakes, and drug taking under high-risk conditions. Occasional, low dosage use of any of the popular recreational drugs under low-risk conditions does not appear to contribute to the type of problems discussed in this book and should not be the target of prevention efforts. There is no reason to believe that the mother who drinks an occasional glass of wine with her dinner or consumes marijuana at a party is placing the health of her unborn child or the welfare of her children at risk. I believe society should not waste its time acting as morals police in trying to eliminate such behavior.

The knowledge-attitudes-behavior (KAB) model, which holds that all one need do is provide the appropriate knowledge in order to shape attitudes and ultimately change behavior, has long held sway in the field of drug abuse prevention. Unfortunately, the success of such efforts has been unimpressive (Gerstein & Green, 1993). Meta-analyses, such as those by Bangert-Drowns (1988) and by Bruvold and Rundall (1988), have found that such programs generally achieve their greatest effects on knowledge, less effect on attitudes, and virtually none on behavior.

Scare tactics have dominated drug education in America since the early efforts of the temperance movement in the late 18th and 19th centuries. This remains true today despite the fact that we have known for decades that these tactics not only don't work, but often actually have a boomerang effect in encouraging drug use and enhancing the barriers to help-seeking. This reliance on scare tactics is closely allied to the tendency to lie. Since the realities seem insufficiently frightening to discourage drug use and abuse, the scaremongers invent "prophylactic lies" the better to frighten their audiences. Soon they are telling such egregious lies as the famous television public service announcement (PSA) that likens using drugs to frying your brains like an egg.

Every proposal that I have read for educational interventions with this population has relied entirely on the KAB model and a dose of scare tactics. They have proposed nothing more than telling mothers about the possible damage to the fetus that can result from maternal alcohol, tobacco, and other drug use. Furthermore, most have given a grossly exaggerated picture of both the likelihood and the severity of damage to the developing fetus and infant. All have offered the advice that a woman should totally abstain from all drugs at all times unless she knows for certain that she isn't pregnant—one can scarcely imagine the reaction if we declared that all men must not drink a beer or take an aspirin unless they were certain their wife wasn't pregnant. From what we have learned conducting drug education for adolescents, it seems unlikely that these programs will do any appreciable good.

Worthwhile primary prevention of drug abuse by parenting-age women would be targeted on reducing the risk factors that result in drug abuse and on strengthening alternative resources for dealing with problems. Concerns of depression (Beckman, 1980; Helzer & Pryzbeck, 1988), low self-esteem (Jones, 1971), lack of social skills (Fillmore, Bacon, & Hyman, 1979; Jones, 1971), and previous histories of abuse (McMahon & Luthar, Chapter 6 in this volume) that play major roles in the etiology of alcohol and other drug abuse in parenting-age women would need to be confronted in realistic ways, and these women would need to be empowered to cope with these issues without reliance on drugs. The informational component of a primary prevention program would need to be accurate and presented in a balanced manner that would allow women to assess their true risks and to make choices about any drug use within the limits of reasonable safety, rather than prescribing an absolute standard of abstinence.

The largest low-impact prevention effort in this area has been the requirement for warning labels on cigarette packages and alcoholic beverage containers. In both instances, one of the labels warns women against use during pregnancy. Specific effects of the warning labels during a period of historic decline in use of both alcohol and tobacco are difficult to measure and even more difficult to specify for women of childbearing age. One ongoing study in Detroit

(Hankin, 1994; Hankin et al., 1993) has attempted this difficult task. It surveyed 3,572 inner-city women who sought prenatal care at an urban clinic over a period of 28 months, beginning 5 months before the labeling law went into effect. The study found that a sharp downward trend in alcohol use by the subjects began about 8 months after the warning label was implemented. Those women who were at greatest risk due to heavy drinking were, however, the least affected by the warning labels. Thus the impact of this program on the incidence of birth defects or abused children remains uncertain and doubtful.

Another form of primary prevention that has received a high degree of publicity is the criminal prosecution of women who use illicit drugs, especially crack cocaine, during pregnancy. Such prosecutions are seen as "sending a message" that drug abuse will not be tolerated during pregnancy. This strong societal message as well as fear of imprisonment is expected to prevent pregnant women from using drugs and to encourage drug-abusing women who become pregnant to seek treatment. There is no evidence, however, that any such effects actually flow from these highly publicized but relatively rare prosecutions. Their major effect seems to have been to discourage drug-abusing women from seeking prenatal care, thus increasing the risk to the fetus far more than their drug use did (Norton-Hawk, in press).

Early Intervention for Drug Abuse
in Pregnant and Parenting Women

The next level of intervention would be secondary prevention of AOD abuse among pregnant and parenting women, which would also achieve primary prevention of child maltreatment by AOD-abusing mothers. Our present efforts in this regard are not achieving great success, apparently reaching only about 10% of all substance-abusing women (Kumpfer, 1991). In part, this is due to inadequate service provision—few programs make allowance for the child care and other special needs of parenting clients, and fewer still will admit pregnant women who may need treatment (Chavkin, 1990; Miller, 1989).

Even more of a problem is the widespread reluctance of such women to enter drug abuse treatment. Hankin points out that heavy-drinking mothers typically tend to ignore general public health warnings about the dangers of drinking during pregnancy (Hankin, 1994). Beyond this, their unwillingness to enter treatment grows out of their realistic awareness that, "Asking for help . . . puts them in real jeopardy of losing custody of their children. Paradoxically, continuing their chemical dependency without seeking help does not, in general, have this effect" (Blume, 1992, p. 803). These facts suggest that we cannot rely on mothers presenting themselves for treatment and must engage in active case-seeking.

Minor and Van Dort (1982) have emphasized the critical importance of intervention by prenatal caregivers in this process. In its recommendations regarding AOD abuse and AIDS, the Expert Panel on the Content of Prenatal Care (1989) of the U.S. Public Health Service urged as a national standard for prenatal care

1. offering all women tests for HIV and drug toxicology during pregnancy;
2. educating all women about risks of alcohol and other drugs during pregnancy;
3. advising abstinence from AOD during pregnancy;
4. increasing the ability of professionals to recognize AOD abuse; and
5. assuring that appropriate referrals for treatment are made.

While the Expert Panel placed emphasis on testing for drugs in the blood and urine of pregnant women, such tests cannot distinguish an abuser from a user. This is crucial, not only because there is no reason to believe that a social user of alcohol or any drug is in need of an intervention, but also because we simply could not afford to provide treatment each year to all of the 34 million women who drink some alcohol and the 6 million who use some illicit drug during their pregnancy. As Blank (1996) has pointed out, intervening with every drug using woman is a tempting proposal but entirely unfeasible.

Moreover, the toxicological exam will fail to detect many abusers. The abuser may escape detection by undergoing a voluntary period of abstinence before medical exams. In many cases this can also be achieved by drinking large volumes of water and urinating frequently before the exam—the latter a natural enough phenomenon in a pregnant woman anyway.

The use of screening questions to identify possible alcohol abusers has been well established. This includes screening instruments such as the T-ACE and the TWEAK that were specifically developed for use with pregnant women (Russell, 1994). Russell et al. (1996) examined the relative effectiveness of a number of widely used screening instruments for use with pregnant women. They found that while the CAGE, MAST (Michigan Alcoholism Screening Test), TWEAK, and T-ACE were all effective in distinguishing risk drinkers from non-risk drinkers, the TWEAK and the T-ACE were more sensitive, detecting more risk drinkers among their pregnant subjects.

Once possible cases have been identified through toxicology and screening questions, a *DSM* diagnostic interview should be conducted to verify the presence of a substance abuse disorder. The intervention that should follow has been described by Jessup (1990) as consisting of five steps:

1. state the indicators of a drug or alcohol problem;
2. educate the mother regarding possible effects on the fetus and the benefits of abstinence;
3. express concern;
4. refer for treatment; and
5. offer advocacy in helping the mother to get treatment and other needed services.

One piece of good news comes from Messer, Clark, and Martin (1996), who found that those mothers who were most in need of treatment seemed to be the ones most likely to enter treatment. This gives grounds for hope that we may be doing better than our 10%-in-treatment finding would suggest.

Another positive sign for the future comes in the form of studies showing that mothers may be more willing to report indicators of excessive drinking on self-administered questionnaires or computer interviews than to their physicians (Lapham, Kring, & Skipper, 1991; Russell & Bigler, 1979). This could lead to the locating of computers in obstetrician's waiting rooms with a programmed version of the TWEAK or the T-ACE and a follow-up AOD history-taking program. As a routine feature of every obstetrician's waiting room, such an arrangement could detect many AOD abusers who currently go undetected and unaided.

Preventing Child Abuse by Drug-Abusing Mothers and Their Male Partners

Many in our society make the assumption that all AOD-abusing parents are necessarily abusive or at least neglectful in the treatment of their children. Hogarth's famous print, Gin Alley, with its depiction of an infant falling from the arms of its stuporously drunken mother and the literary images conveyed in the first chapter come readily to mind. Powell, Gabe, and Zehm (1994) assert this view in stating that,

> Parents in the addicted home naturally focus their resources on the addiction, keeping it central to the family. . . . In addicted families, the rules are governed by the addiction and help the family manage around the addiction. The addiction, not the family members, is central to life. (p. 1)

Under such family circumstances the needs of children, and especially the numerous needs of an infant, go unfulfilled.

There is no doubt that AOD dependence adversely affects the family system (Jackson, 1954; Moos & Billings, 1982). Active alcoholism, for instance, increases family conflict and decreases cohesiveness and expressiveness in the family (Moos & Billings, 1982). Using participant observation methods, Jackson (1954) found that families, or at least the spouse, went through predictable phases in attempting to cope with the alcoholic parent's behavior, beginning with denial and minimization and ending with reorganization once the alcoholic had achieved sobriety.

On the other hand, Clair and Genest (1987) found that while adult children of alcoholics reported greater family conflict, the conflict did not necessarily reach harmful levels. Instead they found that some families could maintain stable functions despite conflict generated by an alcoholic family member. Unquestionably, a drug abuser is not the most desirable parent, but a drug abuser is not necessarily a neglectful or abusive parent. I know of instances where children, and even infants, have been left unattended while their mother went out in search of drugs, but I also know of mothers who went through painful withdrawal because there was no one they could trust to care for their child while they sought drugs. I have known addicted mothers who were every bit as caring and attentive as June Cleaver. While they are not the norm, they show that AOD abusers need not be child abusers.

Child abusers are typified by ignorance of child development and of effective child-rearing practices (Bays, 1990). Abusers commonly expect their child to behave in ways that are not age appropriate. Ordinary infant and toddler behaviors, such as resisting bedtime, diaper soiling (especially right after being changed), throwing food, and so on, are interpreted by abusing parents as willful misbehavior meriting punishment. A baby's persistent crying or refusal to eat may be interpreted by the abusive parent as a rejection of his or her efforts and a criticism of parenting ability. Compensating for their own inadequate childhood, such parents often look to their children as a source of emotional nurturance, expecting a smiling, happy baby to cheer them up and show that their life has meaning. When the baby is fussy and crying and smells of burped-up formula, it can seem like a betrayal to these parents who don't understand the needs and abilities of infants.

Education on human development ought to be part of every child's education, but it isn't. Even if it were, some would never learn, and others would forget the lessons. Prenatal care should include education about early child development. Well-baby visits should include education on the next phase of infant development as well as an opportunity to ask questions about the current phase. AOD-abusing mothers should be identified and targeted for such educational interventions.

Along with education about child development, these parents need to be taught parenting skills. Many were themselves reared in dysfunctional families where they learned the wrong way to raise children—often experiencing neglect and abuse themselves (Briere & Zaidi, 1989; Cohen & Densen-Gerber, 1982). They need to be taught how to care for their child properly. Once again, a variety of methods should be targeted on AOD-abusing parents to teach them these commonly missing skills.

Child abuse is usually triggered during a period of stress, when the parent is faced with too many demands and has too few resources. AOD-abusing parents typically possess few internal resources or social supports for their performance of the maternal role (Bays, 1990). These demands may be all the greater for the alcohol-abusing mother whose child may suffer from fetal alcohol syndrome. Based on their 10-year follow-up of 11 infants, Streissguth, Clarren, and Jones (1985) conclude that even if the mother is attached to the child and well motivated to care for it, she is likely to have inadequate resources and social supports to enable her to attend to the special needs of an alcohol-affected child.

Effective prevention may include both the provision of resources, such as day care or a foster grandparent, and education about ways to access resources and to schedule demands. Self-help groups may have value for these parents by providing a support group. Enrolling them in the local YWCA or other community center may provide a connection with people who will help them care for kids instead of help them use drugs. Provision of a crisis nursery for AOD-abusing mothers could save many infants and children from injury by allowing the mother a few hours of respite when she is overwhelmed by circumstances.

For example, Rhode Island's Women and Infant's Hospital operates a model program for pregnant and postpartum substance abusers that has served more than 225 women during its 5-year history. The services of Project Link are fully integrated into the primary care system at Women and Infant's Hospital, thus assuring both that the medical needs of mother and infant are met and doing so in a fashion that avoids any public labeling of the mother as a substance abuse patient visiting a drug clinic. Each participant in Project Link is assigned both a clinical manager and a case manager. The clinical manager sees to it that the mother receives needed individual, group, and family therapy. Treatment groups in which mothers participate include: early recovery, parenting education, relapse prevention, and parenting skills. Meanwhile, the case manager sees to the nontreatment needs of the mother and infant in such vital life areas as food, housing, clothing, transportation, education, and employment. Case managers also schedule regular infant developmental assessments, conduct home visits, monitor the infant's pediatric care schedule, and provide direct personal support and encouragement to the mothers. These services act as primary prevention of abuse of the child while home visits and regular well-baby care also serve to identify any failures of primary prevention and bring quick response for any infant that is abused.

Conclusion

With well-planned and adequately financed primary prevention programs of the types outlined above, we can prevent a great deal of damage to the next generation. If we fail to invest in primary prevention now, the future costs in crime, drug abuse, mental illness, and domestic violence will be far greater in the future. If we invest our primary prevention resources unwisely, we will at best have lost an opportunity and at worst may have contributed to the problems we sought to prevent.

References

Bangert-Drowns, R. L. (1988). Effects of school-based substance abuse education: A meta-analysis. *Journal of Drug Education, 18,* 243-264.

Bays, J. (1990). Substance abuse and child abuse: Impact of addiction on the child. *Pediatric Clinics of North America, 37*(4), 881-904.

Beckett, K. (1995). Fetal rights and "crack moms": Pregnant women in the war on drugs. *Contemporary Drug Problems, 22,* 587-612.

Beckman, L. J. (1980). Perceived antecedents and effects of alcohol consumption in women. *Journal of Studies on Alcohol, 41,* 518-530.

Blank, R. H. (1996). Mandating treatment for pregnant substance abusers: Attractive but unfeasible. *Politics and Life Sciences, 15,* 49-50.

Blume, S. B. (1992). Alcohol and other drug problems in women. In J. H. Lowinson, P. Ruiz, & R. B. Millman (Eds.), *Substance abuse: A comprehensive textbook* (2nd ed.). Baltimore, MD: Williams & Wilkins.

Briere, J., & Zaidi, L. Y. (1989). Sexual abuse histories and sequelae in female psychiatric emergency room patients. *American Journal of Psychiatry, 146,* 1602-1606.

Bruvold, W. H., & Rundall, T. G. (1988). A meta-analysis and theoretical review of school based tobacco and alcohol intervention programs. *Psychology and Health, 2,* 53-78.

Chavkin, W. (1990). Drug addiction and pregnancy: Policy crossroads. *American Journal of Public Health, 80,* 483-487.

Clair, D., & Genest, M. (1987). Variables associated with adjustment of offspring of alcoholic fathers. *Journal of Studies on Alcohol, 48,* 345.

Cohen, F. S., & Densen-Gerber, J. (1982). A study of the relationship between child abuse and drug addiction in 178 patients: Preliminary results. *Child Abuse & Neglect, 6,* 383-387.

Duncan, D. F. (1988). *Epidemiology: Basis for disease prevention and health promotion*. New York: Macmillan.

Duncan, D. F. (1997). Use and misuses of epidemiology in shaping and assessing drug policy. *Journal of Primary Prevention, 17,* 375-382.

Expert Panel on the Content of Prenatal Care, U. S. Public Health Service (1989). *Caring for our future: The content of prenatal care.* Washington, DC: Government Printing Office.

Fillmore, K. M., Bacon, S. D., & Hyman, M. (1979). The 27-year longitudinal panel study of drinking by students in college (Contract # ADM 281-76-0015). Washington, DC: National Institute on Alcoholism and Alcohol Abuse.

Gerstein, D. R., & Green, L. W. (1993). *Preventing drug abuse: What do we know?* Washington, DC: National Academy Press.

Hankin, J. R. (1994). FAS prevention strategies: Passive and active measures. *Alcohol Health and Research World, 18,* 62-66.

Hankin, J. R., Sloan, J. J., Firestone, I. J., Ager, J. W., Sokol, R. J., & Martier, S. S. (1993). A time series analysis of the impact of the alcohol warning label on antenatal drinking. *Alcoholism: Clinical and Experimental Research, 17,* 284-289.

Helzer, J. F., & Pryzbeck, T. R. (1988). The co-occurrence of alcoholism with other psychiatric disorders in the general population and its impact on treatment. *Journal of Studies of Alcohol, 49,* 219-224.

Jackson, J. K. (1954). The adjustment of the family to the crisis of alcoholism. *Quarterly Journal of Studies on Alcohol, 15,* 562-586.

Jessup, M. (1990). The treatment of perinatal addiction: Identification, intervention, and advocacy. *Western Journal of Medicine, 152,* 553-558.

Jones, M. C. (1971). Personality antecedents and correlates of drinking patterns in women. *Journal of Consulting and Clinical Psychology, 36,* 61-69.

Kumpfer, K. L. (1991). Treatment programs for drug-abusing women. *The Future of Children, 1*(1), 50-60.

Lapham, S. C., Kring, M. K., & Skipper, B. (1991). Prenatal behavioral risk screening by computer in a health maintenance based prenatal care clinic. *American Journal of Obstetrics and Gynecology, 165*(3), 306-314.

Messer, K., Clark, K. A., & Martin, S. L. (1996). Characteristics associated with pregnant women's utilization of substance abuse treatment services. *American Journal of Drug and Alcohol Abuse, 22,* 403-422.

Miller, G. (1989). Addicted infants and their mothers. *Zero to Three, 9,* 20-23.

Minor, M. J., & Van Dort, B. (1982). Prevention research on the teratogenic effects of alcohol. *Preventive Medicine, 11,* 346-359.

Moos, R., & Billings, A. (1982). Children of alcoholics during the recovery process. *Addictive Behaviors, 7,* 155-163.

Norton-Hawk, M. (in press). Career of a crisis: Cocaine babies and the interrelationship of professional, political and ideological forces. *Drugs and Society.*

Powell, R. B., Gabe, J., & Zehm, S. (1994). *Classrooms under the influence: Reaching early adolescent children of alcoholics.* Reston, VA: National Association of Secondary School Principals.

Reinarman, C., & Levine, H. G. (1994). The construction of America's crack crisis. In L. Bollinger (Ed.), *De-Americanizing drug policy.* Frankfurt am Main, Germany: Peter Lang.

Russell, M. (1994). New assessment tools for drinking in pregnancy: T-ACE, TWEAK, and others. *Alcohol Health and Research World, 18,* 55-61.

Russell, M., & Bigler, L. (1979). Screening for alcohol-related problems in an outpatient obstetric-gynecologic clinic. *American Journal of Obstetrics and Gynecology, 134,* 4-12.

Russell, M., Martier, S. S., Sokol, R. J., Mudar, P., Jacobson, S., & Jacobson, J. (1996). Detecting risk drinking during pregnancy: A comparison of four screening questionnaires. *American Journal of Public Health, 86,* 1435-1439.

Streissguth, A. P., Clarren, S. K., & Jones, K. L. (1985). Natural history of the fetal alcohol syndrome: A 10-year follow-up of 11 patients. *Lancet, 2,* 85-91.

Susman, E. (1996). Cocaine's role in the womb has virtually no effect on early childhood development. *The Brown University Child and Adolescent Behavior Letter, 12*(9), 1-3.

Author Index

Subject Index

About the Editors

Thomas P. Gullotta, M.A., M.S.W., is CEO of the Child and Family Agency. He currently is the editor of the *Journal of Primary Prevention*. For Sage, he serves as a general series book editor for **Advances in Adolescent Development,** and is the senior book series editor for **Issues in Children's and Families' Lives.** He serves as the series editor for **Prevention in Practice.** In addition, he holds editorial appointments on the *Journal of Early Adolescence, Adolescence,* and the *Journal of Educational and Psychological Consultation.* He serves on the Board of the National Mental Health Association and is an adjunct faculty member in the psychology department of Eastern Connecticut State University. He has published extensively on adolescents and primary prevention.

Robert L. Hampton received his A.B. degree from Princeton University, and his M.A. and PhD from the University of Michigan. He is Associate Provost for Academic Affairs and Dean for Undergraduate Studies and Professor of Family Studies and Sociology at the University of Maryland, College Park. He is a Gimbel Mentoring Scholar. He has published extensively in the field of family violence. His works include four books: *Violence in the Black Family: Correlates and Consequences, Black Family Violence: Current Research and Theory, Family Violence: Prevention and Treatment,* and *Preventing Violence in America.* He is completing a second edition of *Family Violence: Prevention and Treatment* for Sage Publications and is one of the founders of the Institute on Domestic Violence in the African American Community. His research interests include interspousal violence, family abuse, male violence, community violence, stress and social support, and institutional responses to violence.

Vincent Senatore lives in East Hampton, Connecticut, and has been involved in the issues of youth, drugs, and violence for more than 25 years. As the former executive director of a residential treatment facility for substance-abusing adolescent females and as the former executive assistant to the Commissioner of the Connecticut Department of Children and Families, he has implemented and coordinated substance abuse programs for youth and helped sponsor the state's first legislation for substance-abusing pregnant women and their children. He currently is the Associate Director of Child and Family Agency of Southern Connecticut, Inc. Besides administering child welfare, mental health, and home-based and school-based services, he is the program chair for the 1996 Gimbel Child and Family Program, which works with selected individuals from the federal and state governments and with scholars and practitioners from across the nation to help bridge the field of child welfare and substance abuse.

About the Contributors

Martin Bloom obtained a PhD in social psychology from the University of Michigan in 1963 after receiving a diploma in social study from the University of Edinburgh (1958). He has been teaching in schools of social work for most of his career. Among his publications are *Primary Prevention: The Possible Science* (1981), *Configurations of Human Behavior* (1984), *Life Span Development: Bases for Preventive and Interventive Helping* (1985, 2nd ed.), *Introduction to the Drama of Helping* (1990), and *Evaluating Practice: Guidelines for the Accountable Professional* (1995, 2nd ed.). His current preoccupations include primary prevention, longitudinal research, and his first grandson—not necessarily in the order presented.

Suzanne M. Colby, PhD, is a project director at the Center for Alcohol and Addiction Studies and an investigator in the Department of Psychiatry and Human Behavior at Brown University. She has worked in the field of addictive behaviors research for the past 10 years. The focus of her most recent research includes the development of innovative approaches to removing barriers to treatment and improving success rates for interventions with pregnant smokers. In addition, she is currently directing several federally funded research projects designed to test the efficacy of preventative interventions for health-risk behaviors among adolescents in health care settings.

David F. Duncan, DrPH, is currently Senior Public Health Epidemiologist for the Rhode Island Department of Health and director of that state's Unified Needs Assessment Project for Substance Abuse Prevention and Treatment. He is also Clinical Associate

Professor of Medical Science at Brown University and Adjunct Professor of Biology at Community College of Rhode Island. His previous position was Research Fellow at Brown University's Center for Alcohol and Addiction Studies. Before that he held academic positions as Professor of Health Education and Coordinator of Community Health Programs at Southern Illinois University, Visiting Professor of Health and Environmental Research at the University of Cologne (Germany), and Associate Professor and Chair of the Department of Health Science at the State University of New York at Brockport. He has extensive clinical and community experience in the areas of mental health, drug abuse, child protection, and law enforcement. He is the author of more than 150 papers in scientific journals and of textbooks, *Drugs and the Whole Person* and *Epidemiology: Basis for Disease Prevention and Health Promotion.*

Marianne Eismann, a former journalist, is completing a dissertation on literature, violence, and Victorian society for the University of Chicago. She has taught at Chicago, Wake Forest University, and the University of Maryland, where she currently works for the Dean for Undergraduate Studies as assistant to the Dean for Publications and Special Projects.

Laura Feig, M.P.P., is a social science analyst in the Office of the Assistant Secretary for Planning and Evaluation (ASPE), U.S. Department of Health and Human Services. She has worked for ASPE since 1989, analyzing policy issues regarding the provision of services to children, youth, and families. She specializes in issues regarding children and families affected by substance abuse, and regarding child welfare services generally.

Stephen E. Gardner, D.S.W., is Associate Director for Program Development and Special Projects, Division of Demonstrations for High-Risk Populations/Center for Substance Abuse Prevention (CSAP), in Rockville, Maryland. He was previously the Chief of the High Risk Youth Branch. CSAP has recently begun a prevention initiative targeting violence related to alcohol and other drugs.

Brenda Jones Harden is Assistant Professor in the Institute for Child Study/Department of Human Development at the University of

Maryland, College Park. She has worked in the child welfare field
since 1978 as a clinician, program planner, and administrator. She
is currently conducting research on children exposed to substances
in utero, maltreated and foster children, and children exposed to
community violence. As part of each of these research initiatives,
she has implemented and evaluated programs to address the needs
of these populations of children and their families.

Suniya S. Luthar, PhD, is Associate Professor of Psychology and
Education at Teachers College, Columbia University, and she is the
Director of Child and Family Research at The APT Foundation in
New Haven, Connecticut. She completed her doctoral training in
clinical and developmental psychology at Yale University. In recent
work with families affected by substance abuse, she is using conceptual and methodological strategies from the field of developmental psychopathology to expand understanding of the problems
these families face across generations. Studies currently in progress
are examining risk and protective factors affecting the psychosocial
development of children living with a drug-dependent mother. She
is also exploring parenting issues common among substance-abusing women, and she is developing a group psychotherapy designed
to address the personal and parenting needs of drug-dependent
mothers.

James Maffuid, M.F.T., is a licensed marital and family therapist.
He is also a Clinical Member and Approved Supervisor of the
American Association for Marriage and Family Therapy. For the
past 3 years, he has been the coordinator of home-based services
for Child and Family Agency of Southern Connecticut, Inc. Prior
to that, he served as the agency's emergency services liaison for a
home-based program focusing on neglecting and abusing families
engaged in substance use. Besides his work at Child and Family
Agency, he is an elected board member of the Connecticut Association for Marriage and Family Therapy as well as the cochairperson
of that organization's managed health care committee. He also is a
founding partner of Colchester Counseling Associates, where he
provides family therapy training/supervision, community-based
workshops, and outpatient mental health services.

Micah L. McCreary, M. Div., PhD, is Assistant Professor of Psychology, Department of Psychology at Virginia Commonwealth University. In this capacity, he teaches, conducts applied research, and supervises students in family psychology emphasizing the influences of culture and development. As a licensed clinical psychologist, he also operates an independent practice in Richmond, Virginia.

Thomas J. McMahon, PhD, is currently Assistant Professor in the Department of Psychiatry at the Yale School of Medicine where he is both a faculty member of the Child and Family Research Team within the Division of Substance Abuse and the Director of Children's Services at a satellite clinic of the Connecticut Mental Health Center. He completed his doctoral training in child and school psychology at New York University in 1994. As a clinician and researcher, he is interested in the psychosocial development of children living with a drug-dependent parent and the delivery of clinical services to substance-abusing parents and their children. He is presently examining parenting issues of concern to substance-abusing men, he is attempting to identify factors contributing to both positive and negative outcomes among children living with a drug-dependent mother, and he is involved in several initiatives designed to promote awareness of parental substance abuse within school and child welfare systems.

Wilbert Murrell received his B.A. and M.H.E. from Morehead State University and did three years' post-master's work in counseling psychology at the University of Kentucky. He is a Certified Clinical Chemical Dependency Counselor through the Ohio Credentialing Board, The International Certification Reciprocity Consortium/ Alcohol and Other Drug Abuse, Inc. He studies the relationship among substance abuse, family violence, cultural competence, and children. He is currently the Executive Director for Lima-Urban Minority Alcohol and Drug Abuse Outreach Program (UMADAOP), funded by the Department of Alcohol and Drug Addiction Services, the United Way, and other agencies; these services intervene with court-mandated batterers, children in the homes of violence, student violence in schools, outpatient drug/alcohol treatment, and primary and secondary prevention of violence in K-6 grades in the public school. He has authored and coauthored *Domestic Violence* *in the African-American Community* and *Bridging the Gap Between Child Welfare and Substance Abuse Professionals.* He is currently considering a doctoral program.

Hank Resnik, M.A., is a writer and editor who has written extensively about youth, education, and community-based substance abuse and violence prevention strategies. He is a senior writer for the CDM Group in Chevy Chase, Maryland, and is the editor of *Partnership Perspectives,* bulletin of the Center for Substance Abuse Prevention Community Partnership Demonstration Grant Program.

Carl M. Rogers has devoted his professional life to improvement of social services for children, youth, and families. He received his B.A. from Park College (Parkville, Missouri) and his master's degree and PhD in psychology from George Peabody College. Currently vice president of the National Council on Child Abuse and Family Violence, he previously served as the associate director of the Division of Child Protection at Children's Hospital National Medical Center in Washington, D.C., and as cofounder and executive director of the Center for Child Protection and Family Support, Inc., also located in Washington, D.C. He has served as a scientific and public policy consultant to numerous governmental and nongovernmental organizations, including the National Center on Child Abuse and Neglect and the Office of Community Services (ACF/DHHS). His other accomplishments include serving as a founding member of the Board of Directors of the American Professional Society on the Abuse of Children (APSAC) and authoring more than 30 professional publications.

Toni A. Stepter is a doctoral student in the counseling psychology program at Virginia Commonwealth University, Richmond, Virginia.